What is Architecture?

Architecture can influence the way we feel, sometimes helping us along as we go about our lives, and sometimes sabotaging our habitual ways of doing things. The essays collected here challenge, and help to define, a view of architecture that ranges from the minimal domesticity of Diogenes' barrel, to the exuberant experiments of the contemporary avant-garde. Architecture is always more than building, representing as it does a folding together of buildings and culture, so that the buildings come to have meaning as they are caught up in a way of life – architecture is best appreciated as part of an art of living.

Andrew Ballantyne's substantial essay 'The Nest and the Pillar of Fire' introduces the collection, which explores some themes and problems generated by architecture, from the everyday to the extraordinary, by looking at architecture and what people have to say about it. Collected here, there are reflections on everyday life and the posthumanist subject, and on both the words and deeds of philosophers such as Wittgenstein, Heidegger and Deleuze. There are essays by philosophers, architects and art historians, including Roger Scruton, Bernard Tschumi, Demetri Pophyrios, Kenneth Frampton, Diane Ghirado and David Goldblatt. They consider what architecture should be, what it does, and how it is involved in our lives, whether by reminding us of lofty ideals, or exasperating us by generating housework. Philosophy has a role to play, either by helping to make an exacting and inclusive analysis, or by being deployed as a means of seduction.

What is Architecture?

Edited by Andrew Ballantyne

London and New York

First published 2002
by Routledge
11 New Fetter Lane, London EC4P 4EE

Simultaneously published in the USA and Canada
by Routledge
29 West 35th Street, New York, NY 10001

Routledge is an imprint of the Taylor & Francis Group

Typeset in Frutiger Light by Wearset Ltd, Boldon, Tyne and Wear
Printed and bound in Great Britain by T.J. International, Padstow, Cornwall

British Library Cataloguing in Publication Data

A catalogue record for this book is available from the British Library

Library of Congress Cataloging in Publication Data
What is architecture? / edited by Andrew Ballantyne.
    p. cm.
  Includes bibliographical references and index.
  1. Architecture–Philosophy. I. Ballantyne, Andrew.

NA2500 .W47 2001
720–dc21

                                                    2001040812

  ISBN 0-415-25626-7 (hbk)
  ISBN 0-415-25627-5 (pbk)

for Gerard Loughlin

Contents

Contributors

Andrew Ballantyne is Professor of Architecture at the University of Newcastle upon Tyne. He has taught at the universities of Sheffield, Bath and Newcastle, and is the author of *Architecture, Landscape and Liberty*.

Michel de Certeau, who died in 1986, was a polymath who wrote about a wide range of topics, including two volumes of essays on *The Practice of Everyday Life*. There is a recent compilation of his work and commentaries on it: *The Certeau Reader*, edited by Graham Ward.

Kenneth Frampton is Ware Professor of Architecture at the University of Columbia, New York. He has written extensively on twentieth-century architecture including *Modern Architecture, a Critical History*, and *Studies in Tectonic Culture: The Poetics of Construction in Nineteenth and Twentieth-Century Architecture*.

Diane Ghirardo is Professor of Architecture at the University of Southern California. She has edited the *Journal of Architectural Education* and been President of the Association of Collegiate Schools of Architecture. Her books include *Out of Site*, *Building New Communities*, and *Architecture After Modernism*. She was the translator of Aldo Rossi's *The Architecture of the City*.

David Goldblatt is chair of Philosophy at the University of Denison, Ohio. He has written many articles on aesthetics and the arts, and edited a reader, *Aesthetics: a Reader in the Philosophy of the Arts*. His next book will be on ventriloquism.

Neil Leach is the author of *The Anaesthetics of Architecture*, and *Millennium Culture*. He edited *Rethinking Architecture, a Reader in Cultural Theory*, and *Architecture and Revolution*. He divides his time between teaching at the Architectural Association and a chair at the University of Bath.

Kathleen McHugh is Associate Professor of Comparative Literature at the University of California, Riverside. She has published extensively on aspects of film, and is the author of *American Domesticity: From How-To Manual to Hollywood Melodrama*.

Demetri Porphyrios is a practising architect and theorist, who has taught at the Architectural Association and the Royal College of Art in London, and been Jefferson Professor at the University of Virginia, and Davenport Professor at Yale University. His books include *Classicism is Not a Style*, and *Classical Architecture*, as well as monographs of his architectural work.

Joyce Henri Robinson is an art historian and curator, at the Palmer Museum of Art, Philadelphia, who has taught at the University of Virginia, Davidson College and the American University in Paris.

Roger Scruton is a philosopher, critic and novelist who has held academic positions in Cambridge, London and Boston. He is the author of over twenty books, including *The Aesthetics of Architecture* and *The Classical Vernacular*.

Bernard Tschumi is Dean of Architecture at the University of Columbia. His books include *The Manhattan Transcripts*, *Architecture and Disjunction* and *Event-Cities*. His architectural work is widely published, and his best-known project is the Parc de la Villette, one of the *grands projets* commissioned for the French bicentennial in 1989.

Acknowledgements

The people whose work is included here are warmly thanked for their contributions and their help. It should not go without saying that the essays were all included because I admire something about them, and I have been delighted with the contact that the project has brought about.

Direct intellectual debts are acknowledged in the references, but there are others, more oblique or personal that equally deserve mention. The book grew out of work that began while I was at the University of Bath, when I was working with Vaughan Hart and Robert Tavernor. That work continues at the University of Newcastle, with Simon Guy. The book would not have been begun without the influence of Richard Woodfield, and I am very grateful to him and to the philosophers I have met through the British Society of Aesthetics, especially Carolyn Wilde, Nick McAdoo, Ed Winters and Ian Ground. I want also to thank all my colleagues and friends, but shall hold back from naming them, as the list would either be long or involve omissions, but thank you all for your help and forbearance.

Andrew Ballantyne

The editor and publishers gratefully acknowledge the following for permission to reproduce material in the book.

Every effort has been made to contact copyright holders for their permission to reprint material in this book. The publisher would be grateful to hear from any copyright holder who is not acknowledged here and will undertake to rectify any errors or omissions in future editions of this book.

VISUAL MATERIAL

Andrew Ballantyne, 1.1, 1.4, 10.2, 10.3
Barnes Foundation, 6.1
Bibliothèque Royale, Brussels, 6.3
British Film Institute, 3.1, 3.3, 3.4, 3.5
Caisse Nationale des Monuments Historiques et des Sites, Paris, 6.5

Eisenman Architects, C.6, C.8, 9.1, 9.2, 9.3, 9.4

Hulton Getty Archive, C.1, C.4, 1.2, 1.3, 3.2, 5.1, 5.2, 5.3, 5.4, 5.5

Margherita Krischanitz, C.2

Digne Meller Marcovicz, 4.1, 4.2, 4.3, 4.4

Musée des Arts Décoratifs, Paris, 6.6

Musée d'Orsay, Paris, 6.7

Österreichische Nationalbibliothek, C.3

Michael Nedo, C.7

Demetri Porphyrios, 7.1, 7.2, 7.3, 7.4

Roger-Viollet, 6.4

Bernard Tschumi, 10.1, 10.4

WRITTEN MATERIAL

A version of one section of 'The Nest and the Pillar of Fire' was published in *ARQ* (*Architectural Research Quarterly*), 4, 4, 2000, Cambridge University Press.

Roger Scruton, 'Architectural Principles in an Age of Nihilism', © 1994, Roger Scruton, was first published in *The Classical Vernacular: Architectural Principles in an Age of Nihilism*, by Roger Scruton, Carcanet Press Limited, Manchester.

Diane Ghirardo, 'The Architecture of Deceit', © 1984, Diane Ghirardo, was first published in *Perspecta: The Yale Architectural Journal* 21.

Michel de Certeau, 'Spatial Stories', from *The Practice of Everyday Life*, translated and edited by Steven Rendall, chapter IX, copyright © 1984 The Regents of the University of California.

Neil Leach, 'The Dark Side of the *Domus*', was first published in *The Journal of Architecture*, 3, 1, © 1998, *The Journal of Architecture*.

Kathleen McHugh, 'The Metaphysics of Housework', from *American Domesticity* by Kathleen McHugh, © 1999, Oxford University Press, Inc. Used by permission of Oxford University Press, Inc.

Joyce Henri Robinson, 'Hi Honey, I'm Home' was first published in *Not at Home*, edited by Christopher Reed, published by Thames and Husdon, London and New York. Text © 1996, Joyce Henri Robinson.

Demetri Porphyrios, 'From *Techne* to Tectonics', was first published in *Classical Architecture*, by Demetri Porphyrios, Academy Editions, London. © 1991 Demetri Porphyrios.

Kenneth Frampton, 'Bötticher, Semper and the Tectonic: Core Form and Art Form', from *Studies in Tectonic Culture: The Poetics of Construction in Nineteenth and Twentieth-Century Architecture*, by Kenneth Frampton, edited by John Cava, MIT Press. © 1995 Massachusetts Institute of Technology.

A version of David Goldblatt, 'The Dislocation of the Architectural Self', appeared in *The Journal of Aesthetics and Art Criticism*, 49, 4, Fall 1991. We are grateful to Blackwell Publishers for permission to reprint this essay.

Bernard Tschumi, 'The Pleasure of Architecture,' from *Architecture and Disjunction*, by Bernard Tschumi, MIT Press. Copyright © 1994 Massachusetts Institute of Technology.

Introduction

Philosophers always want us to live simply and modestly. This can hardly come as a surprise, because if someone tells us to be extravagant and showy then we know that this is not a philosopher. It simply does not sound at all high-minded to insist on luxury as a matter of principle. The 'type' of the philosopher's dwelling is the barrel or tub adopted by the Cynic philosopher Diogenes, whose kennel-like abode was as minimal as could be (Figure I.1). His adoption of this

Figure I.1
Diogenes in his *pithos* at the Metroön of Athens, in an illustration from the nineteenth-century architect Gottfried Semper's book *Der Stil*. It is based on a heavily restored marble relief at the Villa Albani in Rome.

dwelling dramatised a renunciation of worldly values – it did not go unnoticed, but has resonated through the centuries, and now that all the Cynic texts are lost, it is the principal gesture on which Diogenes' philosophical reputation is based. The Cynics, who were sceptical of all received wisdom, dropped out of the civil society of ancient Athens, and declared themselves citizens not of the state but of the cosmos – scepticism and cosmopolitanism are their legacy.

This book has its starting point in conversations between architects and philosophers who were thinking about architecture. What we want of architecture and what we expect of it is not universal, but there are various ways of trying to understand what it is that architecture does and what we want it to do. The essays that are collected here, written by architects, philosophers and art historians, represent a variety of viewpoints, not all of them compatible with one another in the minds of their authors. It is not designed as a polemic to promote one particular view, but as a presentation of various views which all have a legitimate claim on our attention when we think about architecture. The question is not so much whether the views are right or wrong – of course they are all correct up to a point – but to decide how much each view might influence the way we think about architecture in particular circumstances. At a practical level, we do not expect the same things of all architecture at all times. Many problems in the discussion of architecture arise from the fact that we use one word, 'architecture', to encompass more than one agenda that we have for buildings. On the one hand we want most buildings most of the time to be comfortable and reassuring – nest-like buildings, in which we feel secure – but on the other hand we give particular approbation to the architects who fly in the face of this commonplace merit, and achieve spectacular buildings against all the odds. They are inspiring, and many an architecture student aspires to play such a role, whereas on the whole that is not what philosophers want architects to do – they would rather have a rational self-effacing sort of person designing the world that we are all to inhabit.

Architecture is part of the art of living, and is at its most successful when it seems to give expression to the life that inhabits it. The seventeenth-century French *homme de lettres*, Michel de Montaigne, had his library in a tower from which he could see across his lands. It was here that he invented the essay, in a room where the walls and beams carry painted lettering, that fuses the thoughts of ancient authors into the building's fabric. The novelist Marcel Proust had a cork-lined room, where he wrote his carefully balanced and exquisitely nuanced sentences. Here he could cocoon himself away from the world, so that his neurotic sensibility could vibrate at its pitch of perfection. In these uncommon rooms, it is impossible to escape awareness that there is a rapport between the building and the mind that is at work in it. In less considered rooms, certain thoughts could not take shape, certain deeds could not be done. A bustling life would cut them out. We might dream the same dreams wherever we are, but we feel more at home in places that seem to give expression to the values we care about. There is art in the arrangement of buildings, and art also in the life that they enable and that they frame. Our feelings can be influenced by the form of a building – whether or not it looks beautiful, or appropriate, or exciting – whether it seems solid and dependable or flashy and insincere. We can applaud or object to the kinds of things it seems to imply about its place in the world, and our place in the world, and whether it does what we want it to do, or seems to trap and frustrate us. Dwellings are caught up with our lives, and shelter our most intimate moments, whereas monuments endure and show us the kind of things that great civilizations can do at their most inspired. And philosophy can help us to analyse what is going on, so that we can unpack the cultural contents of buildings, and realise how it is that they have the effect they do.

In comparison with the problems set by physicists or logicians, architecture is always complex, with many interacting forces at work on it. The problems posed in architecture cannot be solved technically, because there are simply too many interdependent variables, and in practice – since the problems must be solved more or less immediately, and well enough for the time being – various factors are either neglected or else they are taken care of by drawing on the experience offered by tradition and precedent. When our ways of doing things are properly ingrained, they becomes habitual and we call them 'common sense'. This is not to say that architecture cannot have certain sorts of simplicity, such as visual simplicity, but the building's appearance is only one of the ways in which the building can have an impact on the life within, and usually it is not the most important way. For example, perhaps in order to have a visually striking house the occupant has borne an extravagant cost, which might make it necessary to take on unpalatable paid work. The beautiful building might bring about the moral ruin of its owner. Perhaps, because we wanted to make the most of spectacular views, with large areas of opening windows, a house will be impossible to heat on the coldest days of the year – and perhaps this is not a problem, because it is to be used only in the summer. Perhaps the open spaces and polished surfaces effectively enslave the person who lives there by making it imperative that it be continually tidied and cleaned. A different decision about the order of priorities might have made for a more ordinary house and a happier life. But for someone who is delighted by the house, the pleasures will outweigh the inconveniences. If an exorbitant cost brings exalted social status, then it can seem to be a cost worth paying, whatever Diogenes might have thought, and however irrational it might look to the accountant. Perhaps the cleaning can be delegated to an employee who is grateful for the work and who gets to live in the house. And so on. Already it is plain enough that there are political and cultural dimensions to what is going on, which can, if we choose, be excluded from a discussion by insisting that all that really matters is the purely visual effect of the three-dimensional form. While it is impossible to find practical examples of buildings which completely isolate a single issue, nevertheless occasionally a single issue is given prominence and everything else is neglected or made subservient. Such buildings are informative and philosophically interesting, because they can be seen to be testing an idea, and they therefore tend to be discussed and revisited in commentaries, even if they are not particularly beautiful or good to live in. They are valuable because we can learn something from them.

The essays collected here are not concerned with the rival claims of different architectural styles, but with questions of how we relate to buildings and shape them. Questions of style are not unconnected with these concerns, but they take over and become supremely important only when all other questions have been begged, or perhaps when they have been answered, but that would be exceptional. One of the themes that can be pursued in reading the essays is the role of philosophy in discussions about architecture and in the architects' formulation of their ideas. It is possible to pick up from philosophy a habit of clear thinking and clear articulation of ideas, but this is not always apparent where links between philosophy and the arts are concerned. Bernard Tschumi for example writes very clearly about the use of philosophical texts as a means of seduction, which is in effect how these texts often are used in practice, when their actual arguments are less important than their general air of profundity. Any philosopher with a shred of integrity will deplore such practice, but yet it accounts for a significant part of the architecture-world's consumption of philosophical writings. Architecture looks very different from the viewpoint of the architect who has gone through a specialised education and from the viewpoint of the general population, which can include philosophers. There is a corresponding difference between what philosophy looks like to professional philosophers and to the general public – which in this respect includes architects. Analytic philosophy often seems from outside to be preoccupied with questions generated by philosophy, and with their solution by means of fine-grained arguments and mathematical logic.[1] The agenda is established, and careers are devoted to solving the problems which it generates. Meanwhile in the arts, these questions do not seem to inspire, but the more metaphysical questions of Continental philosophy do. This fills analytic philosophers with dismay. 'Arid technicalities,' said Thomas Nagel, 'are preferable to the blend of oversimplification and fake profundity that is too often the form taken by popular philosophy.'[2] I have taken pains to avoid fake profundity in the text that follows, and hope that the necessary simplifications have not tipped over and become the oversimplifications which invalidate arguments. There should be enough detail to allow the argument to be framed, but not so much that my train of thought runs off in all directions (your own train of thought is not mine to control and will do what it likes). The general approach is one of trying to articulate and perhaps solve problems which relate to the understanding of architecture, rather than looking for metaphysical foundations. The issues around which the following essays turn all have practical consequences for the ways in which we design, inhabit and think about architecture. I have tried to relate the more abstract ideas back to these practical concerns, rather than try to pursue the arguments about abstract ideas to some sort of conclusion – which would take me into philosophy. Sometimes I have preferred to leave questions open rather than

4 ☐

suggest that there is a conclusion, which seems preferable to resorting to the kind of simplification that fudges the issue. Even so, there is certainly 'simplification' in Nagel's sense, but on the other hand in opening up some questions even as far as I have done, I will be seen, by experienced architects who work with a background of long experience and solid common sense, to be introducing unnecessary complication. The point is that by taking things apart and seeing how the different forces act on one another, one begins to see how things could turn out differently – a small change in the balance between forces can produce dramatically different long-term effects. For example our cities would be very different today had the explosive properties of petrol not been harnessed, if oil had remained nothing more than a sticky substance which occasionally found its way out of the ground. The state of society as a whole would be very different if Nietzsche's books had sold well and he had enjoyed a contented suburban life.[3] I have found the philosophers of the pragmatist tradition particularly helpful in finding a way through this material, as is evident from my footnotes. They do not normally figure in architectural discussion, but I hope that this exposure will help to draw them into the arena, because they have much to offer. The Italian pragmatist Giovanni Papini described pragmatism as being in the midst of our theories, allowing us to move between them like the corridor in a hotel.[4] Not only is this an impeccably architectural metaphor, it also shows a way to move between the theories (which he envisaged developing in the different rooms) in a way which allows for a degree of coherence much greater than that to be found in the hit-and-run eclecticism which marks some of the current usage of philosophy by architects. I see my introductory essay as such a corridor between the rooms of the other essays by diverse hands which make up this collection. Each essay generates a space of its own, and has its own coherence. Each essay shows an aspect of architecture, but it is perhaps not immediately clear how these aspects can all be aspects of the same thing ('architecture'). It is by strolling along the corridor and spending time in each of the rooms that one begins to sense how it is that the different aspects fit together. The philosopher Nelson Goodman's *Ways of Worldmaking* (1978) suggests another image of the same state of affairs. He supposes that each perspective generates its own perceptions and values and therefore makes, as it were, its own world, which is more or less incommensurable with the worlds of others – especially here other cultures' worlds, which might mean the worlds of bankers or beggars, as well as the worlds of architects and philosophers. Each of the following essays in effect is symptomatic of its world, and implies a view with a particular horizon, giving priority to a certain range of concerns. We do well to have a multiplicity of ways of thinking and responding, so that we can respond to the circumstances we find, and value what we find there. The nineteenth-century critic John Ruskin called architecture's guiding principles *The Seven Lamps of Architecture* (1849), and architects' principles are like headlamps that can illuminate the way ahead, but can, on the other hand, also dazzle and confound. There are times when it seems as if there is a collective madness that entrances people with the terrible beauty of those headlamps, like little animals about to meet their doom. It is the aim in what follows to show some of the allure of architects' ideas without surrendering rationality.

Andrew Ballantyne

NOTES

1   A good introduction is Clark Glymour, *Thinking Things Through: An Introduction to Philosophical Issues and Achievements* (Cambridge, MA.: MIT Press, 1992). I have not taken up questions which seem to have importance only within the world of philosophy. For example the question of whether architecture is an art or a craft, is importantly problematic for readers of R.G. Collingwood, *The Principles of Art* (Oxford: Clarendon, 1938) chapter 2, but not for others. Where architecture is concerned it is the normal expectation that the design would be made by one person and the building work be carried out by another, so that the craftsmanship in a building is not to be directly attributable to the architect, whereas presumably the 'architecture' of the building is, so we do not find architects spending time on this question. Likewise, architecture and sculpture belong to different cultures. I assume that buildings are useful, but they do not stop being buildings when they stop being useful. Similarly sculpture remains sculpture, even if we find a use for it. The major work of analytic philosophy which takes architecture as its central concern is Roger Scruton, *The Aesthetics of Architecture* (London: Methuen, 1979). See also Nelson Goodman, 'How Buildings Mean' in *Critical Inquiry* (June 1985: 642–53); Arnold Berleant, *The Aesthetics of Environment* (Philadelphia: Temple University Press, 1992), the essays collected in *Architecture and Civilization*, Michael Mitias (ed.) (Amsterdam: Rodopi, 1999) including T.J. Diffey, 'Architecture, Art and Works of Art'; and the following essays collected in *The Journal of Architecture*, vol. IV, no. 1 (Spring 1999): Edward Winters, 'Architecture and Human Purposes' (pp. 1–8); John Haldane, 'Form, Meaning and Value' (pp. 9–20); Derek Matravers, 'Revising Principles of Architecture' (pp. 39–46) and Edward Winters, 'Architecture, Meaning and Significance', in *The Journal of Architecture*, vol. I, no. 1 (Spring 1996) pp. 39–47.

2   Thomas Nagel, *Other Minds* (Oxford University Press, 1995: 8–9); cited by Gary Gutting, *Pragmatic Liberalism and the Critique of Modernity* (Cambridge University Press, 1999: 2). Of course Nagel's own work is not mere arid technicality, as his colourful rhetorical style shows. See also Thomas Nagel, *The View From Nowhere* (Oxford University Press, 1986).

3   The idea of a contented Nietzsche is floated by Richard Rorty, 'Derrida and the Philosophical Tradition', in *Truth and Progress* (Cambridge University Press, 1998: 327).

4   Giovanni Papini, '*Il Pragmatismo Messo in Ordine*,' in *Leonardo* (Milan: April 1905: 47); cited by William James, 'What Pragmatism Means', in *Pragmatism: A New Name for Some Old Ways of Thinking* (1907) published in a single volume with its sequel, *The Meaning of Truth* (Cambridge, MA.: Harvard University Press, 1975: 32).

Commentary

The Nest and the Pillar of Fire

Andrew Ballantyne

> Whoever you are, go out into the evening,
> Leaving your room, of which you know each bit;
> Your house is the last before the infinite,
> Whoever you are.
>
> (Rilke, 1902: 21)

> There is some of the same fitness in a man's building his own house that there is in a
> bird's building its own nest. Who knows but if men constructed their dwellings with
> their own hands, and provided food for themselves and their families simply and
> honestly enough, the poetic faculty would be universally developed, as birds universally
> sing when they are so engaged?
>
> (Thoreau, 1854: 30–1)

> They set out . . . and all the time the Lord went before them, by day a pillar of cloud to
> guide them on their journey, by night a pillar of fire . . .
>
> (Exodus, XIII: 21–2)

WHAT IS IT, THIS 'ARCHITECTURE'?

'You think philosophy is difficult enough,' said Wittgenstein, 'but I can tell you it
is nothing to the difficulty of being a good architect' (Rhees, 1984: 126). This is
what architects have long suspected, and of all philosophers Wittgenstein has a
special place in their affections, because when he tried his hand at architecture
he took it seriously and worked, not as if he were an amateur indulging a merely
personal desire to build, but as a determined student out to discover the principles of the art. From his personal point of view his most important finding was
that architecture was not his vocation:

> Within all great art there is a WILD animal: tamed. [. . .] All great art has primitive
> human drives as its ground bass. They are not the melody [. . .] but are what gives the
> melody its depth & power.

[. . .] my house for Gretl is the product of a decidedly sensitive ear, good manners, the expression of great understanding (for a culture, etc.). But primordial life, wild life striving to erupt into the open – is lacking.

(Wittgenstein, 1980a: 43e)

For the reader of Wittgenstein's philosophical remarks there is sometimes a very clear sense of a wild animal lurking somewhere behind them – they have a trans-fixing intensity – and part of Wittgenstein's appeal as a personality is that he seems to have been so barely tamed by society and good manners (Figure C.1). With a few terse remarks, often stranded without the support of a formal argu-ment, he can strike at the nub of a matter, and one finds with the passage of time that the idea has lodged itself in the mind. He was sensitive to the effects of architecture and knew the *frisson* that can be felt on contact with great architec-ture, but he found that it simply was not there in the house which he had designed, with painstaking care, and so – characteristically – he walked away from the practice of architecture. So far as he was concerned, there was simply no point in him being an architect if he was not going to be a great architect.

Figure C.1
Ludwig Wittgenstein,
1889–1951.
Photo: Hulton-Getty.

Wittgenstein had the rare advantage for an architect of having fabulously wealthy relatives. The house for his sister Gretl was a palace – when she moved into it, she left a seventeenth-century mansion by Fischer von Erlach (Figures C.2 and C.3) – and it was in building the house that Wittgenstein had his architectural education, adjusting and reconsidering details on site, even after they had been built. Most architects learn in less extravagant ways, over a longer period, emerg-

Figure C.2
The house on the
Kundmanngasse that
Wittgenstein (working
with Paul Engelmann)
designed for his sister,
1926–8.
Photo: Margherita
Krischanitz.

Figure C.3
Johann Bernhard Fischer
von Erlach, Palais
Batthyány-Schönborn,
1698–1705. The house in
which Wittgenstein's
sister was living when she
commissioned his design.
Photo: Österreichische
Nationalbibliothek.

ing from their education with more modest expectations of what they might achieve, and persisting in architectural practice in the hope that eventually they will find the right sorts of commissions to allow them to develop their creative potential, perhaps hoping that one day a project as free and as well-endowed as Wittgenstein's first and only commission might come their way, but perhaps having given up on such a hope. In the meantime it is to be hoped that what they manage to do is to produce 'well-mannered' buildings – as a society, we would on the whole be pleased with them if they did. Such buildings might not be great architecture, and there might even be doubt about whether they would be architecture at all. 'Architecture is a gesture,' said Wittgenstein. 'Not every purposive movement of the human body is a gesture. Just as little as every functional building is architecture' (Wittgenstein, 1980a: 49e). This is precise and accurate. Buildings do not turn into architecture because they are big, or because they are expensive, but because they have some sort of cultural content – some sort of meaning. Diogenes' barrel was gestural, and so it can happily be counted as belonging to the realm of architecture, even though it was a very minimal dwelling indeed. I can eat in order to stop feeling hungry, or can offer a meal as a gesture of hospitality. In just the same way I can live conveniently but indifferently in an undistinguished house, or I can live in a house which says something about my values – about what kind of person I am. The second kind of house is clearly gestural, but, as Diogenes showed, the first can also be gestural if we have a mind to make it so. The Cynics identified with dogs, and his gesture in effect said that he placed himself no higher in the world than a dog. Few of us would care to follow him quite that far, but there is no doubt that his choice of dwelling said much about his personal values, and that was what it was intended to do. It is certainly possible for legally accredited architects to design properly functional buildings which have far less cultural significance than Diogenes' barrel, and which have less of a claim to be considered to be architecture; but on the other hand Wordsworth showed how the cottages of agricultural labourers in Westmorland could be understood as gestures. In such poems as 'The Ruined Cottage' (1797) and 'Michael' (1800) he presented the cottages as relics of the lives of their hard-working but poor inhabitants; and once they could be seen as the dwellings of heroic characters who every day set out to overcome the obstacles which nature sets in their way, then they changed from being scarcely noticeable hovels into 'vernacular architecture' – buildings which were understood as gestures of tenacity and determination (Figure C.4). What we think of as architecture at any given time will depend on our perspective, and what our culture has prepared us to expect.

The most famous attempt concisely to separate the buildings that count as architecture from the buildings which do not is at the opening of Nikolaus Pevsner's *Outline of European Architecture* (1943), where he said that

Figure C.4
Agricultural cottage,
1857, from *William
Grundy's English Views*.
Photo: Hulton-Getty.

A bicycle shed is a building; Lincoln Cathedral is a piece of architecture. Nearly everything that encloses space on a scale sufficient for a human being to move in is a building; the term architecture applies only to buildings designed with a view to aesthetic appeal.

(Pevsner, 1943: 15)

So his 'outline' is introduced as a story about high-status buildings – 'art' buildings – special buildings which are out of the ordinary run of things. It clearly excludes 'vernacular architecture' which may not have been designed with concerns for aesthetic appeal firmly in mind, even though we now, after Wordsworth, discover that for us vernacular buildings do have aesthetic appeal (Figure C.5). It was not the case that Pevsner did not appreciate 'ordinary' buildings; he certainly did, and the great undertaking that became the series *The Buildings of England* shows it. But by saying that the series documented 'buildings' rather than 'architecture' he avoided the problem set up in his earlier work, and had no need to judge which buildings qualified. He could put in whatever was of interest, whether or not he thought it was properly architecture. The *Outline of European Architecture* for the most part documents a succession of cathedrals and palaces.

By contrast, when Spiro Kostof set out to write a global history of architecture, he ended up with a much broader definition. Architecture as he defined it included everything which had been built, and so his history of architecture became 'the study of what we built' (Kostof, 1985). He included 'ordinary' buildings as well as special ones, but of course it was impossible to include every building – he still had to make judgements about what to put in and what to leave out. So the buildings which are included must have seemed to be in some

Figure C.5
A bicycle shed designed by Aldo Rossi. At an elementary school, Fagnano Olona, 1972. Illustration from *Aldo Rossi: Architect* (1987). Photo: Luigi Ghirri.

way culturally significant, either because they were special and remarkable (like the Great Pyramids in Egypt, or Hagia Sophia at Constantinople) or because they were typical and so helped to give a general idea of the ordinary buildings in a culture (represented for example by a public housing project under construction in Brooklyn). So we can hold on to the idea of cultural significance as something which separates 'mere' buildings from architecture – the actual fabric of buildings is not sufficient to make architecture of them, but the buildings turn into architecture when we feel that we should notice them and treat them with respect, and this can happen to any building. Architecture on this view is not something inherent in the buildings by themselves, but is a cultural matter which involves the buildings. We certainly think of some buildings of our own culture as being too ordinary to be worth noticing, but if we look at the same buildings from outside they might seem to be valuably ordinary – characteristic of our culture. If we have been a long way away from home for a while and return, then the general surroundings can have a new significance, which then fades as they revert to being the familiar background that we hardly notice but which is always there.

Kostof's definition of architecture was broad, but not the broadest possible. George Hersey has broadened it still further, by including not only what 'we' built, but also much else besides – anthills, beehives, various body parts and some molecules (Hersey, 1999). There is no reason why non-human 'buildings' should not have some cultural significance in architectural circles. If we can see an anthill as an expression of the amazing possibilities which result from collective ambition, then we can see it as a gesture, so we can see it as architecture. It does not matter what the ants thought, or even if they thought at all, any more than it matters what Wordsworth's heroes thought when they were building. By extension one can go on with Hersey to include the body parts, molecules and viruses, when they are seen in an 'architectural' way. If one hesitates to adopt his definition it is not because there is any illogicality in it, but for the practical reason that the category 'architecture' becomes unwieldy. At the point where it seems as if anything at all can be included, then the category becomes useless, which is to say meaningless. However if we talk about a beehive, say, as being architecture then there is a clear signal that we are thinking about the beehive in a particular way. Then, the category 'architecture' becomes not a pigeonhole into which we can put a set of objects, but something more like a point of view from which we can see a certain aspect of anything whatever (for beehive paranoia, see Ramírez, 1999). Hersey uses the word 'architecture' in this way. It is not meaningless for him (as it would be for Pevsner, if he were keeping to his definition) to speak of 'the architecture of the human body', for example – it involves conceptualising the body as if it were something designed, and gestural, and culturally significant, and one can certainly do that.

If Wittgenstein walked away from architecture on account of being unable to do any more with it than manage to be polite, then that is no reason for the rest of us to give up on the enterprise. Few of the buildings around us meet the demands which Wittgenstein sought (and failed) to exact from his own designs. Good manners are not civilisation's highest achievement, but they allow for admission into social discourse and are not to be despised. They should be expected as routine, but Roger Scruton, in his essay 'Architectural Principles in an Age of Nihilism' (Chapter 1) makes it clear that they are not to be taken for granted. His title carries an echo of Rudolf Wittkower's book *Architectural Principles in the Age of Humanism* (1949) about Renaissance architecture, which put mankind securely at the centre of the universe and value-systems. When did 'the age of nihilism' begin? Perhaps in 1882, when Nietzsche declared the death of God, as 'the greatest recent event' (Nietzsche, 1882: 279). For Nietzsche, nihilism – the awareness of the inherent meaninglessness of things – was not an end point for philosophy to reach, but a clearing of the decks so that philosophy could begin. The meaning which things have, is something that we humans have invested in them, and does not have the consequence of undermining the meaningfulness of humanity. Nietzsche presented the death of God as the lifting of a shadow, inaugurating the 'gay science', the joyous affirmation of Nietzsche's philosophy. It does not, on the face of it, seem immediately hostile to humanity as such, or to human values.

The principles set out in Scruton's essay might seem to be reactionary to avant-gardists in schools of architecture, but they will seem to be fairly common-sensical to most other people. The British planning system regulates the development of buildings, and is concerned with many things other than architectural style. However, where ordinary buildings in established settlements are concerned, it does its best to enforce a policy which is virtually described in Scruton's text, and – assuming reasonable levels of competence on both sides – the presentation of a design which met with his criteria would be understood and welcomed. Scruton's voice is not crying in the wilderness, but it would be lonely in a school of architecture. When architects' proposals for buildings are challenged, they usually feel that planning consent is being withheld from them by capricious philistines, but the planning system is supposed to be in place in order to represent the interests of the community (and one way in which architects can be persuasive is to demonstrate that the community supports a proposal). Nevertheless, a question which arises is: how can it be that the values of architects have grown to be so distinct from those of the wider community? Clearly the ideas of specialists who devote their lives to thinking about buildings might be more developed than the ideas of people who only think about buildings occasionally, but we would not expect them to be fundamentally out of kilter. It is understandable that people who think about how buildings are built will develop a different range of ideas from those who only use buildings and look at them, just as we expect that a joiner will have ways of thinking about timber that we do not have if we only make use of his furniture. But some aspects of current architectural culture so completely confound the expectations of common sense that it is clear that architects can have a radically different agenda. For example there was a story which circulated concerning the convention centre which was

Figure C.6
Peter Eisenman,
Convention Center,
Columbus, Ohio.
Photo: Eisenman
Architects.

built in Columbus, Ohio, to the designs of Peter Eisenman (who is the subject of Chapter 9, by David Goldblatt) (Figure C.6). Its walls are often not quite vertical, and its floors not quite horizontal – by design – the intention being to put in suspension the sense of the pull of gravity. It had the unanticipated effect of making people vomit. Now this might have been an unfortunate accidental side-effect of an architectural game which had been carried a little too far, but in fact the story is more interesting than that. When a journalist tried to track down somebody who had actually been made sea-sick by the building, and persisted in his inquiries, the architect eventually cracked and admitted that he had invented the story (Pollan, 1997: 68n.). The curious thing here is that the architect was circulating an untrue story which one might have thought that he would be trying to suppress. By some scale of values he was actually enhancing the reputation of his building by letting it be known that it was hostile to humanity.

Plainly this is an advanced and virulent case of nihilism. If Nietzsche could feel that the death of God liberated new, more human, values, then that moment was the dawn of a new stage of humanism (superhumanism, perhaps). But it was also – for those who were not persuaded by him – a moment which undermined crucial certainties, and it is for this group that nihilism takes hold from this point. However Eisenman's nihilism is of a different order altogether, seeking not to promote but to negate human values, not creating new meaning, but dramatising meaninglessness. There will be more to say about him later. We could see Nietzsche, formed by an older age and older values, inaugurating an age of nihilism, and Eisenman as a child of that age, being formed by its values.

Through it all, however, architecture remains gestural, whether the gesture signifies stability or meaninglessness, tenacity or flexibility. As the price of admission into polite society, we can – by way of the planning committees – exact decent manners, but in the best architecture we expect to find more than that: we should sense that beyond the politeness there is raw vitality, passionate and instinctive – the wild animal, tamed. The building which is shaped merely by the exercise of refined taste is feeble and innocuous. The sense of the wild in buildings comes from them carrying cultural memories of caves and shells, primitive huts and cliff faces. At one end of the scale we have the nest, as a modest and comforting place to snuggle down and feel at home; at the other we have the extravagant pyre which consumes vast resources, and fills us with awe. This is the inspirational architecture which does not sustain us, but consumes whatever we can feed it. We admire it and stand back in amazement, and probably do not stop to think why it is that these achievements are so exceptional, but in their development they fly in the face of the everyday common sense that informs the economical nest. It is as if this sort of architecture has its sights on a further horizon, and takes its guidance not from the circumstances close at hand, but from a visionary guide, such as the pillar of fire that guided the Israelites through the desert. Each end of the scale needs its own set of values, and each needs to be in touch with its own wild primordial life.

DASEIN AND DECEIT

In architecture the link between life and art can be so strong that one can see them as fused so that we learn to see buildings as good when they make possible the good lives of their inhabitants. This has been a strong and persuasive line of thought, from Winckelmann's eulogies of ancient Greek culture, to Wittgenstein's assertion that ethics and aesthetics are one and the same (Wittgenstein, 1961: 71, 6.421). David Hume had made "taste" the basis of both his critical and his moral theory – it 'gives the sentiment of beauty and deformity, vice and virtue' (Hume, 1777a: 294). Heidegger's lyrical evocations of simple tasks make it clear that he too belongs in this company. He is an important influence on current architectural debate, but when we turn our attention to his great practical misjudgement in joining the Nazi party, we may be motivated to try to dissolve the link, so that we do not feel obliged to repudiate the philosophy on account of the politics. Some architects, for example Philip Johnson, have sought to argue that architectural aesthetics and politics are distinct from one another, but this argument is untenable because, if a perception of the political aspect of a building colours my feelings about the building, then it is part of my aesthetic response, whatever the architect's intentions and convictions might have been. When we encounter buildings then we find them in connection with the life that inhabits them, and an aesthetic response seems less than satisfying if it does not acknowledge the existence of that life and the building's role in it. However, the relationship between the building and the life within is not a relation of cause and effect. The building is a tool, for which a variety of uses might be found.

The question then turns into the problem of whether it is possible to design buildings which cannot be put to use in malign ways, and the answer is probably no, because the uses cannot be anticipated by the designer. The relationship is a particular instance of a more general principle developed by Gilles Deleuze, who not only saw ideas as tools, but who valued 'nomadism', by which he meant moving between sets of ideas, being inhabited by new *personae*, continually developing and making afresh. A rhetoric of mobility and often playful invention encourages a revaluation which can allow the free play of ideas, including even Heideggerian ideas, while effectively resisting the lure of Heidegger's 'blood and soil' nostalgia.[1]

Heidegger wrote his essay 'Building, Dwelling, Thinking' in 1951 (published 1954) when Europe was in ruins and modernism was firmly established among architects as the way forward for post-war reconstruction in Europe. The architects' concerns, in expressing their enthusiasm for an architecture which was 'universal' in its avoidance of the idiosyncrasies of local cultures, could hardly have been more different from Heidegger's concerns in his essay, which drew on his rootedness in the rural culture of south-west Germany – Baden-Würtemburg – in addressing the questions: 'What is it to dwell?' and 'How does building belong to dwelling?'. He answered to the effect that one dwells when one is properly engaged with one's place in the world, having a sense of the heavens and the earth, gods and mortals. The modern world in his view had lost its sense of dwelling, so that modern urban life had lost its 'authenticity'. '*The real plight of dwelling* does not lie merely in a lack of houses,' he wrote, 'The real dwelling plight lies in this, that mortals ever search anew for the nature of dwelling, that they *must ever learn to dwell*.' And learning to dwell is primarily about thinking, rather than having a house, because 'as soon as man *gives thought* to his home-lessness, it is a misery no longer' (Heidegger, 1954: 161). 'Homelessness' here is not a condition of being without a roof, but of not feeling 'at home' in the house which one has. 'Dwelling' is something that mortals do, and can fail to do despite having a house. For an example of an authentic building he turns to an old farmhouse from the region where he himself belonged:

> The nature of building is letting dwell. Building accomplishes its nature in the raising of locations by the joining of their spaces. Only if we are capable of dwelling, only then can we build. Let us think of a farmhouse in the Black Forest, which was built some two hundred years ago by the dwelling of peasants. Here the self-sufficiency of the power to let earth and heaven, divinities and mortals enter in simple oneness into things, ordered the house. It placed the farm on the wind-sheltered mountain slope looking south, among the meadows close to the spring. It gave it the wide overhanging shingle roof whose proper slope bears up under the burden of snow, and which, reaching deep down, shields the chambers against the storms of the long winter nights. It did not forget the altar corner behind the community table; it made room in its chamber for the

hallowed places of childbed and the 'tree of the dead' – for that is what they call a coffin there: the Totenbaum – and in this way it designed for the different generations under one roof the character of the journey through time.

(Heidegger, 1954: 160)

The word 'building' is used in his essay in a way which seems to make it carry some of the connotations of 'home' (as distinct from 'house') so that the act of authentic 'building' which brought the farmhouse into being is informed by a knowledge of 'dwelling', in a way which would not be normal in, say, the commercially produced housing of the city. The inauthentic building gives rise to an unhomely house, which is not quite a dwelling. Heidegger's particular word for human 'being' was *Dasein* – which was formed from the more general 'Being' or '*Sein*'. Whereas '*Sein*' straightforwardly translates into English as 'Being', '*Dasein*' has no direct one-word equivalent, but translates as 'being-there', having in it an idea of place – so '*Dasein*' has connotations of being-in-the-world, of having been culturally shaped and being in society, being in position, being at home, dwelling (Heidegger, 1926).[2] In 1923 Heidegger had an isolated cabin built at Todtnauberg in the Black Forest, which is where he habitually went to write. It was traditional in form, and he took no close interest in the design, leaving the project in his wife's hands (Safranski, 1994: 129). What mattered to him was that he experienced as perfect the fit between the house and what went on in it. The house participates in dwelling. The life and the built fabric work together, to make a state of mind, a state of human being – *Dasein*, 'being-there', rooted in the culture of the place (Figures 4.1–4.4).

Heidegger's ideas are caught up with politics in a particularly problematic way, because despite having a reputation as one of the twentieth century's greatest philosophers, he nevertheless supported the Nazis, which inevitably leads one to question how close is the link between the philosophy and the politics.[3] Politics encompasses all relations between people, at any scale of operation. The same attitudes that we develop in dealing with people at a personal level can be put into play in institutional structures where they can have a more far-reaching effect – the personal is political. Would Heidegger's philosophy, translated up to the scale of the state, have evil results? Many people whose politics are not what Heidegger's were have found his ideas fruitful, notably and crucially Hannah Arendt (Safranski, 1994). However if one insists on the complete separation of the philosophy from politics then one is left asking: *what is the point* of a philosophy that does not guide one away from the most terrible evils? It is not *necessary* to move from Heidegger's philosophy to his politics, but plainly there is nothing in his philosophy to *prevent* one from making that move, and indeed the whole tenor of the writing is to make links between universal principles and everyday activity, so that the sky and the earth are caught up in the most mundane actions, such as pouring water from a jug.

Where architecture is concerned a similar question arises, because Hitler had clear ideas about what sort of architecture he wished to encourage, and when it was not grandiloquently monumental (as in Speer's projects for Berlin) then it was vernacular – *volkstümlich* – from exactly the same mould as the architecture which Heidegger found 'authentic'. What we absolutely cannot say is that vernacular architecture leads the people who occupy it towards Nazi politics: elsewhere vernacular architecture was romanticised in comparable ways, but the effects were perfectly benign. Nevertheless the Nazis have become so emblematic of evil that it can sometimes be the case that anything they approved can be portrayed as bad. So can there be a link between aesthetics and politics?

The term 'aesthetics' derives from Alexander Baumgarten's book *Aesthetica* of 1750, and the root of its meaning is in the Greek word for perceptions and feelings. From early in its modern career 'aesthetics' has encompassed not only beauty but also the sublime – which is awe-inspiring and thrilling, but is closely related to pain and perhaps fear (Ashfield and de Bolla, 1996; Burke, 1757; Dixon, 1995). A discussion about the aesthetics of buildings is a discussion about the perceptions which buildings prompt us to have (which may or may not be pleasurable) and an analysis of why it is that we have them. The reasons why particular buildings prompt particular feelings may be relatively straightforward, but they are often made complex because a number of factors interfere with one another, so that our pleasure in one aspect is set in opposition to our distaste for another. The case of politics is considered, for example, in Diane Ghirardo's essay, 'The Architecture of Deceit' (Chapter 2), in which she argues that in the design studio the resolution of architectural form should not be discussed in isolation from politics. Decisions about the form of buildings certainly can have political consequences, but they are often unforeseen. We can enjoy the broad straight boulevards of Paris, and the life they support, without necessarily noticing that some of them were introduced in order to prevent the setting up of barricades. Nevertheless, the political content is there if we take note of it. While one cannot say that the more 'politically correct' a building is, the better it is as architecture, nevertheless if a building's political role is repugnant, then that can interfere with the appreciation of the building's formal qualities so as to complicate our response. It is certainly possible to insist that political concerns be entirely excluded from consideration in responding to the building. We might or might not perceive them, depending on whether or not we have learnt about them, and so we can certainly exclude them from discussion. However if we do know about them, and do perceive them, then they can colour our feelings in significant ways, and deliberately excluding them seems to cauterise a perfectly proper and immediate response. The attitude is at least uncomfortable, and perhaps very immoral, not on account of the form of the buildings, but on account of their political 'content', which has a real effect on the way people feel about buildings. When it does so, then it is therefore a necessary part of an account of their aesthetics, but equally clearly the interpretation is not inherent in the buildings. It can shift, as happened in Dublin, where Georgian buildings were once seen as a legacy of British imperial rule, and were neglected, but now that they are seen as the craftwork of Irish builders, they are carefully restored and maintained

We can never know the thing which is purely 'the building in itself', because we approach it by way of the mental apparatus which we already have established and which we bring to bear on it – this is something we can learn from Heidegger – and if in my mind there is an idea which brings about a will to repudiate the building then that idea really is there and cannot be denied me. If my mind is configured in this way, then the feeling will be immediate and will feel instinctual. *Dasein* is always inflected by the circumstances of its acculturation: human being is experienced by way of the categories through which we have our experiences, and if we have developed a sense of 'the political' then this is one of our categories of experience. The sense of primordial 'oneness' – the sense of the connectedness of every part of life, of which Heidegger speaks, and which he associated with ancient Greece – is deeply satisfying, and was first drawn into aesthetics by Winckelmann in his rapturous appreciation of every aspect of the life and art of ancient Greece, when (he imagined) educated men lived in close daily contact with nature (Winckelmann, 1774). Although it has its roots in Neoclassicism, the way of thinking has been allied with various architectural styles, and has been inspirational, for example, in the nineteenth-century Gothic Revival and modernism (Watkin, 1977); and something of the sort certainly appealed to Wittgenstein (Wittgenstein, 1961: 71, 6.421). However, while this appreciation of oneness seems to belong to a state of heightened awareness, there is often, in practice, no noticeable connection, so we feel comfortable with admiring the forms of the ruins of Imperial Rome, without necessarily wanting to adopt the way of life of the ancient Romans.

We are ready enough to separate the political and aesthetic in considering works of the remote past, but still feel uncomfortable with an architect who positively declares himself prepared to embrace evil in order to be able to put up buildings that he believes can be aesthetically good. 'I'd work for the devil himself,' said Philip Johnson (Cook and Klotz, 1973: 36); and moreover by his account it was the aesthetic appeal of blond young men in black leather which led him to join the Nazis in the 1930s, and not the politics, of which he seems to have been quite ignorant (Schultze, 1994: 90). Johnson's example forcibly makes the point that the political plane and the aesthetic plane can be seen as distinct. The paradox we face with Heidegger is that whereas his ideas tend to make inseparable the architecture and the politics, nevertheless the unacceptability of the politics leads one into feeling the will to make some such separation in the case of his ideas, constructing a firewall between one and the other as Johnson did; but were one to do so then one would be rejecting Heidegger's vision of the unity of art and life.

Heidegger's romantic attachment to the life of the Black Forest peasant corresponds with Winckelmann's no less romantic account of the life of the ancient Athenian aristocrat, in which the inseparability of different aspects of the ancient Greek way of life meant that even commonplace activities acquired a sacred grace. The gymnastic exercises, which gave young men their grace of movement, and the physique which so caught Winckelmann's imagination, have a parallel in the daily wood-chopping in which Heidegger engaged when he was at his cabin. He hardly ever travelled outside his own region, but supposed that the ancient Greeks had similar feelings to his own in response to their landscape. The Greek temple plays an important role in his essay 'The Origin of the Work of Art', in which it is seen as instrumental in shaping experience of the world (being-in-the-world, *Dasein*).

> The temple, in its standing there, first gives to things their look and to men their outlook on themselves. This view remains as long as the work is a work, as long as the god has not fled from it. It is the same with the sculpture of the god, votive offering of the victor in the athletic games. It is not a portrait whose purpose is to make it easier to realize how the god looks; rather, it is a work that lets the god himself be present and thus is the god himself.
>
> (Heidegger, 1950: 43)

Heidegger was so intensely involved with a romantic idea of Greece that when he had the chance to go there, he twice cancelled the arrangements, in case a visit to the real Greece broke the spell (Safranski, 1994: 401–3). He did eventually visit, but not until 1962, long after his views on the place had been formed, and by the time he did so it was less to learn about the place, than to see whether it lived up to his expectations – and much of it did not. Heidegger came knowing he should experience certain feelings, and when he did not feel them, he blamed the invasion of modern activity. However he was thrilled with the island of Delos – the name of which translates as 'the manifest, the apparent' – mainly because it was deserted, and he could sense the *absence* of the fled gods (Safranski, 1994: 402). His close knowledge of Greek philosophy helped him to sustain an impression of intimate rapport, in the same way that Winckelmann managed to sustain and communicate his rapt enthusiasm for an illusion of ancient Greek life, formed on the basis of knowledge of Roman statues. Heidegger's mystical evocations of the spirit of place came from Romanticism, and are not to be found in ancient writings, but he projected these ideas back on to the ancients, and when he went to Greece he found what he had determined to find.[4] The idea that buildings have a rapport with 'earth' – which in Heidegger is an important and loaded term – is not inherently dangerous; but in Heidegger's world, in his day, the idea of a culture being rooted in earth carried with it ideas of racial purity. For example, explaining what painting should be about, F.A. Kauffmann, a Nazi art theorist, wrote:

> When there is so much sensibility related to the earth in which we are rooted, it is only natural for us to see our occupation with landscape as the purest of artistic endeavours. . . . For us today the landscape represents the territory of the Reich which demands our dutiful dedication. . . . German painting today attempts to emphasize healthy physical roots, the biological worth of the individual and the renewal of nation and spirit.
>
> (Kauffmann, 1941)

To transfer this agenda into architecture results very straightforwardly in a preoccupation with the links between the people and the soil, and Heidegger's rumi-
nations start to alarm because they were completely in tune with Nazi ideology.
It is easy to set aside misgivings about Roman politics in our appreciation of
Roman architecture, because the Roman gods fled long ago, and there is no
question that they would return if we tried to behave like Romans. The same
cannot be said in the case of the Nazis – their ideas if acted upon today might
still have the same effects – and therefore we feel more anxiety. Theodor Adorno
attacked Heidegger's *Sein und Zeit* as a mystification of the prejudices which
gave rise to Nazism (Adorno, 1964). Romanticism nourished Nazi ideology, and
gave grounds for the suspension of reason in favour of intuition and commitment. But this was not a necessary consequence: other nations had their versions
of romanticism, and did not follow a similar line of development. 'It is nothing
new,' said Adorno, 'to find that the sublime becomes the cover for something
low' (Adorno, 1964: xxi), but Heidegger in his cabin certainly found the wild
primordial life of which Wittgenstein so keenly felt the lack in the polished neighbourhoods of Vienna.

In 1914 Wittgenstein had built himself a house, as small and as remote as
Heidegger's would be. It was perched on a steep slope above a Norwegian lake,
and could be reached only by water. It was the only house he ever owned (Figure
C.7). He moved into it in the spring of 1914 and had left it by July, his return
postponed by war and other wanderings (Wijdeveld, 1994: 30). It is clear that
Wittgenstein's involvement with his house was very different from Heidegger's;
in practical ways he was rather more involved with it – designing details himself –
but it did not become absorbed into his thinking to anything like the same
degree. He seems to have chosen the spot because there were no distractions
there and he could think about his philosophical work. It was remote from the
Viennese *haute-bourgoisie*, in whose culture he had been formed, and there is
no sense of him going there in order to be more fully 'at home' in any sense
(Wijdeveld, 1994: 30). Indeed when he returned there in 1937 he could not face
the prospect of staying there alone. He had found it charming before, but now it
was alien and *unheimlich* (Monk, 1991: 374). He stayed in nearby lodgings until
the prospect of the arrival of his friend Francis Skinner made it possible to face
the idea – a year after his first arrival – and had left Norway four months later.
He briefly returned shortly before his death, but again spent more time in the
lodgings (Monk, 1991: 574). The relationship with the dwelling was not comfortable and contented – indeed in Heidegger's terms Wittgenstein never did
learn to dwell. He could, had he chosen, have lived in a palace along the lines of
the one he designed for his sister, but instead he gave his money away and lived
ascetically – a gesture which has given him an almost saintly reputation. In the
house for his sister he was obsessive about the details of the architecture – refin-
ing proportions, radiators, and the mechanisms for opening doors and windows
– but not about the building's 'grounding', which was so important to Heidegger (*Grund/Boden*). If we read his behaviour as gestural, then nothing indicates a

Figure C.7
Wittgenstein's house in
Norway.
Photo: Michael Nedo.

search for rootedness, but for something more mobile. He certainly wanted to be free from distractions and encumbrances when he was working but nothing in his actions looks like 'bonding' with a particular place.

Michel de Certeau (Chapter 3) uses the terms 'place' and 'space' in a way that helps to articulate this distinction.[5] Both Heidegger and Wittgenstein chose similar places for their small isolated dwellings, but their spatial practices were different. The 'place' is the physical fabric – of the land and the building – whereas the 'space' involves activity (including mental activity). So places are physical whereas spaces are phenomenal, and so on. The fabric of a building is in itself a place, but a building as experienced is spatial. Both 'building' and 'dwelling' in Heidegger's terminology are spatial in de Certeau's sense. Clearly there is a link between places and spaces – each place allows or prevents certain sorts of activity, so there is a limit to the variety of kinds of spaces it can be – and places can be designed and modified in order to accommodate an anticipated range of practices. The distinction is useful in considering architecture because it allows us to separate out things that are normally fused together when we use a building. The house is an instrument, which is designed in order to make possible a certain way of life, but as with any implement, the house can be used in ways that were not anticipated at the time it was made. A place can be used in new spatial practices (some of them perhaps not imagined until long after it was built) as can any tool. For example Kenneth Halliwell murdered the playwright Joe Orton by smashing his skull with a hammer, but that does not make hammers per se murderous. The hammer is, in de Certeau's sense, a 'place', whereas hammering nails and skulls are very distinct spatial practices, with very different emotional investments and practical consequences. In just the same way the peasant's cabin in the woods is a place, whereas its Nazification is a spatial practice. The ethics of spatial practices do not inhere in a building, any more than they inhere in a hammer, but there is ethical content in spatial practice, and there are spatial practices in dwelling. Moreover, although the building (place) is not the same thing as the spatial practices in which it is implicated, nevertheless it is not entirely separate from them. It makes them possible.

If a building were designed precisely so as to make possible spatial practices which we abhor, then it is the normal practice to feel that the building itself is tainted, and rather than convert the building to another use, we might feel that something inhered in the building which would make it preferable for the building to be demolished. For many people, Albert Speer's projects for Berlin are tainted in this way – not all have been demolished, and the most grandiloquent were never built (Canetti, 1976; Dovey, 1999). On the other hand we have buildings such as Schinkel's Altes Museum, which was pressed into service by the Nazis to provide a backdrop appropriate to rallies. Speer hero-worshipped Schinkel, but neither Schinkel nor his buildings have – in the long run – been irredeemably tainted by the association (Sereny, 1995: 144; Wilson, 1992: 42–4).

It is unlikely that it would be possible to develop an architecture which simply could not allow itself to be pressed into the service of evil. It might be possible to put obstacles in the way of some types of behaviour, but one could not anticipate every possibility, and in any case the particular form of a building can be unimportant in the scheme of spatial practices. Heidegger's cabin was not exceptional, but was rooted in a local culture in much the same way as many other traditional buildings around the world, and enforced deracination would cause more problems than it solved. Nevertheless there is something to be said for sacrificing Heidegger's poetic sense of grounding, to aim for something more like Wittgenstein's cosmopolitanism, which escaped the claims of territory and possessions.

Jean-François Lyotard has argued along these lines in '*Domus* and Megalopolis' (Lyotard, 1988; see also Chapter 4, especially p. 92). We cannot abolish 'places', but we can cultivate a cosmopolitan relationship with them. Places do not move, but *we* can. However, when we move we often take our spatial practices with us – as does the business traveller, who goes around the world staying in four-star hotels, or as did Elvis Presley in his years of decline, when he would tour, staying in hotels, but the rooms would be remodelled in advance of his arrival, so as to make the same configurations of space as he had at home – the Graceland mansion. His furniture would arrive, and he could unwind after his performances in surroundings which were completely familiar and comforting.[6] Few people have the resources for such an enterprise, which seems self-indulgent, even before we find out that the room in question, 'The Jungle Room', was an example of particularly lurid *kitsch*. This mobile 'place' sprang from a sentimental base close to Heidegger's 'dwelling', but is remote from any normal idea of 'authenticity'. The repeatedly reconstituted Jungle Room was developed from a grounding in a popular value-system, working beyond its normal limits only because it could draw on resources which were vast in comparison with what was normally available to Tennessee *volk*.

A more radical sort of nomadism would be to change our spatial practices, and then it is possible to become nomadic after a fashion while remaining in one place – as the philosopher Gilles Deleuze did. Deleuze's philosophical work represents a thoroughgoing repudiation of many of Heidegger's values. *Anti-Oedipus*, which he wrote with Félix Guattari, can be read as inculcating an ethics of resistance to fascism (Foucault, in Deleuze and Guattari, 1972: xiii). Deleuze advocated intellectual 'nomadism', but actually lived in the same apartment in Paris for many years. The type of nomadism that was important to him did not entail changing his physical position, but was a matter of living with ever-changing concepts, rather than adhering immovably to a permanent core of *dogmata*. What counts here is not so much a mobility between places, as a mobility between cultures and identities, so that, for example, philosophical *personae* are adopted and abandoned. His idea of the philosopher is of someone looking for wisdom, in contrast with the oriental sage, who possesses and dispenses wisdom (Deleuze and Guattari, 1991). Deleuze's preoccupation with freedom and invention contrasts starkly with Heidegger's sage-like demeanour, described in Karl Jaspers' report to the committee which examined whether or not Heidegger should be allowed to lecture after 1945:

> Heidegger's mode of thinking, which seems to me to be fundamentally unfree,
> dictatorial and uncommunicative, would have a very damaging effect on students of the
> present time. And the mode of thinking itself seems to me more important than the
> actual content of political judgements [. . .] I think it would be quite wrong to turn such

a teacher loose on the young people of today [. . .] First of all the young must be taught how to think for themselves.

(Karl Jaspers, quoted by Ott, 1994: 339 and Safranski, 1994: 341)

The mode of thinking is the issue; not the ideas themselves, but the ways in which they were put to use. 'A theory is exactly like a box of tools,' said Deleuze (in Foucault, 1977: 208) and he saw the crucial practice of the philosopher as being the invention of concepts (Deleuze, 1962: 107; Deleuze and Guattari, 1991: 2). His practice in his books was to show historically how concepts had been formed, because it is at the moment of their invention that one understands them most clearly (one sees at that point what it was that they were invented to do). He would then show how they could be freed from their original context and put to use in other ways. He would also invent new concepts, and claim that this was the oldest and most traditional role of the philosopher – it was what Plato did (though he taught the opposite – Deleuze and Guattari, 1991: 6). Deleuze developed this view from reading Nietzsche, who said that philosophers 'must no longer accept concepts as a gift, . . . but first make and create them' (Deleuze and Guattari, 1991: 5; Nietzsche, 1901: 409). The view of the instrumentality of concepts is equally associated with the 'pragmatism' of Charles Sanders Peirce and William James, for whom likewise theories became instruments, rather than permanent answers to eternal problems. Rather than teaching final truths, James would give directions as to how to find truths – perhaps how to *make* truths (James, 1907: 32).

If we try to apply this kind of thinking to ethical and political ideas about architecture then we can see that there could certainly be ethical and unethical ways to build, and ethical and unethical ways to dwell. But it is not possible to say that the fabric of the building is of itself ethical or unethical, because in the plane of ethics it does nothing – it is an instrument which might or might not be useful, and which could be used to good or bad ends. The *production* of a building could be unethical, for example if it depended on slave labour, but an identical building produced by ethical means would be no better *in itself* – as a place it would be indistinguishable. One would want to reform the spatial practices of production, rather than the form of the building. However, if it were expressly designed to support a reprehensible way of life, then 'places' and 'spaces' would seem to collapse together and the interaction of fabric and activity could seem to be so much more important than the distinction between them that it would in practice seem pedantic, frivolous or immoral to insist that the distinction can be made. In the circumstances it would not be the most pressing point to make. We are faced with such questions when we re-use historic buildings. It seems to be beside the point to ask about the working conditions of the original builders, and we would in no way feel obliged to demolish and start afresh because they took risks which would be unacceptable under current legislation for health and safety at work. It is more ethical, more 'green', to re-use a sound old building than start again with new materials.

The same distinction can be made between the building's fabric and the practices of dwelling, but if we make the kind of link which Heidegger did between places and spaces, in asserting the oneness of *Dasein*, seeing 'dwelling' as the spatial practice of being-in-place, then they are indeed fused and the practices are phenomenally experienced as part of the place. The separation is maintained, however, in the nomadic or cosmopolitan experience – one's identity is not then permanently implicated in the place, but is mobile and can be practised wherever one happens to be; and it is not necessary actually to move about from one place to another in order to maintain this way of living. One lives in any-place-whatever, which might, for practical purposes, as chance has it, always happen to be the same place. It saves the business of having to move from one dwelling to another, which is troublesome, given the way our society is constituted. Perhaps the clearest gesture of immobile deracination was that made by Jean-Paul Sartre in choosing to live in a hotel room and work in cafés. He did not as a matter of principle move round from one hotel to another, but demonstrated a cosmopolitan mode of dwelling, as surely as Diogenes had done.

The lyric charge that Heidegger found in the practices of dwelling and everyday life is certainly to be valued; but in his rhetoric it was associated with the romance of blood and soil which are implicated in finding legitimacy in the autochthonous. Heidegger considered dwelling and building as spatial practices, and saw them as implicated in and formed by culture, so that they lacked authenticity if they became disconnected – particularly if they lost touch with the primordial. In Richard Rorty's view, much of Heidegger's thought can be read as pragmatic and instrumentalist (Rorty, 1991) but with Rorty and other Pragmatists, especially John Dewey, there is a very clear link between their philosophical ideas and politics of emancipation and liberation, and so the writings work to encourage the qualities that Karl Jaspers found to be lacking in Heidegger. Gilles Deleuze also saw philosophy as a matter of creation and invention, rather than disclosure, and developed fluid ways of thinking about personal and interpersonal identities (micropolitics) and about nomadic engagements with our surroundings. This can translate into a culture of mobility and diversity, which involves changing ourselves as much as it involves changing the places we happen to occupy. In such thinkers one finds ways of thinking that are as sophisticated and as developed as Heidegger's, indeed sharing many ideas with him; but in their presentation the ideas come with some means of resistance to his political shortcomings.

DOMESTICITIES

When we look at a culture from outside then it is the most ordinary things that seem most noteworthy and significant for the understanding of that culture, because they are so closely involved with the way of life. The instructions for household cleaning that punctuate Chuck Palahniuk's novel *Survivor*, for example, are sometimes astonishingly meticulous, and sometimes deadpan outlandish. 'I move all the furniture a little and put ice in the little divots left in the carpet. As the ice melts, the matted divots will fluff back up' (p. 219). 'To get blood off piano keys, polish them with talcum powder or powdered milk' (p. 269). The cleaning instructions are used as a means to build an atmosphere of menace, suggesting unseen violence as part of the domestic scene, that is both lurid and commonplace. In my own culture I am for the most part unaware of the daily habits of my routine, and they are all the more revealing for the fact that I perform them unselfconsciously. As children, it is only when we visit a household other than our own, that we realise with fascination that things could be other than they are at home. The different types of vernacular architecture from around the world have developed partly as a response to different climates and the local availability of different materials, but also, importantly, in connection with their own varied cultures – different ways of life, different bodies of knowledge and value-systems (Oliver, 1997; Rapoport, 1969). A culture does not need to be on the other side of the world from us for it to seem exotic. All that is required for it to be noticeably separate is that people do things differently there, so the past is equally a foreign country (Hartley, 1953), and distinct cultures can grow up in different ranks of society occupying the same geographical region – as Disraeli colourfully showed in *Sybil; or, The Two Nations* (1845) where the rich and the poor led such completely different kinds of lives. Indeed now that we live in a self-consciously 'multicultural' society, we expect to come into contact with different cultures in the course of our daily lives, and to be able to recognise characteristic patterns of behaviour in the different settings which we move between. Having once noticed that other ways of living are possible, we can turn back and reflect on the ways in which our own lives are ordered by our habits and contact with familiar surroundings.

The philosopher C.S. Peirce analysed three active elements in the world: chance, law and habit (Brent, 1998: 4), and we can see how, in different cultures, chance circumstances and laws have interacted with patterns of behaviour to shape the habits of a culture. These unconsidered, more or less automatic responses, play a very significant role in our lives. If we live entirely within the repertoire of our accustomed ways of behaving, our familiar spatial practices, then we will feel securely 'at home' – we will not be faced with puzzles which we have to figure out before we can get on with our lives; we will not feel challenged, and we will not really have to 'think' at all, but will be able to deal with each situation as it arises on the basis of the ingrained and unconscious memory of other similar experiences. This is the basis of 'common sense', which feels perfectly normal and everyday. The everyday environment in which we live is constituted through repetition and recognition. We know how to behave because we have successfully behaved in that way before; our habits can become entrenched, and when they do so then they shape our behaviour as firmly as solid walls. Our habitat is habit-generated: there are things we do, and things we don't – barriers we respect and others which some people seem to respect but we don't. Indeed not only our surroundings but also our identities are constituted by habit: 'we are habits, nothing but habits – the habit of saying "I"' (Deleuze, 1953: x). We have a habit of forming habits. At a personal level we would describe habitual behaviour as routine – and we need to have some elements of our lives as routine, so that we are not exhausted and disorientated by ever-shifting circumstances in which we would never be able to act with confidence. Immanuel Kant was particularly notorious for the exactness of the repetitions in his routine, which presumably left his mind free to be exhilarated by the boldness of his intellectual speculations (Scruton, 1982: 5–6; De Quincey, 1863). If we ask ourselves what we have done, then we tend to think of the exceptional things – travel to extraordinary places, bereavements, falling in love – and neglect to think of our routines, remembering only the points of crisis when they are suspended or disrupted. Everyday life is the part of our life about which we think least, but it does much to constitute us, by way of habits of behaviour and the habits of mind, which exclude some possibilities and enforce others. If we organise our lives in the way that Kant organised his, then we hardly have to think about our routine at all. Montaigne described very eloquently how habit insinuates itself and turns into something inflexible which can become oppressive.

> Habit is a violent and treacherous schoolteacher. Gradually and stealthily she slides her authoritative foot into us; then, having by this gentle and humble beginning planted it firmly within us, helped by time she later discloses an angry tyrannous countenance, against which we are no longer allowed even to lift up our eyes.
>
> (Montaigne, 1588: 122)

However, if we also inculcate the habit of not 'lifting up our eyes', and accept the habit, then the strictest rules can be the most liberating, simply because one does not spend time thinking about whether or not they might be obeyed – they must be obeyed, there is no question of it. St Benedict's rules for monastic life are either intolerable, or else they bring peace of mind on account of their precise instructions about what the monks must think and do without murmuring (Benedict, 547). The buildings with which we are most closely involved in a routine way are domestic, and the feelings which we have about our own dwellings are very strong, but in the ordinary course of events they generally pass unconsidered. It is when the routine of everyday life is disrupted that the attachment becomes most evident to us. If a stranger crosses the threshold uninvited then we feel that something important has been violated and it will take a while to feel altogether secure once again, even if the stranger came and went while we were out, and stole nothing. Anyone who has been burgled knows that it is not the loss of goods which is really affecting, but the sense of insecurity, which can undermine self-confidence and change the way we behave – for a while at least. It is the received wisdom of our age that moving house is one of the most stressful life events which most people undergo, exceeded only by divorce. Why is it that we feel this way? Presumably on account of the fact that we have been in such close contact with the house, especially if we have chosen the way it is furnished and decorated, and if we are responsible for its state of cleanliness and tidiness. All sort of attitudes and anxieties are brought to bear on household cleaning, and they are highly personal – for example obsessive cleanliness can be read as an equivalent of sexual frigidity – and they are in place at a level much deeper than reason, so the attitudes are difficult to shake off (Horsfield, 1997). The individual may behave in a reasonable manner, but may be haunted by guilt and shame when housework is neglected, and rewarded with a glow of satisfaction when it is done. Nigella Lawson claims that a habit of baking turns one into – or at least makes one feel like – a domestic goddess, reinventing the role of the fulfilled housewife as a source of deep-seated pleasure, making it sound hedonistic and camp (Lawson, 2000). Kathleen Anne McHugh explores such experiences in her book *American Domesticity*, from which 'The Metaphysics of Housework' is extracted (Chapter 5). She mentions a film, *Semiotics of the Kitchen*, in which the uses of kitchen implements are demonstrated to camera in a violent and exaggerated way, 'abstractly expressing the rage generated by housework' (McHugh, 1999: 179).[7] The household's maintenance exacts a strong emotional investment – and because it does so, a strong emotional bond develops. The things we love most tend to be the things which cost us most, if not in cash then in effort. It is possible to make links between the architecture of a house and the work which is generated in it. A dwelling like Mies Van Der Rohe's house for Edith Farnsworth at Plano, Illinois, is plainly exacting in the demands it makes – its floor to ceiling wrap-around windows and the spareness of the furnishing make it imperative that it be kept immaculately clean and tidy. Any clutter anywhere would be visible and intrusive, and neglect of the window cleaning would change the degree of transparency and the way the whole building looked. By contrast an over-furnished Victorian drawing room could accommodate a great deal of additional clutter without the overall aesthetic being compromised in the least, and although it would take much more cleaning to maintain it as absolutely sterile, it would never actually have been kept at that pitch of cleanliness, which was not so critically necessary to the way it looked. The grate would be blacked, the mahogany and silver would be kept gleaming and so on, but in the days before vacuum cleaners and dry cleaning it would be left to the patterns on the carpet and the upholstery to disguise the shortcomings of the domestic staff. Wittgenstein, as might be suspected, had a horror of household dirt, and would clean his floors by sprinkling damp tea-leaves on them, and then sweeping them up. It meant that he could never live with carpets in his rooms (Monk, 1991: 377–8). Suddenly we see the empty surfaces of the house for his sister in a new light. Our most mundane practices can have important aesthetic outcomes.

The laborious activity of maintenance of the household, along with the emotional investment of anxiety and pain, is expended in an attempt to achieve serenity, in order to make the dwelling into the place of recuperation for the man of the household, which Joyce Henri Robinson describes in 'Hi Honey, I'm Home' (Chapter 6). The dwelling here is seen by way of late nineteenth and early twentieth-century texts, which presented the home as an oasis at which to recover from the debilitating effects of mentally exhausting work outside the dwelling. The idea of 'neurasthenia' was invented, turning the businessman's need for rest into a medical condition, to which his wife would minister by the appropriate constitution of the home. The furnishing would be chosen for its affective qualities – its tendency to produce an atmosphere of calm and serenity. The kinds of paintings which were therefore seen to be appropriate for this kind of dwelling were Arcadian landscapes, such as those of Puvis de Chavannes. Successfully chosen paintings would be comforting rather than challenging, languid rather than energetic, and anaemic rather than stimulating. When conceived in this way and managed with these values in mind, the home is conservative rather than avant-garde, though the same impulse undoubtedly drives the elimination of visual clutter in the domestic architecture of Mies Van Der Rohe and more recent minimalists (see Pawson, 1996; Sudjic, 2000). The aim is domestic serenity, and it is achieved in very many undistinguished dwellings, not by visual incident being reduced to a minimum, but by visual incident being completely predictable, and therefore achieving a kind of invisibility in the way that a habit becomes an unthinking pattern of behaviour. Individually such buildings have no particular claim on our attention, but collectively they certainly have cultural significance, which is unrelated to the forces that brought them into being. For example the persistence of mock-Tudor and neo-Georgian styles in English domestic architecture of the twentieth century is remarkable, given the architectural profession's general unwillingness to have anything to do with them, and now that their origins are more or less forgotten. They persist on account of their familiarity, which makes them reassuring as images of homeliness.

The image of the nest is often used in connection with the home, especially the kind of dwelling which aspires to an ideal of 'homeliness' rather than social or artistic prestige (Bachelard, 1958: 90–104). The birds' activity in bringing twigs and suchlike together in order to build a safe place in which to lay eggs has its parallel in the way the home is assembled from disparate elements. The tranquil and secure home is lined not with felt-like feathers and moss, but both with furnishings which are literally soft – such as carpets, mattresses and cushions – and also with things which produce a comparable effect on the mind: Arcadian landscapes, music and so on. The nest, which feels absolutely secure from within, is in fact precariously placed, perched among high branches in order to make it inaccessible to predators. It is perceived very differently from inside and outside (Bachelard, 1958: 102–3). If we imagine the nest-like home of a traditional nuclear family, then the carefully constructed dwelling seems to the parents to be a significant achievement in the face of the forces of chaos; whereas to the children who have grown up in this environment, at least by the time they are adolescent, the nest is absolutely self-evidently secure and is under-stimulating; the habits which were cultivated in order to keep parts of the mind free for other things, are seen as obstacles in the way of freedom, as prison bars. Here begins the avant-garde. Something in the *domus* does not want the bucolic (Lyotard,

1988: 196). The idyll by Puvis still hangs on the wall, but its affect shifts. From one perspective it is still productive of a desirable calm, but from another it is experienced as stultifying and repellent. There is no better way to understand the particular kind of household analysed by Robinson than by reading the novels of Ivy Compton Burnett. The various households depicted in her stories have an unvarying range of characters: interchangeable remote fathers, more or less weak mothers, and resilient preternaturally articulate children, with whom we more or less identify. Decorum is maintained at all times, and conversations are usually conducted in so hushed a tone of voice that other people at the same table cannot hear them. Movements around the house are within the range allowed by routine, but the emotional range is that of a Greek tragedy. Agonising chronic torture is meted out by means of control of the supply of fuel for the nursery's fireplace. What might have been an unemotional decision on the part of the remote father – to economise on fuel in a place which did not inconvenience him – is experienced by the children as cruelty and torment. The atmosphere of one book is established in its opening pages by a group of children watching as a group of hens peck at one sickly hen, almost killing it (Compton-Burnett, 1953). The violation involved in opening someone else's letter is felt so keenly that artistically it becomes necessary that the perpetrator should die (Compton-Burnett, 1947). The range of incident is minute, but the range of emotion which it produces is vast. It is households such as this that supplied Freud with his patients, and in order to understand them he too brought Greek tragedy into play.

Caring for a dwelling involves a certain range of gestures: wiping surfaces with a damp cloth, sweeping or vacuuming, dusting and so on involve gestures which are like grooming or stroking, and seem to involve a bond of affection between the cleaner and the house. But when, as in McHugh's example, they are exaggerated slightly they can look violent and threatening, which may be more accurately expressive of the emotion involved. Most accidents happen in the home, and if we are to be murdered then it is very much more likely that it will be a member of our household rather than a stranger who does it. The *domus* does indeed have its dark side. The house's serenity is built on a range of emotions which is far from serene. The internal politics of the house may work more or less happily, but it can also be the locus for the build-up of murderous violence. It is possible that the spatial organization of the house might have a bearing on what kind of atmosphere is generated within it, as people might be thrown together much of the time, or have opportunities for autonomy. It is far more likely that the variations will occur on account of the different ways people develop for dealing with one another, rather than on account of the architecture as such – but there have been attempts to make deterministic 'cause-and-effect' links between the way people behave and the buildings in which they are housed (e.g. Coleman, 1990). The atmosphere of a room may be influenced by the hanging of a picture in it, but what influences the observer's mood is not the picture itself but what it has come to mean; so the Puvis might calm the weary (neurasthenic) businessman, but it might positively enrage his teenage daughter, whom it reminds of patriarchal oppression.

The physical fabric of the house is experienced by way of the things we do, which are on the whole habitual. It is these habits which come to constitute the space of dwelling and which we find reassuring and recuperative. The practices are solidified into an environment, which can be an armature for the development of a flourishing life, or can be imprisoning and debilitating. The practices can also be modified, supplemented or discarded, but that will take a kind of thought which an established habit does not take, and it could involve a changed conception of the kind of person one is (if it involves 'acting out of character'). Our lives and identities are constituted through our habits, and the spatial practices of dwelling are intimately implicated in the places we inhabit. Nevertheless the places do not necessarily determine what the spatial practices are, nor that they be fixed.

TRADITION AND TECTONICS

The habits of dwelling are formed in connection with the house once it is built, but where does the design of the house come from? What gives it the particular form that it has? It takes shape in a regime of practices that is very different from what goes on in the house when it is in use. Some sort of idea is formed, which is then turned into a set of instructions which a builder follows – there may be some discussions so that the builder participates in the designing, but primarily the builder is concerned with the solid substance of the building, while the user is concerned primarily with the space. The architect is concerned with devising a form that the builder can build and which the user can use. This giving of form is the architectural profession's central 'mystery' – to use the word in its medieval sense – its central skill.[8] The operation of this skill need not seem very mysterious in a modern sense, and very often seems to be a matter of common-sense problem solving. Nevertheless the process of design is not the kind of logical process which would take us step-by-step from initial premises to an inevitable outcome. Logical analysis can be used in testing the effectiveness of a design with reference to a given parameter, and it is possible to use an explanation structured in this way to show why a particular design would work well if it were built, but it is not possible to produce the design simply by means of logical analysis – there must also be an imaginative leap at some stage (Lawson, 1980). Not that the imaginative leap need be very great. As a minimum it might involve no more than perceiving that building a house just like the one everyone else has would solve one's current problem (need for a house). That was more or less the case with the various vernacular traditions, which continued unselfconsciously into the nineteenth century; and if everyone designs in this way, by more or less exact repetition of what has gone before, then any individual design will have no cultural significance – at least for as long as one's horizons do not retreat beyond the immediate culture. When we look at the culture from outside, then we start to notice that it is 'a culture' rather than 'the world'. From the point when one becomes aware that alternatives are possible, then the repetition of the local design changes its character, and it could become a matter of some cultural significance that a 'traditional' design is built – as a way of declaring allegiance to the tradition. We live in a society in which architecture is definitely multicultural, in which there is a multiplicity of architectural traditions, and in which no building is quite 'innocent'.

We certainly do not escape tradition by *trying* to escape it – there is, after all, a tradition of the avant-garde to which these attempts belong. Modernism has often been promoted with this in mind – one of the most significant books in disseminating the idea of modernism among architects being Sigfried Giedion's *Space, Time and Architecture: the Growth of a New Tradition* (Giedion, 1941). Its method was not to argue for a fresh start to architecture from a *tabula rasa*, but to point to the historical development of a series of ideas that informed the new architecture. For example, he traced the modern sense of fluid space back to Bavarian Baroque churches, and the display of buildings' engineering qualities back to the engine sheds of Victorian railway stations, so that when we reach Le Corbusier's designs for concrete houses raised above the ground on columns, we are well prepared and see them as a reasonable 'next step' to take. Contemporary buildings belong in a historical context, and are given meaning by being seen to be part of a tradition – even if the tradition has to be invented. Giedion's version of a modern tradition is real enough, even though he invented it, but it is not the only possible one. Colin St. John Wilson has traced another (which he calls 'The Other Tradition') and he argues that it makes closer links between architecture and the life lived in buildings, than did Giedion's version of modernism (Wilson, 1992, 1995). Wilson reveres Alvar Aalto, who made no appearance in the first version of Giedion's text, though he was added to later additions. Others, equally important in Wilson's version of events, never did figure in Giedion's. Hans Scharoun and Sigurd Lewerentz, for example, are crucial to Wilson's conception of the development of modern architecture, and he would like his own work – especially the British Library – to be seen in relation to them. The work of the present will be seen in relation to previous work, and will be understood in the light of it. As the author of the work, one's starting point is to imagine it being understood in relation to one's own tradition. A new work of serious cultural significance will make us revisit earlier work in the tradition and reappraise all of it. This is the basis of the view of tradition set out by T.S. Eliot (1920) which Jorge Luis Borges neatly condensed when he said that 'every writer creates his own precursors. His work modifies our conception of the past, as it will modify the future' (Foucault, 1977).

For many years now, Charles Jencks has been illuminating contemporary architecture by presenting it as belonging to a complex mesh of interwoven traditions (Jencks, 1973). Each 'tradition' here is a way of approaching the designing of buildings, with a range of skills and a set of priorities, which are put into play to produce the finished building. It might happen that the buildings produced by all these different traditions look much the same – that wouldn't be the point. Each 'tradition' could be seen to have its own *ethos*, its own characteristic ethics; so, from the point of view of the architect involved in determining the form of the building, there is indeed a close link between ethics and aesthetics, as Wittgenstein tried to claim: the way the building is shaped, derives not from a strictly logical process working from premises to conclusions, but from a culture which has certain values, that work together to influence judgements. Those values can take account of such things as comfort and structural stability, return on capital, playfulness, novelty or rootedness, all of which can have an impact on one another in the development of a design. Architects find ways of doing things, and doing them in a new way means spending more time working out how they are to be done, so if speed of production is paramount, then innovation will not happen. Different traditions will give these qualities different degrees of importance with respect to one another. The tradition of the 'tectonic' (building construction considered with a view to its cultural content) is examined by Demetri Porphyrios in his essay 'From *Techne* to Tectonics' (Chapter 7), using a Heideggerian method of interrogating language for traces of earlier senses of how practices were conceptualised. The essay is complementary to Heidegger's 'Building, Dwelling, Thinking' which is concerned with ontology – the Being which comes before building (or anything else), and the way in which 'dwelling' shapes human 'being' – *Dasein*. Porphyrios in his essay sees buildings as the outcome of the practice of building, and looks to the buildings to show traces of the way in which they were built – either by literally making visible the means of building, or by a playful use of ornament which signals a cultural memory of an earlier practice. This links with Kenneth Frampton's use of the terms 'ontological' and 'representational' in connection with the tectonic. A representational tectonic would be the ornamental signification of construction, whereas an ontological tectonic would be the display of actual construction. Frampton, in his book *Studies in Tectonic Culture* (1995), traces these ideas from the Greek revival, starting with the Abbé Laugier's idea that the Greek temple's origins lay in a primitive timber hut, made by roofing over the space between four columnar trees – in his illustration they were shown still growing in the ground (Laugier, 1753). The idea would later be elaborated by Quatremère de Quincy, who supplemented this hut with a cave (which he saw as the origin of Egyptian architecture) and the tent (supposedly the origin of Chinese architecture) (Lavin, 1992). It was taken up again by Gottfried Semper, as Frampton explains in the text included in the present volume (Chapter 8). Here the model for conceptualising architecture is a hut from the Caribbean which Semper saw when he visited the Great Exhibition in the Crystal Palace on Hyde Park in 1851. He analysed it into four elements: the hearth, the earthwork, a timber frame and a weatherproof covering, and he kept these four basic elements in mind even when he was designing much larger and more complex buildings, such as his vast institutional museums in Dresden and Zürich (Mallgrave, 1996). Frampton takes the idea further, and sees it informing buildings as diverse as Schinkel's

Altes Museum and the Sydney Opera House. The earthwork, which in the hut is a massive and solid plinth, with steps modelled in it, could develop into cave-like masonry vaults, while the frame work can turn into concrete or steel and be used on a greatly increased scale. The lightweight covering, which Semper imagined as woven fabric, turns into modern 'curtain walls'. There is a clear difference in character between the compactness of the 'earthwork' which seems to have been carved or moulded out of a solid block, and the lighter 'framework' which seems to have been assembled from different elements connected together – typically columns and beams. The same word, 'tectonic', can be used both to refer to 'the poetics of building construction' in a general way, and to distinguish the 'tectonic' frame (which originated in the work of carpenters) from the 'stereotomic' earthwork (which looks as if it is cut from the solid). The idea of the tectonic is very flexible and can inform an understanding of a range of buildings from Greek temples to modern skyscrapers, by encouraging the architect to derive the building's appearance from its means of construction, if not directly ('ontologically') then by signifying it indirectly ('representationally').

There are many buildings which do not draw on the values of tectonic culture, such as those which use decoration without a sense of constructional logic behind it – the buildings in which the elements, in Porphyrios's words, 'do not hang together'. Buildings can work by other means – as the house in Joyce Henri Robinson's article does (Chapter 6) or as the architecture of Adolf Loos did. Loos suppressed any expression of construction in his buildings, coating the walls with wallpaper-like marble. Wittgenstein was not impressed by Loos' 'virulent bogus intellectualism', but was nevertheless influenced by his example in the design for his sister's house.[9] The solid substance of the building is shaped by a range of factors that come into play in the architect's culture. There are craft traditions which would influence which materials might be used and how they might be worked, and under that heading we would today need to include industrial processes, since they can have such a bearing on building products. There are all sorts of utilitarian aspects to the building which would have to be considered – such as how it would be lit, ventilated and heated – and decisions taken about one of these things will often have an impact on the others, so a balance must be struck, and it is not always possible exactly to explain how that balance was struck. Often it is a matter of experience and judgement. Sometimes it can be a matter of measurement, but even then the measurement is rarely more than a reassurance that the judgement is not seriously wrong. Such judgements are influenced by culture and tradition – by what we think our buildings should be, what values they should reflect, and that is caught up in what our own values are, whether we think of ourselves as rational and principled, or as carefree hedonists. It is a matter of asking ourselves: what feels right? Which is plainly a question that belongs to ethics. Looking at a sleek German-designed toaster, the architect James Stirling remarked that it seemed altogether too sophisticated for so primitive a function as scorching bread: a clumsier British design seemed to him to be more appropriate to the task (Banham, 1997: 96). It is this cultural aspect of the design of buildings that makes architecture of them – matching the container to its contents – and it is a crucial problem in dealing with it that our culture is increasingly diverse, so that we cannot all be assumed to have been formed by the values of a single tradition, and expect to find its values reflected back to us in the architecture around us. Roger Scruton's essay (Chapter 1) proposes principles which sound sensible enough, but the architects who are actually in practice today were for the most part educated to see their work as belonging to quite a different tradition – probably one of those outlined by Giedion, Wilson or Jencks – and what looks normative in one tradition can look alien or even inflammatory in another. Nevertheless common ground is there to be found, some of it in the handling of materials. For example they can be finely or coarsely wrought, making them seem more sophisticated or primitive. A very simple, crudely worked house could have a characterful ruggedness and solidity. The problem for tectonic culture would be if the crudely built house were to be wrapped up in a thin coat of decorative finishes which masked what was genuine about the building in favour of status-enhancing signs. This might be embraced as popular culture or derided as kitsch, but it is recognisably the same thing as the factory workers' finery described by Disraeli, the tinsel which 'whatever were its materials, had unquestionably a very gorgeous appearance' (Disraeli, 1845: II, Chapter 9). They go out to a place with exactly parallel characteristics: The Cat and Fiddle, inside which, up some stairs, is a bright green doorway with gilt panels, labelled 'The Temple of the Muses', in which there is tawdry entertainment, much enjoyed by the undiscerning audience (II, Chapter 10). The value-system of tectonic culture is elitist, not in the sense of insisting that only very expensive buildings are good, but in desiring that buildings should in their solid fabric seem to be what they actually are, which has never been a characteristic of populist architecture – from The Temple of the Muses to the Jungle Room. Loos associated ornament and crime, so that decoration became an equivalent of tattooing, which he associated with poverty, criminality and the underdevelopment of civilised traits (Loos, 1929). Peasant taste ran to the most extravagant Baroque, when it could be afforded, as it could be in some memorable eighteenth-century Bavarian churches. The plain unembellished dwelling is therefore the abode of the very poor, who cannot afford decoration, and the very cultivated, such as philosophers in retreat, who have learnt not to want it. Even the least pretentious tectonically expressive building is assimilated in different ways according to the culture in which it is appropriated, but the fabric of the building will have a solidity and stability about it which will make it 'hang together', and even if it is a very impoverished little building, it will have a good character.

ECONOMY AND EXTRAVAGANCE

The ideas in this text have been applied mainly to examples drawn from houses; but just as Laugier and Semper could make points about how to determine the forms of monumental architecture with reference to primitive huts, so the principles associated with the dwelling can apply to other, much larger and more complex buildings, where the kinds of relationship between user and building are similar. At a larger scale the 'user' may not be an individual or a family, but might have a collective character – a corporation could 'dwell' (or fail to dwell) in its headquarters, or might have a more or less cosmopolitan relationship with particular places. A building which was commissioned to house a large company would be expected in some way to reflect and display the company's values – the high-quality, bland but serviceable office buildings which we see around are the exact architectural equivalent of a neatly tailored suit (Sorkin, 1991: 271–2). In fact, as most of the large office buildings now seem to be built speculatively by developers, rather than individually tailored to particular companies' requirements, they equate with a ready-to-wear suit. The word 'economy' comes from the Greek word for a house, *oikos*, but the concept has grown well beyond its origin in the dwelling. The pattern of economy, though, the idea that we should be looking for the best return for our expenditure, is usually evident in the home, and is the basis of much commercial thinking in the modern world – in the global economy.

There is, however, a fundamentally different motive for action which comes into play on occasion, and where architecture can be involved in a highly significant way. This is when the motive is not economy but extravagance. The most memorable buildings throughout architectural history have been created when this impulse has been acting – from Stonehenge and the pyramids to the Empire State Building and the Petronas Towers, the world's great monuments have been built by consuming resources which were vast by the standards of the day. Pevsner's version of architectural history in his *Outline of European Architecture* is more or less a history of this kind of building.[10] In these buildings function and economy are not the principal forces at work, still less is sustainability a consideration. It is much more important that the building is magnificent than that it was done for the minimum cost, and it is in this realm of extravagance and ruinous consumption that architects have traditionally worked – designing buildings which are noble and set apart from the everyday run of things, designing palaces and cathedrals which burn up vast resources. There are many buildings in a society which are designed to support a way of life as efficiently as possible, in order to make it possible to do things, in order to participate in the amassing of resources. On the other hand once the resources are amassed then what can they be spent on? The economist Thorstein Veblen used the term 'conspicuous waste' to describe the displays of consumption made by the 'leisure class' of his own day (Veblen, 1899); and we can see that buildings, being very expensive, can have an important role to play in the consumption of vast resources – if we look to the Guggenheims in New York and Bilbao, the Kimbells in Fort Worth or the Menils in Houston, we can see that the sacrifice of personal wealth for public good (by way of fine art and fine building) does indeed bring renown. If we think of domestic architecture as being guided by the comforting idea of a nest, then what is it that guides monumental architecture, if not a pillar of fire, guiding the initiate through oppidan gloom? In this mode of thought the everyday is simply clutter which gets in the way of seeing the essential, so that it becomes a duty to shut it out. Whereas the nest is anchored, and invites us to stay where we are – to snuggle down into it – the pillar of fire beckons as a destiny and invites us to move. It is a challenge to all that is comfortable, having the character rather of a quest. It is grand and inspiring, and suggests that the art of architecture should take us away from the everyday surroundings that enslave us, guiding us to a better place.

General architectural histories give priority to architecture which has been produced from some such standpoint as this, because it is such an outlook which inspires one to go beyond what had previously seemed possible, to reach out into the unknown and produce the most remarkable buildings – the tallest, the most astonishing, or the most visionary. Would we want a history of architecture which omitted the pyramids, the Parthenon, Chartres Cathedral and the Sydney Opera House? These are the cultural landmarks which give us our orientation, and by which we navigate; they tell us what kind of people we are, at our most splendid, while the lesser achievements take their place within the framework established by them. If these are the works whose begetters were stirred into action by the sight of the pillar of fire, it leaves the rest of the buildings in Stygian gloom, blind to the guidance which was there for the initiates to see. So, if we look back at the architecture of the 1920s with knowledge of what was to inspire the architectural world in the years to come, we see lots of ordinary build-ings which retreat into the shadows, and a few remarkable buildings which seem to have insight into what, for them, was yet to come. Le Corbusier's villas, Mies Van Der Rohe's early works – especially the German pavilion for the international exposition at Barcelona – and Gerrit Rietvelt's Schröder House in Utrecht have had an extraordinary degree of coverage and influence given their size. They would be fine artistic achievements in any age, but that is not the whole reason for their celebrity. They look as if they were 'ahead of their time', which is a logical nonsense, but with the benefit of hindsight it is possible to make a com-pelling visual case for the architects having seen the future and built it early. They are, in effect, presented as having followed the pillar of fire out of the wilderness of ignorance and confusion, and this has given the architects the status of prophets, so that their work seems to enjoy a status which is not accorded to those whose work we admire for more straightforward reasons. This is an effect of hindsight – there were other architects who worked with conviction that other things were important, and they have been selected out of the story, because they cannot be seen to be preparing the way for what was to come. Making the distinction between those who had and those who had not seen the light of the pillar of fire the criterion for inclusion in an architectural history, transfers across to the very idea of architecture. True architecture is then seen to be the work of initiates and visionaries, whereas ordinary building is the work of ordinary people, and is simply beside the point. When architecture is seen in this perspective then certain consequences follow. The 'perceptive initiate' will not be suscep-tible to arguments advanced by people who do not have similar insight, no matter how many of them there are and no matter how uniform their views. These people are simply seen as ignorant or blind, and any value in their argu-ments remains unexamined. They are set on one side because they have not seen the point which should be self-evident to someone who is properly in tune with architecture. The clearest exponent of this kind of view is Howard Roark, the hero of Ayn Rand's novel, *The Fountainhead*, who is presented in this way not in order to show how erroneous he is, but how admirable (Rand, 1943; Saint, 1983). He is one of the most completely 'heroic' heroes in modern literature, and he is admired without irony or reserve. He is of course a fictional character, though he is recognisably based on Frank Lloyd Wright, who was capable of thinking of himself as prophet-like and certainly encouraged his public to do so (Levine, 1996; Wright, 1932). This image of the architect as superhuman, as someone in touch with the forces of nature, who is shaping the physical world, has immense appeal if it is tenable. It appeals to the architect's vanity and sense of significance in the world, and it appeals to people who are looking for guid-ance, who like strong leaders and unshakeable convictions. Unshakeable convic-tions are in practical circumstances much more persuasive than careful reasoning – the person with conviction knows the answers, whereas the people who are debating and reasoning are looking for answers. It is the polarity between the sage and the philosopher returning in the architectural persona – what is the architect: a friend of wisdom, seeking to find it, or a dispenser of wisdom, in possession of it? Is architecture a matter of finding form by way of inquiry and exploration, or is it a matter of having inspiration and conviction?

OVERCOMING ORDINARINESS

So there are two linked issues here: the architect's orientation – the sense of a calling higher than that of dealing with the commonplace world of day-to-day domesticity and business; and the architect's immunity to the appeals of people who are caught up in that world, who do not see the world to which the archi-tect aspires. The architect who deals with the mundane world has a self-image as a professional, and takes pride in dealing effectively with everyday problems, working through consensus for an idea of the general good. The visionary archi-tect has a self-image as an artist, and takes pride in having strong convictions which must be realised at all costs – destroying opposition where possible, com-promising only at the expense of feeling defeat and betrayal by an ignorant and philistine world. The tension between these two self-conceptions has been explored in Mark Crinson and Jules Lubbock's book *Architecture: Art or Profes-sion?* (1994), and Roger Scruton (Chapter 1) makes it clear that architects often do well in the eyes of the rest of society when their aims are set low. Robert Venturi and Denise Scott Brown memorably identified themselves as designers of 'ugly and ordinary' buildings, in contrast with the architects from whom they wished to distance themselves, whom they labelled as 'heroic and original' (Venturi *et al.*, 1977: 93–100). Their labels catch and neatly ironize the approbation which normally attaches to the second group – those lured on by the pillar of fire – while the comfortable nest-builders are treated with less reverence but make themselves useful. They are probably not noticed and are certainly never treated as heroes – they do not invite it – and their practices flourish in a low-key way.[11]

It used to be the case that architects only ever designed temples and palaces, and conferred exalted status on buildings through their involvement. They also, and not incidentally, controlled the expenditure of vast resources. Imhotep, the first architect whose name is known to us, came to be worshipped as a god; but that was not because he designed astonishing buildings. He had high status in the Pharaonic court, and was therefore able to command remarkable building work. Through most of history, architects have had high status on account of their birth and connections, rather than because their architectural skills have won them rank (Stevens, 1998). Nowadays most architects are involved with much more pedestrian buildings which need have only modest aims, and that is mostly the purely logical consequence of the fact that far more people today practise as architects. Sir Howard Colvin has compiled a celebrated dictionary which includes as many as possible of the people whom we would today call architects, but who practised between the end of the middle ages and the foundation of the Institute of British Architects, from which point these matters are documented by other means (Colvin, 1995). It covers the period 1600–1840, a period of 240 years, and lists every British building of importance whose architect can be identified. It is remarkable, then, that altogether it lists approximately two thousand architects; whereas there are approximately twenty-six thousand architects registered as practising in Britain now. If that number were projected across two-and-a-half centuries, we begin to see how much further down the social scale architects must now move if they are to keep themselves in steady employment. They must look beyond the courts of princes and the nobility. From the eighteenth century, which Colvin's dictionary covers, the country gentry started to become an important source of employment, and since then the commercial world has vastly increased in significance. Architects started to design dwellings for poor people in the late eighteenth century – when they tried to persuade the great landowners to build better houses for their labourers. Nineteenth-century architects worked for industrialists on model villages, and twentieth-century architects for local authorities on mass housing schemes, which have now for the most part been replaced by more direct contact with the inhabitants of the dwellings through the 'community architecture' movement.

Architecture that belongs to the tradition of heroism and originality is commissioned by princes, or in the modern world, multi-millionaires. Its threshold is at the point where it is possible to go beyond simple necessities – it begins with some kind of superfluity, some kind of affluence. In designing a palace, for example, there will be a need for the display of power as a way of signalling the influence of the prince, which in turn becomes a way of the prince having influence – we are (collectively) inclined to bow to his will because we are persuaded that it is stronger than our own, and the building is part of the persuasion. This can be managed in ways which may differ very greatly so far as their detail is concerned, but they will have in common a degree of extravagance, which demonstrates that the prince at the focus of the scene has impressive resources at his command. A prince who was thought to have less power than his barons would find himself with practical political problems, and architecture could help him to present himself in the right light. Of course 'the prince' as a public role has profoundly different needs from the person who played that role, and in addition to the extravagantly scaled state rooms for public display, the palace would also have suites of rooms for a more private kind of life – a 'nest' from which to venture out. The architects whose names we remember from the past are for the most part people who worked for kings, pharaohs and emperors. In the parts of their work for which these architects are remembered they set aside the normal requirements for living quietly and contentedly, and necessarily worked to a different set of values, because if they worked by normal domestic values the rooms would be homely instead of magnificent, pleasant instead of impressive, and comforting instead of thrilling.

How does this agenda operate in the contemporary world? Sometimes without any problems at all, if there is the right match between the occasion and the architecture. The people with 'princely' power are now for the most part in business, but the means of impressing others and the role of buildings in the exercise of power has remained – a shift which began in the fifteenth century and which has accelerated since, as the values of commerce have been adopted and institutionalised. The use of displays of extravagance as demonstrations of enlightened patronage continues, at both a personal and an institutional level. For example we find that the dwellings of such figures as Randolph Hearst or the late James Goldsmith were organised more for the sake of display and the accumulation of treasures (and therefore prestige) than they were for accommodation as such – these needs being relatively easily dealt with, they are more or less lost in the overall effect of magnificence. These dwellings do not appear in standard architectural histories, because they do not engage with the development of the architecture of the avant-garde, and are therefore seen to be beside the point in terms of their artistic accomplishments. It is in the case of cultural institutions that we have seen the most remarkable displays of avant-garde extravagance in recent years. The spectacular art gallery in Bilbao, which Frank Gehry designed, has been a great popular as well as a critical success. It seems that it is generally accepted and seen to be culturally appropriate that a new art gallery should have a perplexing appearance, because art can be perplexing. Here it seems that the public is happy to accept an extraordinary degree of novelty. Another recent example is the extension which Daniel Libeskind has designed for the Victoria and Albert Museum in London, which has an extreme and unsettlingly unstable-looking form, expressive of dynamism and complexity. This has been introduced into a sequence of sedate façades in a conservation area, breaking with all the usual guidelines about what can be allowed to happen on such a site. But yet permission has been given for it to be built, because it seems that it is understood that this internationally important institution needs to project an impression of itself which the extension is seen to give. Had the building been a private dwelling then it would certainly not have been allowed – there is a correspondence between the form of the building and the cultural expectations we have of such a building.

The kind of domestic extravagance which is most respected by the avant-garde is the burning up of extravagant intellectual resources. Heidegger did this in support of the peasant's cabin, but it is not possible to present such a building as at the cutting edge of architectural development. Peter Eisenman, who sabotaged everyday expectations in his convention centre in Columbus Ohio, as has already been mentioned, has sought in comparable ways to dislocate the normal domestic agenda. Few of his designs for houses have been built, but one which has – called 'House VI' – achieved notoriety because of the way in which it attacked head-on the usual routines of living (Figure C.8).[12] For example the

Figure C.8
Peter Eisenman, House VI
(Frank House).
Photo: Eisenman
Architects.

dining table has a column running through the middle of it, which makes it impossible to have the usual sort of dinner party where people sit around the table and speak to one another – the column simply gets in the way. There was an eighteen-inch wide slot in the floor of the principal bedroom, running right across the room in between the twin beds. And so on. Why? Because this is no ordinary house – it belongs in the realm of art – being set up in order to provoke new ways of living. The idea is not to make the house uninhabitable, but to make it impossible to inhabit it in a traditional way. Looking back to the Edwardian households described by Joyce Henri Robinson (Chapter 6), the domestic disciplines there which were reified and turned into an imprisoning cage (for some of the inhabitants) are made impossible in Eisenman's design – although it would be possible to institute new domestic disciplines, equally firm. If we constitute ourselves through our actions, particularly through our patterns of repeated behaviour, then such a house should be the means of becoming a new sort of person. The house is a remarkable achievement. It is now better understood than when it was first built, when it seemed to be the product of mere perversity, but it still functions as a referent in discussion over twenty years later. It is starting to look like a kind of classic, but it is unlikely to inspire frequent imitation, as few people want to be challenged so directly in their everyday lives. It is one thing to visit such a house, quite another to invest in it as a principal dwelling. David Goldblatt discusses some of Eisenman's ideas in his essay 'The Dislocation of the Architectural Self' (Chapter 9). It is possible now to see why Eisenman circulated the story about his building making people feel queasy – it signalled the fact that its agenda was profoundly different from cosy domesticity, and that rejection of the domestic – even in the home – has been an aspect of the agenda of most architecture which we have felt inclined to recognise as 'great' (Reed, 1996). If however the aim is 'to retain independence from bourgeois taste' then his degree of success is surely limited. He has distanced himself very effectively from the domestic, and has set himself apart from *petit bourgeois* values; but he is nevertheless in tune with the taste of the part of the *haute bourgeoisie* which funds the architectural art-world. Moreover Eisenman attempts to abolish the influence of humane values (as David Goldblatt describes) in order to confront us with a sense of the absolute – a sense of the sublime. For example at the Wexner Center he hoped to make a building which in some way went beyond the accommodation of human desires (Figure 9.2). Nevertheless it fails to manage this (as it was bound to do) as what it does is to dramatise and enact the idea of arbitrariness. The building does not escape meaning, but very articulately conveys the idea 'meaninglessness'. Eisenman as much as Scruton accepts the diagnosis that we live in an age of nihilism, but Eisenman's efforts are directed to dramatising the idea – in practice actually accepting it as a firm foundation – rather than as something to deplore and overcome.

Trying to escape the centrality of humanity in architecture is futile – it is central to us, and it is only in a human culture that architecture can be noticed and valued. The attempts to escape, like Eisenman's, which have been made seem only to succeed in escaping from a *petit bourgeois* into an elite value system. The brave assault on the centrality of the human turns into something all too human, something rather like intellectual elitism – for which it is possible to make honourable claims, but they are not the claims being made by Eisenman. The desire to escape does make sense, but only if we see ourselves situated in a world which has been so completely domesticated by civilisation that we are in danger of forgetting that there is anything more to the world than human culture. For that perhaps we need to escape into the mountains and forests, rather than look to any kind of buildings. In these terms the principal value of Heidegger's cabin would be not its humane side, making it possible to dwell in a particular spot, but its outside – if it is used as the means of facilitating contact with the inhuman grandeur of nature. Architecture can never be indifferent to human needs, and when it *pretends* to be, it becomes a symptom of the all too human longing of the sentimental nihilist.

THE DISSOLUTION OF FORM

Bernard Tschumi takes a different approach in his essay 'The Pleasure of Architecture' (Chapter 10). Like Eisenman, he has worked with the philosopher Jacques Derrida and has used philosophically-derived ideas in his designs. In making 'pleasure' his focus, he has humanity firmly in his sights, but in theorising the production of pleasure in architecture as an 'erotics' of architecture, he looks not to domestic chintz, but to the ropes and chains of a sado-masochist's dungeon. The pleasure of architecture which he is trying to cultivate is not the everyday domestic affection, which gives one confidence in dealing with the world, but the kind of sublime grand passion in which the world fades from one's attention. He holds back from supposing that there is a link between architectural erotics and actual sexual practices. It is true of an architectural act that if it manages to slide between conflicting sets of expectations and requirements without being deflected from its graceful gesture, then we can be thrilled by the skill and bravura with which the deed has been done. Tschumi says this more memorably: 'the more numerous and sophisticated the restraints, the greater the pleasure' (Figure 10.1).[13] The title of Tschumi's essay alludes to Roland Barthes' *Le plaisir du texte* (1973) and Barthes is particularly associated with the idea that a text is can be treated in a 'readerly' way, neglecting any intentions which the author might have had for it, in favour of seeing how it could be deployed in new discourse – the idea of the death of the author. With Tschumi the focus is similarly on the activities going on in relation to a building rather than on the substance of the building itself, which tends to be lost in the background. For him the point under discussion is not what the building is, but what one can make of it – in what kinds of practices can it engage?

The tenor of Tschumi's essay is intense and passionate rather than cool and reasonable. The persuasiveness of its rhetoric depends relatively little on the connectedness of his argument and rather more on excitement generated in the reader. One responds to the wild animal within (which in this case is not so much tamed as bound). It has the quality of a manifesto, exhorting us to change the way we behave, to join in with the game whose rules are here declared. It involves looking at architecture in terms of the actions and events in which it is implicated – transitory events and actions which may be repeated or may be unique. The shaping of buildings as such ceases to be the focus of concern: if we relate to buildings by way of actions and events then perhaps, if we focus on them, we can make buildings which are remarkably effective. The way of seeing is neatly encapsulated in the term 'event-cities', which is the aggregation of such actions and events conceived in spatial terms (Tschumi, 1994b). Tschumi's voice is not alone, and there are echoes in the concerns of others, such as Rem Koolhaas, who suggests that we experience a corresponding formlessness when faced with buildings of very large size. When faced with even the largest monuments of the western tradition, the parts tend to be related to the whole in such a way that we have a sense of pervading reason and we can relate our own position in the building to our sense of the whole. That at least would be the aim. However with very large contemporary building projects this sense is lost, and Koolhaas has leapt a fence and seen that this is something that can be celebrated (Koolhaas *et al.*, 1995; see also Bois and Krauss, 1997). If one ceases to expect to be able to relate to the whole, then its form becomes unimportant. One responds to events which are at hand, picking up signals from other things nearby which might next engage one's attention. Once the idea of coherence has been sacrificed, anything can happen anywhere, and the stimulation which the building provides as it is 'sampled' is a matter of chance juxtapositions and transitions, as the result of freely chosen movements, rather than the carefully controlled drama of sequenced spaces which has been cultivated in the academies.

Such qualities are associated with a stimulating urban environment, which we may well warm to for its being lively with activity, despite being without the appearance of having been visually ordered (Sennett, 1970, 1991). The abandonment of such traditional concerns as coherence and form has its parallel in the way in which the idea of the body has reappeared in the context of architectural design in recent years. It is no longer the carefully measured body of the Renaissance, which was reduced to a series of mathematical proportions, which could then inform decisions about the design (Rykwert, 1996; Tavernor, 1998). Rather the body is configured in terms of stimulus and response: luxuriating in pleasure, being racked with pain, or being involved in dynamic processes of consumption and expulsion. The body is still a microcosm, but whereas in the Renaissance it was made of harmonious numbers, it seems now to be made of blood, nerves and mucous membranes, and there has been a remarkable growth in the number of books making connections between architecture, gender and sexuality. If we see the body as well as buildings, and cities, in terms of their actions and passions, then the precise configuration of the form ceases to seem to be of primary importance. If today we see the body as a society of dismembered parts, then this can translate through into an architectural composition involving random scatter, or arbitrary placement.[14] This highly visceral agenda has developed hand in hand with architects taking an interest in Continental philosophy (and strangely little interest in the work of philosophers working in English) which runs in parallel with the way that social scientists and others have found the texts fruitful.[15] The philosophical texts tend not to be used so as to construct arguments, but associatively, in fragments, lending themselves to the process of seduction of which Baudrillard speaks:

> Distinctive signs, full signs, never seduce us. Seduction only comes through empty, illegible, insoluble, arbitrary, fortuitous signs, which glide by lightly, modifying the index of the refraction of space. . . . As such the signs of seduction do not signify; they are of the order of the ellipse, of the short circuit, of the flash of wit [*le trait d'ésprit*].
>
> (Baudrillard, 1988)[16]

If we are in pursuit of the sensual and immediately gratifying, rather than underlying coherence, then we can readily link the density and obscurity of Heidegger's language with the abandonment of any feeling that coherence is possible, let alone desirable, in the contemporary world (Sokal and Bricmont, 1997). This is a world of buzz-words and sound-bites, which translates into architecture in the world of commercial activity. It is stimulating and immediately engaging, but it does not last, and it leaves us feeling enervated rather than restored. It is a world in which our resources are used up, and from which we go home to recover. The discotheque and the shopping mall are replete with seductive signs – empty, illegible, insoluble, arbitrary, fortuitous signs – which are also temporary signs: they cease to be so seductive when they become familiar. The kind of environment which is generated by these concerns is playful, entertaining, and can have a powerful emotional charge. Although signs could be solidly integrated with buildings, as they were at times in the past, it then becomes more difficult to replace them when their effectiveness has expired, so we are left with more or less mute frameworks, to which transient signs attach, and in these conditions architecture escapes from the realm of the solid monument and the preoccupations of tectonic culture, to become at its best an absolutely enchanting mirage (Leach, 1999a; Thakara, 1988; Venturi *et al.*, 1977).

It might be possible to see Bötticher's core-form as a building's equivalent of its *Dasein* – an invariant sort of innermost being, which is never directly encountered, but which is experienced only by way of one art-form or another. All the buildings that we recognize as belonging to a 'type' would share a core-form. Indeed it is the usual definition of a 'type', that we would be able to recognize a generic character across the group, just as the logic of a particular argument might be embodied in any number of essays – some of them polished and literary, others rough-hewn. The structuring argument would be the same in all, but would be encountered by way of one essay or another. Core-form, then, becomes something like the structure of a building, or a building-type. It is always present in what is built, but is never encountered directly, because it

always needs to be finished in some way in order to allow the building to function. It is at this point that the idea of 'authenticity' becomes problematic in the
way that Leach describes. Everything which is in the world has its own authenticity, so how can we claim that some authenticities are more *authentic* than
others? What feels most authentic is merely that with which we are most closely
bonded, on account of some deep familiarity at a formative age, or dispersed a
cultural nostalgia. On this scale of value, the aspiration to authenticity becomes
sentimental and reactionary, whereas the opposite move, aspiring to the furthest
possible development of culture and civilisation becomes admirable. With the
banishment of the real world we have abolished the unreal world (Nietzsche,
1889). The question then becomes, not 'what is the world?' but 'what can I
make of the world?' or, 'what is it *for me*?' (Barthes, 1973: 13).

The surrender of rigour in argument is exactly akin to the neglect of the
tectonic in architecture. Without the structure of logical connectedness, one's
argument is weak (more exactly, one does not actually have an argument)
and if it carries the day it does so on its subsidiary characteristics, like the charm
of the speaker, the rhetorical skill, the authority of the tone of voice, and the
predisposition of the audience to be won over. Nevertheless, as a model of persuasion, Tschumi's seduction has more to recommend it at a practical level than
a logical argument that takes us to a conclusion we are unwilling to hear. If adequate attention is not given to the materiality of the building, to solidity of the
structure and its appropriate treatment for the role it is to play, then it can no
doubt be rescued as a serviceable building, by applying as an afterthought the
right sorts of signs. A well structured argument or a well disposed building can
be taken and handled without panache, but it will at least have good character
to recommend it – at such moments ethics and aesthetics can work together as
one. The performances in which we take the greatest delight, however, are
those extravagant moments when a sound basis is taken and developed further
than we had previously thought possible. It is in those moments that a tradition
flowers, that a culture develops and grows, and that humanity flourishes. And as
with all delights, we can sustain only fleeting moments of such pleasure: a
society which tried to make these moments the routine part of everyday life
would burn itself out in no time at all.

SO, WHAT IS ARCHITECTURE?

The various essays in this collection draw on a variety of ways of thinking about
architecture, and I have set up the nest and the pillar of fire as opposite poles
which can act as guiding principles. These two poles generate very different sets
of values, both of which are well represented in architecture as practised today.
The comforting nest-inspired architecture is the everyday building which most of
us inhabit and use most of the time. Whatever its style it is the modest sort of
undemanding architecture which most of us want most of the time, but it is also
the very kind of architecture which is excluded from the most traditional

accounts of architectural history. The procession of cathedrals and palaces which fills most general architectural histories, tells a story in which practising architects who read it will want to feel they they can locate their own work. They know that they are architects because they have certificates to prove it. And if their conception of architecture has been informed by reading architectural history then they know that it is elevated above a concern for everyday things. To design simply and straightforwardly would lead them into approaching the design of a modest building as if it were a bicycle shed. It would be inoffensive in character, but in the eyes of the community of architects, it would not be architecture. In these circumstances the architect is bound to feel misunderstood by one group or another. In order to step outside of the problem we need to see how the different ideas in it have been shaped. The distinction between architecture and 'mere building' is useful in some contexts, and unhelpful in others. It is a useful way of saying that some buildings matter to us and others don't – something which manifestly is the case: I am indifferent to the fate of some buildings, would gladly see others pulled down, and would fight to save those which I really care about. The works of the past – like Lincoln Cathedral – which are now unequivocally called 'architecture' tend to be works of extraordinarily high status, which were produced at enormous cost. The types of projects which we are stirred by most – cathedrals, palaces, castles, pyramids, etc. – were exceptional in their day, and were designed by very few people. The number of architects we have today means that they cannot possibly all be employed in the design of projects of this degree of extravagance, and most – the overwhelming majority – must settle for work which is modestly resourced and has a routine character of a domestic or commercial kind. Unfortunately this type of project calls for different attitudes from those required for the design of palaces and cathedrals, and those attitudes may be seen to be inimical to architecture, as opposed to mere building. The architecture that is studied in schools of architecture tends, for the most part, to belong to the category which is led on by the pillar of fire, which is exciting, creative and heroic. The architecture which most of society wants most of the time is, by contrast, nest-like: familiar, reassuring and comfortable to be in and be near. It is undemanding and reliable, and no-one expects or wants it to be interesting or thought-provoking. The definition of architecture has serious consequences for human happiness and the quality of our surroundings. In practice if we make a distinction between building and architecture then our idea of architecture is informed by a great pageant of wonderful buildings which are exceptions to the general rule of the society in which they were built. If what we want architects to do is to design mainly ordinary buildings, then an entirely different kind of history is needed, involving a revaluation of all values – an ethics which would be new to architecture – which would see modest repetition as praiseworthy, and extravagance as something to be condemned.[17] In such a history small, efficient buildings which might not have any visual distinction would be models of excellence, and the 'great' monuments of the past would be criminally eccentric.[18] Initially they might be included as examples of past evils, but they would soon fade from the picture altogether. From the point of view of a traditional architectural culture this agenda might seem radical and barbaric, but some such revaluation is what would be needed if architects were to accept with enthusiasm the agenda which society in general would seem to want. In this perspective the showy monuments of the avant-garde belong to an antiquated and unsustainable tradition, while a thoroughgoing revolution is needed for us to be able to value the orthodox.

What I want to propose by way of conclusion is that we should put behind us the habit of thinking that some useful buildings are architecture while others are not, and that the two groups of buildings can be separated out in a definitive way. 'I had realised before now,' said Proust, 'that it is only a clumsy and erroneous form of perception which places everything in the object, when really everything is in the mind' (Proust, 1913–27: VI, 275). Proust's cork-lined room was like a cloud-chamber, in which a very precise atmosphere was maintained, so that when the trivial incidents of his former life in fashionable bourgeois society were introduced into it (as mental events) they left shimmering vapour trails suspended in the air. Buildings are solid objects, there is no doubt about that, but they are never in themselves architecture. Architecture is dependent on the observer's culture, and the ideas that are brought to bear on the building, so that we either recognize it as gestural, or else we don't. More clearly, one might say 'that building produces in me a feeling of architecture'. It would sound so odd that we would not ordinarily let ourselves say it, but architecture is in the mind of the beholder, in just the same way that beauty is, and has been since the eighteenth century at least (Hume, 1777b, 230). Depite the passing of generations since that realisation, it has not passed into common sense, so we still have not developed a habit of saying 'that object produces in me a feeling of beauty'. What we still say is: 'that object is beautiful', even though we know it's only a manner of speaking. This isn't to say that architecture is altogether personal and without objectivity, because within any given culture we can expect a degree of consensus in the responses, and one can design with the expectation that some gestures will be recognized – there is an element of unpredictability involved, but we can set in place the conditions that favour an appropriate response. The play of arbitrariness and predictability is dramatised in a work by the artist Walter de Maria – his *Lightning Field* – which is an extensive grid of steel poles in New Mexico (Web-site: http://www.diacenter.org/ltproj/lf/lf.html).[19] It is often more or less invisible – in bright sunlight it is hardly noticeable – but when there are stormy conditions, the steel rods tend to induce lightning strikes. The installation does not make thunderstorms, but makes it likely that if there is a storm, the lightning will strike one of the rods rather than an arbitrary point elsewhere in the vicinity. The architecture-system works along these lines. We can control the form of buildings, which are the equivalent of the rods, but we cannot control the culture of the people who come into contact with the buildings – the equivalent of the atmospheric conditions. The bright, even conditions are those of everyday philistinism, cheerily unnoticing of the buildings' potential charge, whereas the storm clouds' brooding angst is an active and dynamic culture, ready to spark with thousands of volts of enthusiasm when appropriately triggered. The lightning's line of flight is, then, the moment of recognition of architecture, or the aesthetic charge. It is not in the rod, nor exactly in the cloud, but is produced when the two come into proximity, like the shock of recognition when we make reciprocal eye contact with a wild animal. It is real, but not in the object, and it was not in us, before we came into contact with the object, so the feeling seems to have come from outside. Architecture's epiphanies are produced when we have both a building and a culture, but the two are not tethered together, and culture can shift and recompose itself, drifting like a cloud in the night.

NOTES

1   The approach that I have taken in this chapter, and the language that I have used, owe more to the Pragmatist than the Heideggerian tradition. See Rorty, 1989, 1991.

2   It has been argued that we should not read it as 'being in a particular spot' (Mugerauer, 1997) even though such a reading would seem to be sympathetic to Heidegger's actions, and is how it often has been read by his advocates. My reading here is that he meant something like 'being in a particular culture', which has its parallel in my reading of Deleuze moving nomadically between 'cultures,' rather than 'places' per se (which is how Leach reads him in his essay). However Heidegger does seem to have imagined his own indigenous culture to be rooted in a particular region, and his meaning therefore slides very readily into 'being in a particular spot,' despite the theoretical distinction. Moreover, the view is certainly prevalent in many traditional communities, whether or not it was Heidegger's view, and it is the idea rather than the man that is of interest here.

3   Heidegger did not support the Nazis' worst excesses, but in the early 1930s he did find them plausible agents for change, and joined the party. He was disappointed that things did not develop as he had hoped, but even after 1945 he did not speak out to recant his earlier involvement, and it is his apparent failure to be changed by his experience that seems now to condemn him, as it did in the eyes of Karl Jaspers, in remarks quoted below. There are now many books which deal with this problem; see, for example: Farias, 1987; Ott, 1994; Safranski, 1994; Ward, 1995; Wolin, 1993.

4   Rykwert (1996: 379–81) points to factual inaccuracies in Heidegger's account of the Doric temple, and Van Gogh's painting – the only two concrete examples of art works cited in 'The Origin of the Work of Art'.

5   Other people, such as Christian Norberg-Schulz and Suzanne Langer, made comparable distinctions, using different locutions. In this chapter I follow de Certeau's usage, which is reasonably widespread in current discourse, especially among cultural theorists, and have explained it in the text in order to keep confusion to a minimum.

6   Mark Campbell gave a paper on the subject of this room at the Annual Meeting of the Society of Architectural Historians at Houston, Texas, 14–18 April 1999.

7   The film, *Semiotics of the Kitchen*, is by Martha Rosler (1975).

8 The Oxford English Dictionary explains the word's development as a contraction of 'ministry' (a calling). The most familiar usage in this sense now is in the title of the cycles of medieval 'Mystery Plays', which are still performed. The plays were originally staged by the various craft guilds, or mysteries.

9 Wittgenstein to Engelmann, 2 September 1919 (Wijdeveld, 1994: 34). Selections of Loos' writings are available in translation, for example: Loos, 1929. One or two illustrations of buildings by Loos find their way into most histories of architecture which include the twentieth century, and will be adequate to give an idea of the kind of buildings which he proposed. The interiors however turn out to be unexpectedly sumptuous, despite their severe lines (Schezen, 1996).

10 It would be wrong to suggest that Pevsner could not entertain other views of architectural history. The great project of *The Buildings of England* aimed to cover, county by county, all the interesting buildings around the country, of whatever size and whether or not they had any wider significance beyond their charm to recommend them.

11 The real architect who designed the little 'writing hut' for Michael Pollan (Pollan, 1997), for example, contrasts spectacularly with the fictional Howard Roark.

12 The house was built for the Frank family, in Washington, Connecticut, 1975. It is illustrated in later editions of Charles Jencks, *The Language of Postmodern Architecture*; for example in the sixth edition (Jencks, 1991: 97). Suzanne Frank, who commissioned the house, has written a book about it (Frank, 1994).

13 See page 175.

14 Anthony Vidler, 'Architecture Dismembered', in *The Architectural Uncanny*, op. cit.

15 Leach (1997) collects together something rather like a canon of texts (we might call it a loose canon) which have a bearing on this line of development. They are by 23 authors, two of them with English as their first language, the rest mostly French or German. Andrew Benjamin and Fredric Jameson are the English-speakers; there are two Italians – Umberto Eco and Gianni Vattimo (Paul Virilio I take to be French); and one woman – Hélène Cixous.

16 Baudrillard (1988) quoted by Koolhaas (1995: 1128). This seems to be very similar to the claims made by Bennington about Jacques Derrida. Derrida, says Bennington is 'in the position of Moses, proposing an unintelligible liberation in so abstract and forced a rhetoric, a writing so artificial and full of ruses that one would say that it was a foreign language. This writing would be like the Jewish tabernacle, a construction of bands, empty inside, signifier without signified, containing nothing at the center' (Bennington, 1991: 297).

17 There are now architectural history books which deal with buildings of lower status – for example Oliver (1997) – but they tend to be specialised studies rather than a general historical framework, which encourages architects to see themselves as belonging in a line of modest craftsmen, turning out well considered designs which are not in any way attention-seeking. Brenda Vale has suggested linking feminism with a 'green' agenda in the cause of such architecture, which has some plausibility, but this link could be rhetorically counter-productive if the argument from feminist principles distances it from what it expected of men. (If it is the role specifically of

women to lead the way in taking responsibility and being sensible, where does that leave men? Does it leave them free to be irresponsible? It seems to be what one has come to expect.) However she proposes exactly the kind of revaluation of values which is needed to solve this particular problem, and her conclusions lead to practical results which are much the same as Scruton's, but by way of very different reasoning. (Vale, 1996). See also Gorst, 1995; Meiss, 1990; Norman, 1988; Pye, 1978

18   For a vigorous demonstration of the effects of conflating criminality and greatness see Fielding (1743).

19   I am not proposing here that *The Lightening Field* is a work of architecture, only using it as a metaphor.

Chapter 1: Architectural Principles in an Age of Nihilism

Roger Scruton

The search for objective canons of taste has often proved to be the enemy of aesthetic judgement. By pretending to an authority which cannot reasonably be claimed, this search provokes an original rebellion against the Father. Repudiating the dictatorship of one law, the rebellious offspring refuses to accept the advice of any other and opts for an aesthetic anarchy, rather than submit once again to a discipline which had become intolerable to him. At the same time he stands more in need of this discipline than ever: and the greater the rebellion, the more implacable the need.

The tale is familiar, and its lesson is one that man is destined not to learn, or to learn only when the price of disobedience has been paid. But let us, for all that, draw the lesson, since debates about modern architecture are futile otherwise. Just as we should not look for more objectivity in any study than can be obtained from it, so should we not be content with less. The substance of aesthetic judgement lies in feeling, imagination and taste. But this subjective matter is objectively formed: it is brought to the forum of discussion, and given the status and the structure of a rational preference. Hence there is both the possibility, and the necessity, of aesthetic education. The disaster of modern architecture stems from a misunderstanding of this education, and a disposition to discard the true disciplines of the eye and the heart in favour of a false discipline of the intellect.

Of course, the aesthetic preference, like any human faculty, may remain infantile and unexamined. In architecture, however, there is special reason to resist the pleasure principle. The person who builds imposes himself on others, and the sight of what he does is as legitimate an object of criticism as are his morals and his manners. It is not enough for an architect to say: *I like it*, or even: I and my educated colleagues like it. He has to *justify its existence*, and the question is whether he and his colleagues are right.

As I have argued elsewhere, the search for some kind of co-ordination of tastes is forced on us by our nature as social beings. This search may not lead to a single set of principles; nevertheless it involves a common pursuit of an

Figure 1.1
A street in Autun,
Burgundy, looking
towards the basilica.
Photo: Andrew
Ballantyne.

acceptable solution. It may seem strange to describe aesthetic values as solutions to a 'co-ordination problem'. In architecture, however, they are that, and more besides. Through aesthetic reflection we endeavour to create a world in which we are at home with others and with ourselves. That is why we care about aesthetic values, and live wretchedly in places where they have been brushed aside or trampled on. Man's 'estrangement' in the modern city is due to many causes besides modern architecture. But who can deny that modern architecture has played its own special part in producing it, by wilfully imposing forms, masses and proportions which bear no relation to our aesthetic expectations and which arrogantly defy the wisdom and achievement of the past?

What was primarily wrong with modernism was not its rigidity, its moralising, its puritanical zeal – although these were repulsive enough. Modernism's respect for discipline was its sole redeeming feature: but it was a discipline about the *wrong things*. It told us to be true to function, to social utility, to materials, to political principles. It told us to be 'of our time', while enlisting architecture in those insolent experiments for the re-fashioning of man which have threatened our civilisation with such disaster. At the same time, modernism threw away, as a worthless by-product of the past and a symbol of its oppressive rituals, the *aesthetic* discipline embodied in the classical tradition. It had no use for *that* kind of discipline, and no patience towards the few brave critics who defended it as the only discipline that counts.

Postmodernism is a reaction to modernist censoriousness. It 'plays' with the classical and gothic details which were forbidden it by its stern parent, and so empties them of their last vestiges of meaning. This is not the rediscovery of history, but its dissolution. Modernism had the decency to stand condemned by

Figure 1.2
Simla, Northern India.
Photo: Hulton-Getty.

Figure 1.3
Montenegro, which was
in Yugoslavia when the
photo was taken in 1938.
Photo: Hulton-Getty.

history. Postmodernism wishes to stand condemned by nothing, and also to condemn nothing. The details with which it plays are not the ornaments it takes them for: their significance is that of an order which lies crystallised within them, and to use them in defiance of that order is to undo the work of centuries. Such a practice marks a new departure of the nihilistic spirit which is foreshadowed in modernism, and which there takes the belligerent form of a doctrine. Instead of the unbending rectitude of modernism, we are given the self-service lifestyles of the moral playground. But the effect of this transgression is no less destructive than the paternal interdiction which inspired it. We are now even further from the discipline-in-freedom that we need.

Where, then, should we look? In what laws or principles should the aesthetic choice be grounded, and how can those laws and principles be justified

Figure 1.4
Buildings in the market
square, Richmond,
Yorkshire.
Photo: Andrew
Ballantyne.

to the person who does not share them? I have argued in favour of certain traditional principles of design. However, the practice of good architecture depends upon the presence of a motive, and that motive is not given by the philosophy which recommends it. It comes to us through culture – in other words, through a habit of discourse, submission and agreement which is more easily lost than won, and which is not detachable, in the last analysis, from piety. If Ruskin is to be esteemed above all other critics of architecture it is not for his judgements (many of which were wrong, and all of which were eccentric), but for his elaboration of that truth. It is partly the failure to read Ruskin which explains the widespread conviction that the materials, the forms and the work of the builder can be understood by anyone, whatever the condition of his soul.

Nevertheless, all is not lost. It is possible for a civilisation to 'mark time' in the absence of the spirit which engendered it. It is by learning to 'mark time' that Western civilisation has endured so successfully since the Enlightenment, and reproduced that agreeable simulacrum of itself in which the life of the mind goes on. Our civilisation continues to produce forms which are acceptable to us, because it succeeded in enshrining its truth in education. An astonishing effort took place in nineteenth-century Europe and America to transcribe the values of our culture into a secular body of knowledge, and to hand on that knowledge from generation to generation without the benefit of the pulpit or the pilgrimage.

Nowhere was this process more successful than in the field of architecture. All the busy treatises of the Beaux-Arts, of the Gothic, Greek and Classical revivalists, of the critics and disciplinarians of the syncretic styles, had one over-riding and urgent concern: to ensure that a precious body of knowledge is not lost, that meaning is handed down and perpetuated by generations who have been severed from the inner impulse of a justifying faith. And, looking at the

nineteenth-century architecture of Europe and America, who c
success of their endeavour?

The most important change initiated by the modern movemen
unconditional war on this educational tradition. Certain things were *no longer to be studied*, not because they had been examined and found wanting, but because the knowledge contained in them was too great a rebuke to the impatient ignorance of the day. Architects were deliberately *diseducated*, with the result that most who have risen to fame or notoriety since the Second World War have been without the knowledge necessary to their trade. Architects now emerge from schools of 'architecture' unable to draw (either the human figure, on the perception of which all sense of visual order depends, or even the forms of building); they are, as a rule, ignorant of the Orders of classical architecture, with no conception of light and shade, or of the function of mouldings in articulating them, and without any idea of a building as something other than an engineering solution to a problem stated in a plan. That result is a natural consequence of the programme of 're-education' instituted by Le Corbusier and the Bauhaus. We should not be surprised, therefore, if the efforts of the re-educated architect are so seldom attended with success.

I wish to record and endorse some of the principles which informed the education of the nineteenth-century architect, and which I have defended elsewhere, in the course of which they have acquired more nuances than I need here repeat. My procedure will be to lay down eleven *fundamental* principles, and then to throw down a challenge to those who would reject them. Finally, I shall add eleven more specific principles, whose authority is less obvious.

1. Architecture is a human gesture in a human world, and, like every human gesture it is judged in terms of its meaning.
2. The human world is governed by the principle of 'the priority of appearance'. What is hidden from us has no meaning. (Thus a blush has a meaning, but not the flux of blood which causes it.) To know how to build, therefore, you must first understand appearances.
3. Architecture is useful only if it is not absorbed in being useful. Human purposes change from epoch to epoch, from decade to decade, from year to year. Buildings must therefore obey the law of the 'mutability of function'. If they cannot change their use – from warehouse to garage, to church, to apartment block – then they make room for other buildings which can. The capacity of a building to survive such changes is one proof of its merit: one proof that it answers to something deeper in us than the transient function which required it. (This idea gives grounds for hope, for it implies a 'natural selection of the beautiful'.)
4. Architecture plays a major part in creating the 'public realm': the place in which we associate with strangers. Its meaning and posture embody and contribute to a 'civic experience', and it is against the expectations created by that experience that a building must be judged. Of all architectural ensembles, therefore, it is the street that is the most important.

5. Architecture must respect the constraints which are imposed on it by human nature. Those constraints are of two kinds – the animal and the personal. As animals, we orient ourselves visually, move and live in an upright position, and are vulnerable to injury. As persons we live and fulfil ourselves through morality, law, religion, learning, commerce and politics. The reality and validity of those personal concerns can be either affirmed or denied by the architecture that surrounds us, just as our animal needs may be either fulfilled or thwarted. Buildings must respect both the animal and the personal sides of our nature. They must be 'persons suited to the public realm'. If not, they define no place for our habitation.

6. The primary need of the person is for values, and for a world in which his values are publicly recognised. The public realm must permit and endorse either a recognised public morality, or at least the common pursuit of one.

7. The aesthetic experience is not an optional addition to our mental equipment. On the contrary, it is the inevitable consequence of our interest in appearances. I see things, but I also see the meaning of things, and the meaning may saturate the experience. Hence appearance becomes the resting place of contemplation and self-discovery.

8. The aesthetics of everyday life consists in a constant process of adjustment, between the appearances of objects, and the values of the people who create and observe them. Since the common pursuit of a public morality is essential to our happiness, we have an overriding reason to engage in the common pursuit of a public taste. The aesthetic understanding ought to act as a shaping hand in all our public endeavours, adapting the world to our emotions and our emotions to the world, so as to overcome what is savage, beyond us, *unheimlich*. We must never cease, therefore, to seek for the forms that display, as a visible meaning, the moral co-ordination of the community.

9. A beautiful object is not beautiful in relation to this or that desire. It pleases us because it reminds us of the fullness of human life, aiming *beyond* desire, to a state of satisfaction. It accompanies us, so to speak, on our spiritual journey, and we are united with it by the same sense of community that is implied in the moral life.

10. Taste, judgement and criticism are therefore immovable components of the aesthetic understanding. To look at the world in this way, so as to find meaning in appearance itself, is at the same time to demand public recognition for what we see. It is to stand in the forum of rational argument, demanding the acceptance and the sympathy of our kind.

11. All serious architecture must therefore give purchase to the claims of taste. It must offer a public language of form, through which people can criticise and justify their buildings, come to an agreement over the right and the wrong appearance, and so construct a public realm in the image of their social nature.

Here I shall pause to take stock. There have been many opponents of aesthetic value in architecture – utilitarians, constructivists, *marxisants*, philistines. I have affirmed that the aesthetic understanding cannot in fact be eliminated from our lives. But my eleven points constitute no proof of such a view. Moreover, what I have said can be defended only by defending a whole culture, and the way of life that has grown within it. To those who despise that culture, or who have lost all sense of its validity, I can make no appeal. Yet, if they have lost the culture of their forefathers, the onus is on them to replace it, and not on me to persuade them that they are wrong. It is an onus that the critics of civilisation have never discharged. The great discourses of architecture – from Alberti, Serlio, Palladio, Ruskin – were written from a standpoint within the culture to which we are heirs. The discourses of the iconoclasts – Le Corbusier, Hannes Meyer, Gropius – express not some other culture, or some higher set of values, but a disorienta-tion, a 'decultivation' which – however it may be fortified by theory – has no authority against the tradition which it strives to disestablish. The same is true of those styles of criticism which try to undermine our certainties, by calling on some 'science' which 'explains' them. The Marxist theory, which allocates taste to ideology, may undermine my self-confidence. But it is not, for all that, an argument against my tastes. Taste is necessary to the rational being, and its assessments are – like the assessments of morality – internal to itself, neither confirmed nor denied by the 'science' which explains them. The arguments of the structuralists, post-structuralists, deconstructionists, post-deconstructionists, post-post-structuralist-deconstructionists etc., are worthless for a similar reason. Even if true they are of no aesthetic consequence: they constitute a massive *ignoratio elenchi* whose charm is that they promise *power* over a given study without the price of understanding it. But it is a spurious power: the power of the magician, whose spell is broken just as soon as you cease to believe in it.

With that I shall move from my eleven abstract principles to the eleven derivative principles which would form the basis of a pattern book in the Kingdom of Ends.

12.   The problem of architecture is a question of manners, not art. In no way does it resemble the problem which confronted Wagner in composing *Tristan*, or that which confronted Manet and Courbet when they endeav-oured to paint the modern world *as it really seems*. Such artistic problems faced by people of genius demand upheavals, overthrowings, a repudiation or reworking of traditional forms. For this very reason the resulting stylistic ventures should not be taken as prescriptions by those lesser mortals whose role is simply to decorate and humanise the world.

The problem of architecture is addressed to those lesser mortals – among whom we must count the majority of architects. For such people to model their actions on an idea of 'creativity' taken from the great triumphs of modern art is not only a supreme arrogance: it constitutes a public danger against which we should be prepared to legislate. Our problem is this: by what discipline can an architect of modest ability learn the aesthetic decencies? The answer is to be found in aesthetic 'constants', whose value can be understood by whomsoever should choose to build.

13. The first constant is that of scale. To stand in a personal relation to a building, I must comprehend it visually, without strain, and without feeling dwarfed or terrorised by its presence. Only in special circumstances do we take pleasure in buildings of vast undifferentiated mass (like the pyramids of Egypt), or of surpassing height. The spires of a Gothic cathedral, the competing towers of Manhattan: these clusters of stone and glass in flight, which start away from us like enormous birds, are rare achievements, in one case designed, in the other arising by an invisible hand from the pursuit of commerce. They delight us by defying our normal expectations. If the cathedral does not frighten us, it is because it is an act of worship: an offering to God, and an attempt to reach up to him with incorruptible fingers of stone. But that which thrills us in Manhattan also disturbs us: the sense of man overreaching himself, of recklessly extending his resources and his aims. And the massive weight of the pyramids strikes us with awe: time stands still in these blocks of stone, trapped in an airless coffin beneath a terrifying monolith.

Such constructions cannot serve as models for the ordinary builder, in the circumstances of daily life. His first concern must be the viewpoint of the man in the street. A building must face the passer-by, who should not be forced to look up in awe, or to cringe in humility, beset by a sense of his own littleness.

14. Buildings must therefore have façades, able to stand before us as we stand before them. It is in the façades that the aesthetic effect is concentrated. In addition to destroying old-fashioned decencies of scale, modernism also abolished the very concept of the 'face' in building. The modernist building has no orientation, no privileged approach, no induction into its ambit. It faces nothing, welcomes nothing, smiles and nods to no-one. Is it surprising that we are alienated?

15. It follows that the first principles of composition concern the ordering of façades. But to establish such principles we must break with the tyranny of the plan.

The 'diseducated' architect is not, as a rule, sent out into the world to study its appearance. He is put before a drawing board and told to plan. By the use of axonometrics he can then project his plans into three dimensions. The result is the 'horizontal style'; the style, or lack of it, which emerges from composing in two-dimensional layers. This style has generated the major building types of modernism.

Its bad manners can be attributed to four causes, all of them resulting from the tyranny exerted by the ground-plan. First, an unnatural regularity of outline. Second, and consequently, the need for a site that will fit the plan, and therefore for a barbarous work of clearance. Third, the absence of an intelligible façade. Fourth, the denial (implicit in those foregoing qualities) of the street. Such buildings either stand behind a little clearing, refusing to align themselves; or else they shuffle forwards and stare blankly and meaninglessly into space. They appear in our ancient towns like expressionless psychopaths, hungry for power, and careless of all the decencies that would merit it.

16. Composition requires detail, and the principles of composition depend upon the sense of detail. Here, too, matters have not been unaffected by modernist diseducation. The hostility to 'ornament' led to a corresponding neglect of detail, and to an emphasis on line and form as the main variables of composition. It came to seem as if architecture could be understood simply through the study of *geometry*; buildings were conceived as though cast in moulds out of some pliable fluid. (And, in due course, this is exactly how modernist buildings were made.)

    The fact is, however, that words like 'form', 'proportion', 'order', and 'harmony' can be applied to buildings only if they have *significant parts*. Harmony is a harmony among parts; proportion is a relation between perceivable divisions, and so on. The form of a building is perceivable only where there are details which divide and articulate its walls.

17. The true discipline of style consists, therefore, in the disposition of details. Hence the basis of everyday construction must lie in the pattern book: the catalogue of details which can be readily conjured, so as to form intelligible unities. All serious systems of architecture have produced such books (even if they have existed in the heads and hands of builders, rather than on the printed page). They offer us detachable parts, rules of composition, and a vocabulary of form. By means of them, an architect can negotiate corners, build in confined spaces, match wall to window, and window to door, and in general ensure an effect of harmony, in all the varying circumstances imposed on him by the site and the street which borders it.

18. The art of combination relies for its effect on regularity and repetition. The useful details are the ones that can be repeated, the ones which satisfy our demand for rhythm, sameness and symmetry. To invent such details, and at the same time to endow them with character and life, is not given to every architect at every period. On the contrary, it is here that the *great discoveries* of architecture reside. The value of the classical tradition is crystallised in the theory of the Orders, in which beauty is transfigured into a daily discipline, and the discoveries of true artists made available to those ordinary mortals for whom work and application must take the place of genius.

19. As the Orders make clear, the true discipline of form emphasises the vertical, rather than the horizontal line. The art of design is the art of vertical accumulation, of placing one thing above another, so as to create an order which can be spread rhythmically from side to side. It is by virtue of such an order that buildings come to stand before us as we before them, and to wear the human face that pleases us.

20. To endow a façade with vertical order, it is necessary to exploit light, shade and climate, to divide the wall space, and to emphasise apertures. In other words, it is necessary to use mouldings.

The abolition of mouldings was a visual calamity, the effects of which can be clearly witnessed in the modern American city. The real ugliness came not with the skyscraper, but when the skyscraper was stripped of all those lines, shadows and curlicues which were the source of its life and gaiety. Without mouldings, no space is articulate. Edges become blades; buildings lose their crowns; and walls their direction (since movement sideways has the same visual emphasis as movement up and down). Windows and doors cease to be aedicules and become mere holes in the wall. Nothing 'fits', no part is framed, marked off, emphasised or softened. Everything is sheer, stark, uncompromising, cold. In a nutshell, mouldings are the *sine qua non* of decency, and the source of our mastery over light and shade.

21. The building of a human face in architecture depends not only on details, but also on materials. These should be pleasant to the touch, welcoming to the eye and accommodating to our movements. They should also take a patina, so that their permanence has the appearance of softening and age. The duration of a building must, like the building itself, be marked by *life*. It must show itself as mortality, finitude, sadness, experience and decay. Hence concrete, even if it lends itself to massive aesthetic effects like the dome of the Pantheon, is not a suitable material for the ordinary builder.

22. The discipline of such a builder consists in the ability to perceive, to draw, to compare and to criticise details; and thereafter to combine those details in regular and harmonious forms, whatever the shape of the site in which he works, and without doing violence to the surrounding order.

Those twenty-two points do not dictate a style, but only the form of a style. But of course, they are in keeping with the tradition of Western architecture as it existed until the First World War, and they are enacted in the Classical and Gothic pattern books of the nineteenth century. But it is not enough to study a pattern book. Education is needed before you can apply it, and the question remains what form that education should take. I am inclined to say that the aspiring architect should go into the world and use his eyes. He should study the great treatises of architecture and learn to see with the eyes of others. He should learn to draw the shadows that fall on a Corinthian order, cast by the lines, mouldings and ornaments of a whole vertical cross-section. Then, perhaps, he will be ready for his first project: to design a façade between two existing buildings, in such a way that *nobody will be forced against his will to notice it*.

But such an education requires mental effort, and spiritual humility. And whatever things are taught in schools of architecture, those two qualities are not among them.

Chapter 2: The Architecture of Deceit

Diane Ghirardo

The town itself is peculiarly built, so that someone can live in it for years and travel into it and out of it daily without ever coming into contact with a working-class quarter or even with workers – so long, that is to say, as one confines himself to his business affairs or to strolling about for pleasure. This comes about mainly in the circumstances that through an unconscious, tacit agreement as much as through conscious, explicit intention the working-class districts are most sharply separated from the parts of the city reserved for the middle class ... Manchester's monied aristocracy can now travel from their houses to their places of business in the center of the town by the shortest routes, which run right through all the working-class districts, without even noticing how close they are to the most squalid misery which lies immediately about them on both sides of the road. This is because the main streets which run from the Exchange in all directions out of the city are occupied almost uninterruptedly on both sides by shops, which are kept by members of the middle and lower-middle classes. In their own interests these shop-keepers should keep up their shops in an outward appearance of cleanliness and respectability; and in fact they do so ... Those shops which are situated in the commercial quarter or in the vicinity of the middle-class residential districts are more elegant than those which serve to cover up the worker's grimy cottages. Nevertheless, even these latter adequately serve the purpose of hiding from the eyes of wealthy gentlemen and ladies with strong stomachs and weak nerves the misery and squalor that form the completing counterpart, the indivisible complement, of their riches and luxury. I know perfectly well that this deceitful manner of building is more or less common to all big cities ... I have never elsewhere seen a concealment of such fine sensibility of every thing that might offend the eyes and nerves of the middle classes. And yet it is precisely Manchester that has been built less according to a plan and less within the limitations of official regulations – and indeed more through accident – than any other town.

(Engels, 1845: 84–6)

In *The Condition of the Working Class in England in 1844*, Friedrich Engels exposed the effects of capitalism on the laboring classes. In his analysis of Manchester he also offered one of the first sustained critiques of the built environment. Engels discerned a relationship among political intentions, social realities, and building. Although he was not the last to perceive the nature of this relationship, his approach to building has had little influence on the architecture, construction, and real estate industries in the twentieth century.

Both as a profession and as an academic discipline, architecture prefers not to be directly associated with the construction and real estate industries. All three deal with building and enjoy an enormously beneficial symbiotic relationship, and all three share an atrophied social conscience. Architecture offers itself as different from the other two by virtue of being an "art" rather than a trace or a business and to this end contemporary practice – through highly refined mechanisms of dissimulation – conspires to preserve that precarious pretense.

ARCHITECTURE AS ART

William Curtis articulates a particularly cogent version of what amounts to a traditional art-historical position in his *Modern Architecture Since 1900*. Curtis insists on "a certain focused interest on questions of form and meaning." He selects what he believes to be the masterpieces of modern architecture – "I make no apologies for concentrating on buildings of high visual and intellectual quality" – and sets out to write "a balanced, readable, overall view of modern architecture from its beginnings until the recent past." To Curtis, balance implies exorcising political, social, and ideological considerations of the sort that he finds in the versions of history offered by Kenneth Frampton or Manfredo Tafuri and Francesco Dal Co, who "emphasized ideology at the expense of other matters" (Curtis, 1982: 6–11, 389–92).

This critical position – which is by far the dominant one in America – at most admits only passing reference to any larger cultural, political, and social considerations. Instead it involves extended visual analysis, concentrating primarily on a few "important" buildings – the Robie House, the Villa Savoye, the Kimball Art Museum. Such singular masterpieces transcend not only political, social, and ideological contingencies, but their own time as well. In Curtis' words, "To slot them into the Modern Movement is to miss much of their value" (Curtis, 1982: 388). Set like jewels into the diadem of architecture, they become aesthetic objects *par excellence* and above reproach.

However appealing it may seem, a critical position predicated on formal qualities remains problematical. The standards of judgment are reduced to categories – "formal resolution," "integration," and "authenticity" – concepts which are more opaque than most critics will concede. Except on the most general level, none of these categories denote an objectively verifiable criterion, despite an unspoken assumption to that effect. Even if, in the best of both cases, there is a general agreement to canonize a few works, considerable disagree-

Figure 2.1
A city thoroughfare.
Gustave Doré, 1872.

ment usually attends the decision about the particular works to be so embalmed. Indeed, the criteria for selecting one work over another are often arbitrary precisely because judgments based on formal analyses boil down to nothing more than matters of taste. One critic may find a certain degree of mathematical complexity necessary to make a building great; another may focus on the effects of massing techniques; and yet a third may demand an elegant series of references to or comments on the past. Though there is no denying the interest or significance of any of these aspects, it remains clear that assessing them depends as much upon personal taste as do preferences for a particular style.[1]

Edoardo Persico remarked on this situation nearly half-a-century ago, when he surveyed the bitter factional rivalries in Fascist Italy between classicizing traditionalists and Modern Movement rationalists. Persico concluded that, although they appeared to reflect dramatically different positions, the polemics in fact masked an underlying consensus. Since all sides took their cues from Fascism, the stylistic debates that flourished in the architectural press concerned matters of taste rather than substance (Persico, 1934). It was no more than a preference for white walls and ribbon windows competing with a predilection for traditional columns and arches. Persico's critique addressed an unspoken corollary – that both factions fell over themselves to give architectural expression to the ideals of Italian Fascism: to provide luxury apartments for the bourgeoisie, or to design urban settlements that permitted close surveillance of the lowest classes.

Lobotomized history surfaces in contemporary criticism in a variety of guises. Curtis, for example, faults the "whites" (formalists) and the "greys" (informalists) of the 1970s for having nothing to say about the current state of American society; and he does this in a 400-page text devoted to formalist analysis (Curtis, 1982: 355). Other historians laboriously criticize the naïve and utopian visions of early European modernists who associated their architecture with radical opposition to existing political and social systems; at the same time they lament the fate of the Modern Movement under the totalitarian pressures of Stalinist Russia and Nazi Germany.

To be sure, the high aspirations of the European early modernists were often unrealistic, as were their exaggerated claims for the role of the architect in shaping the new societies they envisioned. Further, many critics have correctly diagnosed an authoritarian strain in the social programs of Le Corbusier and others. Yet the extraordinary power of Le Corbusier's architecture sprang in part from their passionate searches for an architecture that would confront contemporary social realities.

ARCHITECTURE AS FASHION

A telling contrast can be drawn between the responses of contemporary architects to the economic decline of the 1970s and the attitude adopted by the radical architects who confronted the economically uncertain aftermath of the First World War. In the immediate post-war period architects turned to dreaming up new worlds to replace the old one; Bruno Taut and Walter Gropius come to mind as architects who attempted to reformulate architecture's role in society, and they are only two of a large and distinguished group active in Weimar Germany.

Conversely, when building opportunities dwindled in the United States in the 1970s, architects turned to drawings – not even designs of a different and better world, but instead a set of increasingly abstract, pretty (and marketable)

Figure 2.2
Warehousing.
Gustave Doré, 1872.

renderings of their own or of antique works and recycled postclassical picturesque sites. Like much building of the decades just preceding, these aesthetic
indulgences simply masquerade as architecture. They reveal architects in full
retreat from any involvement with the actual world of buildings.

ARCHITECTURE AS FEELING

Another approach attempts to evade the trap of taste and fashion by explicitly setting itself apart from the current postmodernist discourse. Christopher Alexander, an ardent advocate of this view, maintains that "the core of architecture depends on feeling." Alexander talks about the "primitive feeling" evoked by a steeply pitched roof; he believes that the pitched roof may be the "most natural and simple" thing to build, and he contrasts it with the arid forms of contemporary architecture, which are prized precisely because they lack feeling. The task of the architect, Alexander argues, is to produce a harmonious work that feels "absolutely comfortable – physically, emotionally, practically," and indeed, "architects are entrusted with the creation of that harmony in the world" (Alexander *et al.*, 1977; Alexander 1979, 1983).

Like the formalists, this group arrogates to itself the power to decide what you and I will find "authentic," "integrated," "natural," and "comfortable." Underlying this archaeology of primitive forms is a desperate search, shared with the formalists, for a universal architecture and a universal standard of value; there is a concomitant aggressive hostility toward critical positions that engage in dialogue with the unresolved, uncomfortable, politically explosive, and unharmonious.

The contemporary discourse on architecture thus fashions the discipline's own neutron bomb, which promises to leave nothing but the vacant buildings intact – an empty *bric-a-brac* landscape in both style and substance, a literally empty reminiscence of a bygone culture.

THE CRITIC'S COMPLICITY

The responsibility for having cultivated this hardy bloom belongs at least as much to critics and historians as it does to architects. Because they assign priority to the unique formal features of individual monuments, historians and critics diminish interest in anything else. Criticism today borrows the already inadequate tools of art history as traditionally practiced, substitutes description for analysis, and turns architecture into a harmless but ultimately meaningless and consumable artifact. As society's arbiters of taste, critics also help to distribute society's rewards – prestige and money – to those architects who are willing to produce fresh new fashions destined for elite consumption.

The architectural profession seems deeply divided between those who conceive it as an art and those who perceive it as a service. Few would argue that either of these components can safely be jettisoned, but exactly what their proper relationship ought to be is not clear – nor is it likely to become so. Moreover, anything beyond purely formal concerns in the work of architecture is seen as sullying architecture's purity and rendering it no more than a billboard for political beliefs or the tool of class conflict and competing ideologies.[2] While banal or badly built work presents less of a problem (Speer's Berlin, for example),

Figure 2.3
Urban poverty.
Gustave Doré, 1872.

a widely acclaimed, complex, and interesting work such as Giuseppe Terragni's Casa del Fascio in Como is deeply troubling, for its explicit and undeniably political matrix cannot successfully be evaded.

Sometimes architecture is an explicit political billboard; at other times it sets itself in opposition to dominant class interests; and still elsewhere it constitutes an unconscious – but no less real – expression of political and social realities and aspirations. Certainly aesthetic and formal considerations come into play in any understanding of a building; but the inescapable truth is that these categories are culturally conditioned, often arbitrary, and only two among a number of components that determine the value of architecture.

ARCHITECTURE AND EVASIVE MANEUVERABILITY

What accounts for the architectural community's pervasive refusal to confront real issues in the realm of architecture and the world that circumscribes it? When so much energy is devoted to maintaining architecture's privilege and its purity, one has to wonder what is being concealed.

Academic politics are so bitter because the stakes are so small; in a case where stakes are immeasurably larger – as in the politics of a building – the apparent strategy is to place something innocuous at center stage in order to divert attention from more important concerns. Formal elements – style, harmony of parts, call them what you will – are sufficiently trivial to be awarded top billing in architectural discourse. It is also far easier and far more tidy to persevere in formalist critiques, thereby avoiding the risk of antagonizing moneyed interest. In turn, architects choose the safer course by designing buildings that evade issues of substance.

The position that only formal elements matter in architecture bespeaks a monumental refusal to confront serious problems; it avoids a critique of the existing power structure, of the ways power is used, and of the identity of those whose interests power serves. To do otherwise might entail opening a Pandora's box of far more complicated issues: racism and white flight, exploitation and the manipulation of land values, prices, resources, building permits, zoning, and taxes on behalf of a small power elite – as well as larger questions about our current cultural situation. At the same time, to suggest that the world contains an ineluctable harmony which an architect need only discover in the realm of forms and feelings is dangerously naïve (Sullivan, 1900: 223). An architecture predicated solely upon such principles finds its objective correlative in a Walt Disney movie: soothing in the promise of happy endings, simplified with clear-cut villains and heroes, and seductive in the presentation of a world that in so many ways simply does not correspond to the one in which we live.

In none of its manifestations does the profession dare question the politics of building: who builds what, where, for whom, and at what price. Although arguably one of the most important issues for all architects to consider – and for the discipline to emphasize – it is addressed by few. Certainly as professionals, architects do little to gain a voice in these important decisions – they do not, for example, organize political action committees; by default they are left with the trivial issues of fashion and taste. The anemic architecture that issues from this acquiescence overwhelms our cities. Nowhere is this more grotesquely apparent than in the tenements of the South Bronx in New York. Officials chose to deal with socially troubled, abandoned, and physically scarred public housing projects by spending thousands of dollars to replace broken and boarded up windows with decorative panels depicting houseplants and window shades, thereby avoiding a serious confrontation with the community's problems. Public officials in effect aped the activities of prominent architects who currently undertake the same kind of window dressing in their own work.

Only when architects, critics, and historians accept the responsibility for building – in all of its ramifications – will we approach an architecture of substance.

NOTES

1   Postmodernists defend the use of formal elements from ancient or Renaissance classicism, for example, with the argument that meaning inheres only in historical forms-that is, pre-modern forms. With this claim they impale themselves on the horns of a dilemma since it leads them to incorporate historical forms into their works in such a way as to drain the forms of their highly precise historical associations. (In the designs of Michael Graves, for example, the keystone is hollowed out to become a window or raised high to become a scupper.) However contradictory the two positions, postmodernists do indeed want it both ways, and the point remains that they stand on the shifting grounds of arbitrary fashion.

2   If we look at the building by Diana Agrest and Mario Gandelsonas in Buenos Aires, for example, we recognize the references to historical forms that avoid banal imitation, and we can appreciate it as a highly intelligent, accomplished structure, with a high degree of sensitivity to the site, to the urban context, to contemporary building practice, and specifically, to building traditions in Buenos Aires. But what if we ask for whom it was built or inquire into its urban context in the political turbulence of Buenos Aires? Altogether too many critics and architects today would dismiss this line of questioning as irrelevant.

Chapter 3: Spatial Stories

Michel de Certeau

Narration created humanity.

(Janet, 1928: 261)

In modern Athens, the vehicles of mass transportation are called *metaphorai*. To go to work or come home, one takes a "metaphor" – a bus or a train. Stories could also take this noble name: every day, they traverse and organize places; they select and link them together; they make sentences and itineraries out of them. They are spatial trajectories.

In this respect, narrative structures have the status of spatial syntaxes. By means of a whole panoply of codes, ordered ways of proceeding and constraints, they regulate changes in space (or moves from one place to another) made by stories in the form of places put in linear or interlaced series: from here (Paris), one goes there (Montargis); this place (a room) includes another (a dream or a memory), etc. More than that, when they are represented in descriptions or acted out by actors (a foreigner, a city-dweller, a ghost), these places are linked together more or less tightly or easily by "modalities" that specify the kind of passage leading from the one to the other: the transition can be given an "epistemological" modality concerning knowledge (for example: "it's not certain that this is the Place de la République"), an "alethic" one concerning existence (for example, "the land of milk and honey is an improbable end-point"), or a deontic one concerning obligation (for example: "from this point, you have to go over to that one"). These are only a few notations among many others, and serve only to indicate with what subtle complexity stories, whether everyday or literary, serve us as means of mass transportation, as *metaphorai*.

Every story is a travel story – a spatial practice. For this reason, spatial practices concern everyday tactics, are part of them, from the alphabet of spatial indication ("It's to the right," "Take a left"), the beginning of a story the rest of which is written by footsteps, to the daily "news" ("Guess who I met at the bakery?"), television news reports ("Teheran: Khomeini is becoming increasingly

Figure 3.1
A metaphor in the
Australian Outback.
*The Adventures of
Priscilla, Queen of the
Desert*, Stephan Elliot,
1994.
Photo: British Film
Institute.

isolated . . . "), legends (Cinderellas living in hovels), and stories that are told (memories and fiction of foreign lands or more or less distant times in the past). These narrated adventures, simultaneously producing geographies of actions and drifting into the commonplaces of an order, do not merely constitute a "supplement" to pedestrian enunciations and rhetorics. They are not satisfied with displacing the latter and transposing them into the field of language. In reality, they organize walks. They make the journey, before or during the time the feet perform it.

These proliferating metaphors – sayings and stories that organize places through the displacements they "describe" (as a mobile point "describes" a curve) – what kind of analysis can be applied to *them*? To mention only the studies concerning spatializing *operations* (and not spatial systems), there are numerous works that provide methods and categories for such an analysis. Among the most recent, particular attention can be drawn to those referring to a semantics of space (John Lyons on "Locative Subjects" and "Spatial Expressions", in Lyons, 1977: II, 475–81, 690–703), a psycholinguistics of perception (Miller and Johnson-Laird on "the hypothesis of localization", 1976), a sociolinguistics of descriptions of places (e.g. William Labov's, see page 76), a phenomenology of the behavior that organizes "territories" (e.g. Scheflen and Ashcraft, 1976), an "ethnomethodology" of the indices of localization in conversation (e.g. Schegloff, 1972), or a semiotics viewing culture as a spatial metalanguage (e.g. the work of the Tartu School, especially Lotman, 1973; Lotman and Ouspenski, 1976), etc. Just as signifying practices, which concern the ways of putting language into effect, were taken into consideration after linguistic systems had been investigated, today spatializing practices are attracting attention now that the codes and taxonomies of the spatial order have been examined. Our investigation belongs to this "second" moment of the analysis, which moves from structures to actions. But in this vast ensemble, I shall consider only *narrative actions*; this will allow us to specify a few elementary forms of practices organizing space: the bipolar distinction between "map" and "itinerary," the procedures of delimitation or "marking boundaries" ("*bornage*") and "enunciative focalizations" (that is, the indication of the body within discourse).

"SPACES" AND "PLACES"

At the outset, I shall make a distinction between space (*espace*) and place (*lieu*) that delimits a field. A place (*lieu*) is the order (of whatever kind) in accord with which elements are distributed in relationships of coexistence. It thus excludes the possibility of two things being in the same location (*place*). The law of the "proper" rules in the place: the elements taken into consideration are *beside* one another, each situated in its own "proper" and distinct location, a location it defines. A place is thus an instantaneous configuration of positions. It implies an indication of stability.

A *space* exists when one takes into consideration vectors of direction, velocities, and time variables. Thus space is composed of intersections of mobile elements. It is, in a sense, actuated by the ensemble of movements deployed within it. Space occurs as the effect produced by the operations that orient it, situate it, temporalize it, and make it function in a polyvalent unity of conflictual programs or contractual proximities. On this view, in relation to place, space is like the word when it is spoken, that is, when it is caught in the ambiguity of an actualization, transformed into a term dependent upon many different conventions, situated as the act of a present (or of a time), and modified by the transformations caused by successive contexts. In contradistinction to the place, it has thus none of the univocity or stability of a "proper."

In short, *space is a practiced place*. Thus the street geometrically defined by urban planning is transformed into a space by walkers. In the same way, an act of reading is the space produced by the practice of a particular place: a written text, i.e. a place constituted by a system of signs.

Merleau-Ponty distinguished a "geometrical" space ("a homogeneous and isotropic spatiality," analogous to our "place") from another "spatiality" which he called an "anthropological space." This distinction depended on a distinct problematic, which sought to distinguish from "geometrical" univocity the experience of an "outside" given in the form of space, and for which "space is existential" and "existence is spatial." This experience is a relation to the world; in dreams and in perception, and because it probably precedes their differentiation, it expresses "the same essential structure of our being as a being situated in relationship to a milieu" – being situated by a desire, indissociable from a "direction of existence" and implanted in the space of a landscape. From this point of view "there are as many spaces as there are distinct spatial experiences"

Figure 3.2
Narrative character-
building.
A Sunday-school class
hears the story of Moses
crossing the Red Sea,
1955.
Photo: Hulton-Getty.

(Merleau-Ponty, 1945: 324–44). The perspective is determined by a "phenomenology" of existing in the world.

In our examination of the daily practices that articulate that experience, the
opposition between "place" and "space" will rather refer to two sorts of determinations in stories: the first, a determination through objects that are ultimately
reducible to the *being-there* of something dead, the law of a "place" (from the
pebble to the cadaver, an inert body always seems, in the West, to found a place
and give it the appearance of a tomb); the second, a determination through
operations which, when they are attributed to a stone, tree, or human being,
specify "spaces" by the actions of historical *subjects* (a movement always seems
to condition the production of a space and to associate it with a history).
Between these two determinations, there are passages back and forth, such as
the putting to death (or putting into a landscape) of heroes who transgress frontiers and who, guilty of an offense against the law of the place, best provide its
restoration with their tombs; or again, on the contrary, the awakening of inert
objects (a table, a forest, a person that plays a certain role in the environment)
which, emerging from their stability, transform the place where they lay motion-
less into the foreignness of their own space.

Stories thus carry out a labor that constantly transforms places into spaces
or spaces into places. They also organize the play of changing relationships
between places and spaces. The forms of this play are numberless, fanning out in
a spectrum reaching from the putting in place of an immobile and stone-like
order (in it, nothing moves except discourse itself, which, like a camera panning
over a scene, moves over the whole panorama), to the accelerated succession of
actions that multiply spaces (as in the detective novel or certain folktales, though
this spatializing frenzy nevertheless remains circumscribed by the textual place). It
would be possible to construct a typology of all these stories in terms of identification of places and actualization of spaces. But in order to discern in them the
modes in which these distinct operations are combined, we need criteria and
analytical categories – a necessity that leads us back to travel stories of the most
elementary kind.

TOURS AND MAPS

Oral descriptions of places, narrations concerning the home, stories about the streets, represent a first and enormous corpus. In a very precise analysis of descriptions New York residents gave of their apartments, Linde and Labov recognize two distinct types, which they call the "map" and the "tour." The first is of the type: "The girls' room is next to the kitchen." The second: "You turn right and come into the living room." Now, in the New York corpus, only three percent of the descriptions are of the "map" type. All the rest, that is, virtually the whole corpus, are of the "tour" type: "You come in through a low door," etc. These descriptions are made for the most part in terms of operations and show "how to enter each room." Concerning this second type, the authors point out that a circuit or "tour" is a speech-act (an act of enunciation) that "furnishes a minimal series of paths by which to go into each room"; and that the "path" is a series of units that have the form of vectors that are either "static" ("to the right," "in front of you," etc.) or "mobile" ("if you turn to the left," etc.) (Linde and Labov, 1975; see also Hammad, 1973).

In other words, description oscillates between the terms of an alternative: either *seeing* (the knowledge of an order of places) or *going* (spatializing actions). Either it presents a *tableau* ("there are . . . "), or it organizes *movements* ("you enter, you go across, you turn . . . "). Of these two hypotheses, the choices made by the New York narrators overwhelmingly favored the second.

Leaving Linde and Labov's study aside (it is primarily concerned with the rules of the social interactions and conventions that govern "natural language," a problem we will come back to later), I would like to make use of these New York stories – and other similar stories (see, for example, Bidoue and Kouie, 1974; Médam and Augoyard, 1976) – to try to specify the relationships between the indicators of "tours" and those of "maps," where they coexist in a single description. How are acting and seeing co-ordinated in this realm of ordinary language in which the former is so obviously dominant? The question ultimately concerns the basis of the everyday narrations, the relation between the itinerary (a discursive series of operations) and the map (a plane projection totalizing observations), that is, between two symbolic and anthropological languages of space. Two poles of experience. It seems that in passing from "ordinary" culture to scientific discourse, one passes from one pole to the other.

In narrations concerning apartments or streets, manipulations of space or "tours" are dominant. This form of description usually determines the whole style of the narration. When the other form intervenes, it has the characteristic of being *conditioned* or *presupposed* by the first. Examples of tours conditioning a map: "If you turn to the right, there is . . . ", or the closely related form, "If you go straight ahead, you'll see . . . " In both cases, an action permits one to see something. But there are also cases in which a tour assumes a place indication: "There, there's a door, you take the next one" – an element of mapping is the presupposition of a certain itinerary. The narrative fabric in which describers

Figure 3.3
The road to nowhere.
Janet Leigh in *Psycho*,
Alfred Hitchcock, 1960.
Photo: British Film
Institute.

(*descripteurs*) of itineraries predominate is thus punctuated by describers of the map type which have the function of indicating either an effect obtained by the tour ("you see . . . ") or a given that it postulates as its limit ("there is a wall"), its possibility ("there's a door"), or an obligation ("there's a one-way street"), etc. The chain of spatializing operations seems to be marked by references to what it produces (a representation of places) or to what it implies (a local order). We thus have the structure of the travel story: stories of journeys and actions are marked out by the "citation" of the places that result from them or authorize them.

From this angle, we can compare the combination of "tours" and "maps" in everyday stories with the manner in which, over the past five centuries, they have been interlaced and then slowly dissociated in literary and scientific representations of space. In particular, if one takes the "map" in its current geographical form, we can see that in the course of the period marked by the birth of modern scientific discourse (i.e. from the fifteenth to the seventeenth century) the map has slowly disengaged itself from the itineraries that were the condition of its possibility. The first medieval maps included only the rectilinear marking out of itineraries (performative indications chiefly concerning pilgrimages), along with the stops one was to make (cities which one was to pass through, spend the night in, pray at, etc.) and distances calculated in hours or in days; that is, in terms of the time it would take to cover them on foot (Kimble, 1938). Each of these maps is a memorandum prescribing actions. The tour to be made is predominant in them. It includes the map elements, just as today the description of a route to be taken accompanies a hasty sketch already on paper, in the form of citations of places, a sort of dance through the city: "20 paces straight ahead, then turn to the left, then another 40 paces . . . " The drawing articulates spatializing practices, like the maps of urban routes, arts of actions and stories of paces, that serve the Japanese as "address books" (Barthes, 1970) or the wonderful fifteenth-century Aztec map describing the exodus of the Totomihuacas. This drawing outlines not the "route" (there wasn't one) but the "log" of their journey on foot – an outline marked out by footprints with regular gaps between them and by pictures of the successive events that took place in the course of the journey (meals, battles, crossings of rivers or mountains, etc.): not a "geographical map" but "history book."[1]

Between the fifteenth and the seventeenth centuries, the map became more autonomous. No doubt the proliferation of the "narrative" figures that have long been its stock-in-trade (ships, animals, and characters of all kinds) still had the function of indicating the operations – travelling, military, architectural, political or commercial – that make possible the fabrication of a geographical plan.[2] Far from being "illustrations," iconic glosses on the text, these figurations, like fragments of stories, mark on the map the historical operations from which it resulted. Thus the sailing ship painted on the sea indicates the maritime expedition that made it possible to represent the coastlines. It is equivalent to a describer of the "tour" type. But the map gradually wins out over these figures; it colonizes space; it eliminates little by little the pictural figurations of the practices that produce it. Transformed first by Euclidean geometry and then by descriptive geometry, constituted as a formal ensemble of abstract places, it is a "theater" (as one used to call atlases) in which the same system of projection nevertheless juxtaposes two very different elements: the data furnished by a tradition (Ptolemy's *Geography*, for instance) and those that came from navigators (portulans, for example). The map thus collates on the same plane heterogeneous places, some *received* from a tradition and others *produced* by observation. But the important thing here is the erasure of the itineraries which, presupposing the first category of places and conditioning the second, makes it possible to move from one to the other. The map, a totalizing stage on which elements of diverse origin are brought together to form the tableau of a "state" of geographical knowledge, pushes away into its prehistory or into its posterity, as if into the wings, the operations of which it is the result or the necessary condition. It remains alone on the stage. The tour describers have disappeared.

The organization that can be discerned in stories about space in everyday culture is inverted by the process that has isolated a system of geographical places. The difference between the two modes of description obviously does not consist in the presence or absence of practices (they are at work everywhere), but in the fact that maps, constituted as proper places in which to *exhibit the products* of knowledge, form tables of *legible* results. Stories about space

Figure 3.4
Exodus to the promised land.
"Climb Ev'ry Mountain",
in *The Sound of Music*,
Robert Wise, 1965.
Photo: British Film Institute.

exhibit, on the contrary, the operations that allow it, within a constraining and non-"proper" place, to mingle its elements anyway, as one apartment-dweller put it concerning the rooms in his flat: "One can mix them up" ("*On peut les triturer*") (Bidoue and Kouie, 1974: 55). From the folktale to descriptions of residences, an exacerbation of "practice" ("*faire*") (and thus of enunciation) actuates the stories narrating tours in places that, from the ancient cosmos to contemporary public housing developments, are all forms of an imposed order.

In a pre-established geography, which extends (if we limit ourselves to the home) from bedrooms so small that "one can't do anything in them" to the legendary, long-lost attic that "could be used for everything" (Bidoue and Kouie, 1974: 57, 59), everyday stories tell us what one can do in it and make out of it. They are treatments of space.

MARKING OUT BOUNDARIES

As operations on places, stories also play the everyday role of a mobile and magisterial tribunal in cases concerning their delimitation. As always, this role appears more clearly at the second degree, when it is made explicit and duplicated by juridical discourse. In the traditional language of court proceedings, magistrates formerly "visited the scene of the case at issue" ("*se transportaient sur les lieux*") (transports and juridical metaphors), in order to "hear" the contradictory statements (*dits*) made by the parties to a dispute concerning debatable boundaries. Their "interlocutory judgment," as it was called, was an "operation of marking out boundaries" (*bornage*). Written in a beautiful hand by the court clerk on parchments where the writing sometimes flowed into (or was inaugurated by?) drawings outlining the boundaries, these interlocutory judgments were in sum nothing other than meta-stories. They combined together (the work of a scribe collating variants) the opposing stories of the parties involved: "Mr. Mulatier declares that his grandfather planted this apple tree on the edge of his field . . . Jeanpierre reminds us that Mr. Bouvet maintains a dungheap on a piece of land of which he is supposed to be the joint owner with his brother André . . . " Genealogies of places, legends about territories. Like a critical edition, the judge's narration reconciles these versions. The narration is "established" on the basis of "primary" stories (those of Mr. Mulatier, Jeanpierre, and so many others), stories that already have the function of spatial legislation since they determine rights and divide up lands by "acts" or discourses about actions (planting a tree, maintaining a dungheap, etc.).

These "operations of marking out boundaries," consisting in narrative contracts and compilations of stories, are composed of fragments drawn from earlier stories and fitted together in makeshift fashion (*bricolés*). In this sense, they shed light on the formation of myths, since they also have the function of founding and articulating spaces. Preserved in the court records, they constitute an immense travel literature, that is, a literature concerned with actions organizing more or less extensive social cultural areas. But this literature itself represents only a tiny part (the part that is written about disputed points) of the oral narration that interminably labors to compose spaces, to verify, collate, and displace their frontiers.

The ways of "conducting" a story offer, as Pierre Janet pointed out (Janet, 1928: 249–94)[3] a very rich field for the analysis of spatiality. Among the questions that depend on it, we should distinguish those that concern dimensions (extensionality), orientation (vectorality), affinity (homographies), etc. I shall stress only a few of its aspects that have to do with delimitation itself, the primary and literally "fundamental" question: it is the partition of space that structures it. Everything refers, in fact, to this differentiation which makes possible the isolation and interplay of distinct spaces. From the distinction that separates a subject from its exteriority to the distinctions that localize objects, from the home (constituted on the basis of the wall) to the journey (constituted on the basis of a geographical "elsewhere" or a cosmological "beyond"), from the functioning of the urban network to that of the rural landscape, there is no spatiality that is not organized by the determination of frontiers.

In this organization, the story plays a decisive role. It "describes," to be sure. But "every description is more than a fixation," it is "a culturally creative act." (Lotman and Ouspenski, 1976: 89). It even has distributive power and performative force (it does what it says) when an ensemble of circumstances is brought together. Then it founds spaces. Reciprocally, where stories are disappearing (or else are being reduced to museographical objects), there is a loss of space: deprived of narrations (as one sees it happen in both the city and the countryside), the group or the individual regresses toward the disquieting, fatalis

Figure 3.5
Re-made in the desert.
Thelma and Louise,
Ridley Scott, 1991.
Photo: British Film
Institute.

tic experience of a formless, indistinct, and nocturnal totality. By considering the role of stories in delimitation, one can see that the primary function is to *authorize* the establishment, displacement or transcendence of limits, and as a consequence, to set in opposition, within the closed field of discourse, two movements that intersect (setting and transgressing limits) in such a way as to make the story a sort of "crossword" decoding stencil (a dynamic partitioning of space) whose essential narrative figures seem to be the *frontier* and the *bridge*.

1. *Creating a theater of actions*. The story's first function is to authorize, or more exactly, to *found*. Strictly speaking, this function is not juridical, that is, related to laws or judgments. It depends rather on what Georges Dumézil analyzes in connection with the Indo-European root *dhe*, "to set in place," and its derivatives in Sanskrit (*dhatu*) and Latin (*fas*). The Latin noun "*fas*," he writes,

> is properly speaking the mystical foundation, which is in the invisible world, and without which all forms of conduct that are enjoined or authorized by *ius* (human law) and, more generally speaking, all human conduct, are doubtful, perilous, and even fatal. *Fas* cannot be subjected to analysis or casuistry, as *ius* can: *fas* can no more be broken up into parts than its name can be declined.

A foundation either exists or it doesn't: *fas est* or *fas non est*. "A time or a place are said to be *fasti* or *nefasti* [auspicious or inauspicious] depending on whether they provide or fail to provide human action with this necessary foundation" (Dumézil, 1969: 61–78, on "Ius fetiale").

In the Western parts of the Indo-European world, this function has been divided in a particular way among different institutions – in contrast to what happened in ancient India, where different roles were played in turn by the same characters. Occidental culture created its own ritual concerning *fas*, which was carried out in Rome by specialized priests called *fetiales*. It was practiced "before Rome undertook any action with regard to a foreign nation," such as a declaration of war, a military expedition, or an alliance. The ritual was a procession with three centrifugal stages, the first within Roman territory but near the frontier, the second on the frontier, the third in foreign territory. The ritual action was carried out before every civil or military action because it is designed to *create the field* necessary for political or military activities. It is thus also a *repetitio rerum*: both a renewal and a repetition of the originary founding acts, a *recitation* and a citation of the genealogies that could legitimate the new enterprise, and a *prediction* and a promise of success at the beginning of battles, contracts, or conquests. As a general repetition before the actual representation, the rite, a narration in acts, precedes the historical realization. The tour or procession of the *fetiales* opens a space and provides a foundation for the operations of the military men, diplomats, or merchants who dare to cross the frontiers. Similarly in the *Vedas*, Visnu, "by his footsteps, opens the zone of space in which Indra's military action must take place." The *fas* ritual is a foundation. It "provides space" for the actions that will be undertaken; it "creates a field" which serves as their "base" and their "theater" (Dumézil, 1969: 61–78).

This founding is precisely the primary role of the story. It opens a legitimate *theater* for practical *actions*. It creates a field that authorizes dangerous and contingent social actions. But it differs in three ways from the function the Roman ritual so carefully isolated: the story founds *fas* in a form that is fragmented (not unique and whole), miniaturized (not on a national scale), and polyvalent (not specialized). It is *fragmented*, not only because of the diversification of social milieus, but especially because of the increasing heterogeneity (or because of a heterogeneity that is increasingly obvious) of the authorizing "references": the excommunication of territorial "divinities," the deconsecration of places haunted by the story-spirit, and the extension of neutral areas deprived of legitimacy have marked the disappearance and fragmentation of the narrations that organized frontiers and appropriations. (Official historiography – history books, television news reports, etc. – nevertheless tries to make everyone believe in the existence of a national space.) It is *miniaturized*, because socioeconomic technocratization confines the significance of *fas* and *nefas* to the level of the family unit or the individual, and leads to the multiplication of "family stories," "life stories," and psychoanalytical narrations. (Gradually cut loose from these particular stories, public justifications nevertheless continue to exist in the form of blind rumors, or resurface savagely in class or race conflicts). It is finally *polyvalent*, because the mixing together of so many micro-stories gives them functions that change according to the groups in which they circulate. This polyvalence does not affect the relational origins of narrativity, however: the ancient ritual that creates fields of action is recognizable in the "fragments" of narration planted around the obscure thresholds of our existence; these buried fragments articulate without its knowing it the "biographical" story whose space they found.

A narrative activity, even if it is multiform and no longer unitary, thus continues to develop where frontiers and relations with space abroad are concerned. Fragmented and disseminated, it is continually concerned with marking out boundaries. What it puts in action is once more the *fas* that "authorizes" enterprises and precedes them. Like the Roman *fetiales*, stories "go in a procession" ahead of social practices in order to open a field for them. Decisions and juridical combinations themselves come only afterwards, like the statements and acts of Roman law (*ius*), arbitrating the areas of action granted to each party (Dumézil, 1969: 31–45), participating themselves in the activities for which *fas* provided a "foundation."

According to the rules that are proper to them, the magistrates' "interlocutory judgments" operate within the aggregate of heterogeneous spaces that have already been created and established by the innumerable forms of an oral narrativity composed of family or local stories, customary or professional "poems" and "recitations" of paths taken or countrysides traversed. The magistrates' judgments do not create these "heaters of action," they articulate and manipulate them. They presuppose the narrative authorities that the magistrates "hear", compare, and put into hierarchies. Preceding the judgment that regulates and settles, there is a founding narration.

2. *Frontiers and bridges.* Stories are actuated by a contradiction that is represented in them by the relationship between the frontier and the bridge, that is, between a (legitimate) space and its (alien) exteriority. In order to account for contradiction, it is helpful to go back to the elementary units. Leaving aside morphology (which is not our concern here) and situating ourselves in the perspective of a pragmatics and, more precisely, a syntax aimed at determining "programs" or series of practices through which space is appropriated, we can take as our point of departure the "region," which Miller and Johnson-Laird define as a basic unit: the place where programs and actions interact. A "region" is thus the space created by an interaction (Miller and Johnson-Laird, 1976: 57–66, 385–90, 564, etc.). It follows that in the same place there are as many "regions" as there are interactions or intersections of programs. And also that the determination of space is dual and operational, and, in a problematics of enunciation, related to an "interlocutory" process.

In this way a dynamic contradiction between each delimitation and its mobility is introduced. On the one hand, the story tirelessly marks out frontiers. It multiplies them, but in terms of interactions among the characters – things, animals, human beings: the acting subjects (*actants*) divide up among themselves places as well as predicates (simple, crafty, ambitious, silly, etc.) and movements (advancing, withdrawing, going into exile, returning, etc.). Limits are drawn by the points at which the progressive appropriations (the acquisition of predicates in the course of the story) and the successive displacements (internal or external movements) of the acting subjects meet. Both appropriations and displacements depend on a dynamic distribution of possible goods and functions in order to constitute an increasingly complex network of differentiations, a combinative system of spaces. They result from the operation of distinctions resulting from encounters. Thus, in the obscurity of their unlimitedness, bodies can be distinguished only where the "contacts" (*touches*) of amorous or hostile struggles are inscribed on them. This is a paradox of the frontier: created by contacts, the points of differentiation between two bodies are also their common points. Conjunction and disjunction are inseparable in them. Of two bodies in contact, which one possesses the frontier that distinguishes them? Neither. Does that amount to saying: no-one?

The theoretical and practical problem of the frontier: to whom does it belong? The river, wall or tree makes a frontier. It does not have the character of a nowhere that cartographical representation ultimately presupposes. It has a mediating role. So does the story that gives it voice: "Stop," says the forest the wolf comes out of. "Stop!" says the river, revealing its crocodile. But this actor, by virtue of the very fact that he is the mouthpiece of the limit, creates communication as well as separation; more than that, he establishes a border only by saying what crosses it, having come from the other side. He articulates it. He is also a passing through or over. In the story, the frontier functions as a third element. It is an "in-between" – a "space between," *Zwischenraum*, as Morgenstern puts it in a marvelous and ironic poem on "closure" (*Zaun*), which rhymes with "space" (*Raum*) and "to see through" (*hindurchzuschaun*) (Morgenstern, 1965: 229). It is the story of a picket fence (*Lattenzaun*)

Es war einmal ein Lattenzaun	One time there was a picket fence
mit Zwischenraum, hindurchzuschaun.	with space to gaze from hence to thence.

A middle place, composed of interactions and inter-views, the frontier is a sort of void, a narrative symbol of exchanges and encounters. Passing by, an architect suddenly appropriates this "in-between space" and builds a great edifice on it:

Ein Architekt, der dieses sah,	An architect who saw this sight
stand eines Abends plötzlich da –	approached it suddenly one night –
und nahm den Zwischenraum heraus	removed the spaces from the fence
und baute draus ein grosses Haus.	and built of them a residence.

Transformation of the void into a plenitude, of the in-between into an established place. The rest goes without saying. The Senate "takes on" the monument – the Law establishes itself in it – and the architect escapes to Afri-or-America:

Drum zog ihn der Senat auch ein.	the senate had to intervene.
Der Architekt jedoch entfloh	The architect, however, flew
nach Afri-od-Ameriko	to Afri- or Americoo.

(Max Knight, trans.)

The Architect's drive to cement up the picket fence, to fill in and build up "the space in-between," is also his illusion, for without knowing it he is working toward the political freezing of the place and there is nothing left for him to do, when he sees his work finished, but to flee far away from the blocs of the law.

In contrast, the story privileges a "logic of ambiguity" through its accounts of interaction. It "turns" the frontier into a crossing, and the river into a bridge. It recounts inversions and displacements: the door that closes is precisely what may be opened; the river is what makes passage possible; the tree is what marks the stages of advance; the picket fence is an ensemble of interstices through which one's glances pass.

The *bridge* is ambiguous everywhere: it alternately welds together and opposes insularities. It distinguishes them and threatens them. It liberates from enclosure and destroys autonomy. Thus, for example, it occurs as a central and ambivalent character in the stories of the Noirmoutrins, before, during, and after the construction of a bridge between La Fosse and Fromentine in Vendée in 1972 (Brunet, 1979). It carries on a double life in innumerable memories of places and everyday legends, often summed up in proper names, hidden paradoxes, ellipses in stories, riddles to be solved: Bridgehead, Bridgenorth, Bridgetown, Bridgewater, Bridgman, Cambridge, Trowbridge, etc.

Justifiably, the bridge is the index of the diabolic in the paintings where Bosch invents his modifications of spaces (Certeau, 1976). As a transgression of the limit, a disobedience of the law of the place, it represents a departure, an attack on a state, the ambition of a conquering power, or the flight of an exile; in any case, the "betrayal" of an order. But at the same time as it offers the possibility of a bewildering exteriority, it allows or causes the re-emergence beyond the frontiers of the alien element that was controlled in the interior, and gives objectivity (that is, expression and re-presentation) to the alterity which was hidden inside the limits, so that in recrossing the bridge and coming back within the enclosure the traveler henceforth finds there the exteriority that he had first sought by going outside and then fled by returning. Within the frontiers, the alien is already there, an exoticism or sabbath of the memory, a disquieting familiarity. It is as though delimitation itself were the bridge that opens the inside to its other.

DELINQUENCIES?

What the map cuts up, the story cuts across. In Greek, narration is called "diegesis": it establishes an itinerary (it "guides") and it passes through (it "transgresses"). The space of operations it travels in is made of movements: it is topological, concerning the deformations of figures, rather than topical, defining places. It is only ambivalently that the limit circumscribes in this space. It plays a double game. It does the opposite of what it says. It hands the place over to the foreigner that it gives the impression of throwing out. Or rather, when it marks a stopping place, the latter is not stable but follows the variations of encounters between programs. Boundaries are transportable limits and transportations of limits; they are also *metaphorai*.

In the narrations that organize spaces, boundaries seem to play the role of the Greek *xoana*, statuettes whose invention is attributed to the clever Daedalus: they are crafty like Daedalus and mark out limits only by moving themselves (and the limits). These straight-line indicators put emphasis on the curves and movements of space. Their distributive work is thus completely different from that of the divisions established by poles, pickets or stable columns which, planted in the earth, cut up and compose an order of places (see Frontisi-Ducroux, 1975: 104, 100–1, 117 etc., on the mobility of these rigid statues). They are also transportable limits.

Today, narrative operations of boundary-setting take the place of these enigmatic describers of earlier times when they bring movement in through the very act of fixing, in the name of delimitation. Michelet already said it: when the aristocracy of the great Olympian gods collapsed at the end of Antiquity, it did not take down with it "the mass of indigenous gods, the populace of gods that still possessed the immensity of fields, forests, woods, mountains, springs, intimately associated with the life of the country. These gods lived in the hearts of oaks, in the swift, deep waters, and could not be driven out of them . . . Where are they? In the desert, on the heath, in the forest? Yes, but also and especially in the home. They live on in the most intimate of domestic habits (Michelet, n.d., 23–4). But they also live on in our streets and in our apartments. They were perhaps after all only the agile representatives of narrativity, and of narrativity in its most delinquent form. The fact that they have changed their names (every power is toponymical and initiates its order of places by naming them) takes nothing away from the multiple, insidious, moving force. It survives the avatars of the great history that debaptises and rebaptises them.

If the delinquent exists only by displacing itself, if its specific mark is to live not on the margins but in the interstices of the codes that it undoes and displaces, if it is characterized by the privilege of the tour over the state, then the story is delinquent. Social delinquency consists in taking the story literally, in making it the principle of physical existence where a society no longer offers to subjects or groups symbolic outlets and expectations of spaces, where there is no longer any alternative to disciplinary falling-into-line or illegal drifting away, that is, one form or another of prison and wandering outside the pale. Inversely, the story is a sort of delinquency in reserve, maintained, but itself displaced and consistent, in traditional societies (ancient, medieval, etc.), with an order that is firmly established but flexible enough to allow the proliferation of this challenging mobility that does not respect places, is alternately playful and threatening, and extends from the microbe-like forms of everyday narration to the carnivalesque celebrations of earlier days (see, for example, on the subject of this ambiguity, Ladurie, 1979).

It remains to be discovered, of course, what actual changes produce this delinquent narrativity in a society. In any event, one can already say that in matters concerning space, this delinquency begins with the inscription of the body in the order's text. The opacity of the body in movement, gesticulating, walking, taking its pleasure, is what indefinitely organizes a here in relation to an abroad, a "familiarity" in relation to a "foreignness." A spatial story is in its minimal degree a spoken language, that is, a linguistic system that distributes places insofar as it is articulated by an "enunciatory focalization," by an act of practicing it. It is the object of "proxemics" (Fabbri, 1968).[4] Before we return to its manifestations in the organization of memory, it will suffice here to recall that, in this focalizing enunciation, space appears once more as a practiced place.

NOTES

1   The map is reproduced and analyzed by Pierre Janet (Janet, 1928: 284–7). The original is in Cuauhtinchan (Puebla, Mexico).

2   See, for example, Marin (1973: 257–90), on the relation between figures (a "discourse-tour") and the map (a "system-text") in three representations of the city in the seventeenth century: a relation between a "narrative" and a "geometric."

3   Particularly in the lectures on "the procedures of narrative" and "fabrication." Médam and Augoyard have used this unit to define the subject matter of their investigations (Situations d'habitat, 90–5).

4   E.T. Hall defined proxemics as "the study of how man unconsciously structures spaces – the distance between men in the conduct of daily transactions, the organization of space in his houses and buildings, and ultimately the lay out of his towns" (Hall, 1963).

Chapter 4: The Dark Side of the *Domus*

Neil Leach

THE NEGATIVE SIDE TO 'DWELLING'

Within recent architectural theory, architecture as 'dwelling' has become something of a dominant paradigm, amid calls for a regionalist architecture and celebration of the concept of *genius loci*. This is an approach that emanates from the work of the German philosopher, Martin Heidegger, which has been pursued by those who have developed his thought – architectural theorists such as Christian Norberg-Schulz and philosophers such as Gianni Vattimo (Norberg-Schulz, 1979; Vattimo, 1990). Many have looked to an architecture of 'dwelling' as a means of combatting the alienation of contemporary society and of resisting the homogenizing placelessness of International Style architecture. What I wish to argue, however, is that taken to an extreme, 'dwelling' itself – the logic of the *domus* – can have negative consequences. There is, I would maintain, a negative side to 'dwelling' – a dark side to the *domus*.

According to Heidegger, one's capacity to live on this earth – to 'dwell' in the phenomenological sense – is an essentially architectural experience. The very Being of being is linked to one's situatedness in the world. This is the thesis that comes out most clearly in his essay, 'Building, dwelling, thinking' (Heidegger, 1954). As the title of this chapter implies, for Heidegger there is a clear link between 'dwelling' and architecture. The whole concept of 'dwelling' is grounded in the architectural. For Heidegger a building should be on and of the soil, of the location on which it is built. He illustrates this with the example of a Greek temple, which sits so naturally within its setting it is as though it has been 'brought forth' by its setting. Throughout Heidegger's thinking there is an emphasis on the soil, on the earth, and this applies especially to the question of architecture. Buildings are not buildings in the abstract, they gain their very sense of presence through being situated where they are, through their *Dasein*.[1] 'Does not the flourishing of any work of art,' he asks, 'depend upon its roots in a native soil?' (Heidegger, 1966. 47). This evocation of the soil, this call for a

88 ☐

'situated' architecture, can be read as an evocation for the *Heimat*, for the homeland. And for Heidegger it is not in the cities but in the countryside – where one is most in touch with nature and tradition – that the sense of homeland may flourish:

> Homeland is most possible and effective where the powers of nature around us and the remnants of historical tradition remain together, where an origin and an ancient, nourished style of human existence hold sway. Today for this decisive task perhaps only the rural counties and small towns are competent – if they recognise anew their unusual qualities, if they know how to draw the boundaries between themselves and life in large cities and gigantic areas of modern industrial complexes.
>
> (Heidegger, 1971a; cited in Zimmerman, 1990: 71)

This appeal to the homeland would appear to be part of a consistent nationalistic outlook in his thought, which is echoed in a series of forced etymological strategies in his writings that attempt to lend authority to the German language, by tracing the origins of certain German words to ancient Greek. All this would seem to imply that there is a potential nationalism that permeates the whole of his thought – a nationalism that, in the context of pre-war Germany, shared something in common with fascism.

It would be wrong to associate Heidegger's thought too closely with the excesses of fascist ideology. There is much to be praised in his work, and one could argue that his philosophy need not necessarily lead to a nationalistic outlook, and that to judge his thought solely at the level of the political would be to do him an injustice. Indeed his work is open to a variety of interpretations, and the complexity of his thought defies any neat categorisation. But equally, the point should be made that his work lends itself to a nationalist outlook, and that his own life was inscribed with a nationalist outlook. Thus it hardly seems inconsistent that a philosopher such as Heidegger should have belonged at one stage to the National Socialist party, a stand for which he has been highly criticized.

It is in 'The self-assertion of the German university', his rectoral address of 1933, that Heidegger most closely associates his thoughts with the aspirations of National Socialism. He unequivocally links the question of Being to the '*soil and blood*' of a *Volk*:

> [S]pirit is the determined resolve to the essence of Being, a resolve that is attuned to origins and knowing. And the *spiritual world* of a volk is not its cultural superstructure, just as little as it is its arsenal of useful knowledge and values; rather, it is the power that comes from preserving at the most profound level the forces that are rooted in the *soil and blood* of a Volk, the power to arouse most inwardly and to shake most extensively the Volk's existence.
>
> (In Wolin, 1993: 29–39)

Similar themes are echoed in Heidegger's speech in honour of the German nationalist hero, Albert Leo Schlageter, who had been executed in 1923 for acts of sabotage against the French army of occupation. Here the 'soil' is specifically identified with the Black Forest:

> Student of Freiburg! German student! When on your hikes and outings you set foot in the mountains, forests and valleys of this Black Forest, the home of this hero, experience this and know: the mountains among which the young farmer's son grew up are of primitive stone, of granite. They have long been at work hardening the will. The autumn sun of the Black Forest bathes the mountain ranges and forests in the most glorious clear light. It has long nourished clarity of heart. As he [Schlageter] stood defenceless facing the rifles, the hero's inner gaze soared above the muzzles to the daylight and mountains of his home that he might die for the German people and its Reich with the Alemannic countryside before his eyes.
>
> (In Wolin, 1993: 41)

And it was precisely in the soil of this Alemannic countryside that Heidegger declared his own thought to be rooted:

> The inner relationship of my own work to the Black Forest and its people comes from a centuries-long and irreplaceable rootedness in the Alemannian–Schwabian soil.
>
> (In Sheehan, 1981: 213)

The very evocation of the soil in Heidegger echoes a consistent trope within fascist ideology. As Klaus Theweleit has argued in the context of pre-war German fascism, this evocation can be understood in psychoanalytic terms as a need to reinforce and protect the ego by identifying with a larger body (Theweleit, 1987, 1989).[2] This larger identity would be constituted in a social order, and would be embodied in a figurehead, and a physical location: *ein Volk, ein Reich, ein Führer*. Identity therefore becomes territorialized and mapped onto a geographic terrain. The individual becomes one with the land in a process of identification that is itself mythic, and this process is often supported by other myths of identification. In this dissolving into nature, difference is suppressed and a new identity is forged with Mother Earth. Thus we find constant references to natural phenomena – storms, blood and soil – in fascist ideology. As Ernst Jünger, a figure who exerted a great influence on Heidegger (Zimmerman, 1990: 66–93), wrote of pre-war German fascism:

> What is being born is the essence of nationalism, a new relation to the elemental, to Mother Earth, whose soil has been blasted away in the rekindled fires of material battles and fertilised by streams of blood.
>
> (In Theweleit, 1989: 88)

And it can be seen that it is precisely in the context of an identity rooted to the soil that those groups not rooted to the soil are excluded. Traditionally, Jews and gypsies are both 'wanderers', although each for different reasons: the gypsies largely by choice, the Jews mainly by necessity. Neither is rooted to the soil. The 'wanderer' does not fit within a concept of situatedness or rootedness to the soil, and therefore does not fit within the philosophy of the *Heimat*. The 'wanderer' is the element that cannot be controlled, cannot be domesticated, cannot be contained within the logic of the *domus*. The 'wanderer' is therefore treated as the 'other', the excluded one, and is perceived as a threat to the nation. Just as nationalism forms a symbolic identification with the soil, so it also generates an antagonism towards all that cannot be identified with the soil. For it is precisely the fear of flows and movements that cannot be stemmed, as Klaus Theweleit has observed, that characterizes the fascist obsession with control (Theweleit, 1987: 229–435).

THE *DOMUS* AND THE MEGALOPOLIS

Heidegger's involvement with the National Socialists has been known to German intellectuals for some time, but it was not until the publication in 1987 of Victor Farias' *Heidegger et le nazisme* that the full extent of his involvement with the organization and his anti-semitism became known to French intellectuals. This

Figure 4.1
Elfride and Martin
Heidegger at
Todtnauberg, 1968
Photo: Digne Meller
Marcovicz.

event fanned the flames of what was to become known as the 'Heidegger controversy'. Those who have attempted to defend him for his political indiscretions have claimed that he was either politically naïve or that his own philosophy is essentially apolitical (Dallmayr, 1993; Lacoue-Labarthe, 1990). Others, such as Jean-Francois Lyotard, have been less charitable towards him. In his book *Heidegger and 'the jews'* (1990), Lyotard uses 'jew' with a lower-case 'j' to signify not just Jews themselves, but all minority groups who might be perceived as the 'other': outsiders, non-conformists, artists, anarchists, blacks, homeless, Arabs and anyone else who might be perceived as alien and potentially threatening. For Lyotard, the crime in Heidegger, and so too in all thought, lies in the forgetting, and the forgetting of the forgetting. It is in what is left out, what is excluded, what is in effect 'repressed', that his thinking is at fault. And this more general forgetting includes the more specific forgetting: the failure on the part of Heidegger to acknowledge and apologize fully for his support of National Socialism.[3]

Lyotard picks up the problem of Heidegger's thought in the context of architecture in his piece '*Domus* and megalopolis' (Lyotard, 1988: 191–204). Lyotard contrasts the traditional *domus* with our present condition, that of the megalopolis. In other words he is contrasting two models of existence, two ideals of living. Although the one, the *domus*, is associated with the simple homestead, and the other, the megalopolis, with the city, he is not contrasting the homestead with the city, so much as the condition of the homestead with the condition of the city. He is contrasting the myth of the *domus* – the phenomenon of 'home' – with the more alienated model of 'city life' within the age of the megalopolis.

The traditional *domus* has been presented as a bucolic idyll, where all you do is serve the *phusis* – the natural order – and place yourself at the service of its urge. The traditional *domus* has its natural rhythm, which contains and controls everything. The domestic hierarchy of the *domus* likewise has its natural order, with the master and mistress (the *dominus* and the *domina*) and the *ancilla* (the female servant). Yet this image of the bucolic idyll, for Lyotard, remains but an image. Since the time of Virgil, the *domus* has no longer been possible. 'Domesticity,' Lyotard comments, 'is over, and probably it never existed, except as a dream of the old child awakening and destroying it on awakening' (Lyotard, 1988: 201). For the current *domus* is but a myth, a product of the megalopolis, the nostalgic yearning for what can now only be a mirage. For Lyotard there can be no more *domus*; the megalopolis has now stifled the *domus*, and has 'gnawed away' at the *domus* and its community. With the advent of the megalopolis the traditional values of the *domus* have been transformed, and the hegemony of the natural order has been supplanted by the artificial.[4] But the crucial point for Lyotard is that the *domus* constitutes a form of myth. It is not that myths – 'the myths we live by' – are in themselves bad, but rather that there is something potentially deceptive about myth, because its own identity as myth is often concealed.

And it is precisely in its reliance on the mythic that Heidegger's own thought is most suspect.

In such a context the values of the *domus* likewise become façades. They can never be invoked, but only mimicked as in the case of the Nazis. Thus, for Lyotard, the 'service' of nature in the original *domus* leads inexorably to the 'service' – *Dienst* – of Heidegger's rectorship address – a hollow and ironic sense of 'service', where 'knowledge service' is treated at the same level as 'labour service' and 'military service' (Lyotard, 1988: 195; Wolin, 1993: 35). The *domus* here has a different 'take'. For in the age of the megalopolis – in an age when the god-nature has been doubled as an anti-god – when there is no 'nature' to serve, service is incorporated within a generalized system of exchange – business – whose aim is profit, and whose governing principle is performativity. Under this new condition the violence of the *domus* is exposed. Everything that was ordered and contained within a hierarchized structure, which served to replicate and repeat the cycle of domesticity, all that was once tamed and controlled – 'domesticated' – within the *domus*, is revealed for what it is in the figure of modern man, *Homo redomesticus* (redomesticated man). To quote from Lyotard:

> The undominated, the untamed, in earlier times concealed in the *domus*, is unleashed in the *homo politicus* and *homo economicus* but under the ancient aegis of service, *Dienst* . . . *Homo redomesticus* in power kills in the street shouting 'You are not one of ours' . . . The ruin of the *domus* makes possible this fury which it contained and which it exercised in its name.
>
> (Lyotard, 1988: 197)

Figure 4.2
Landscape with the
Heidegger house
Photo: Digne Meller
Marcovicz.

What masquerades as the *domus* in fact constitutes 'domestication without the *domus*'. It contains a violence repressed within it. 'The untameable was tragic,' for Lyotard, 'because it was lodged in the heart of the *domus*' (Lyotard, 1988: 202). And here we might recognize a Freudian moment within Lyotard. Indeed the house itself, as Freud suggested, can be taken as a model for repression. The terms that Freud uses in this context – *heimlich* (homely) and *unheimlich* (uncanny) – are terms with clear architectural resonances.

For Freud the *heimlich* contained the *unheimlich* repressed within it: 'For this uncanny is in reality nothing new or alien, but something which is familiar and old-fashioned in the mind and which has become alienated from it through a process of repression' (Freud, 1985).

It is as though the very foundations of the house and of all that is homely are built on the repression of its opposite, the *unheimlich* buried deep beneath the *heimlich*. Yet *heimlich* and *unheimlich*, it would seem, are terms that fold into one another. As Freud comments: 'This *heimlich* is a word the meaning of which develops in the direction of ambivalence, until it finally coincides with its opposite, *unheimlich*' (Freud, 1985: 347). Thus any definition of the term *heimlich* made 'against' the term *unheimlich* is clearly a false one. The very 'opposition' that is posited denies the reciprocal tension that binds the two terms together. This denial constitutes a form of conscious repression, which always threatens to be unleashed in the realm of the unconscious. The 'fury' of the uncanny haunts the home like a ghost.

THE MYTH OF 'PLACE'

The *domus*, then, can be seen as a myth of the present, and it is within this framework that we can now also begin to understand regionalism as a movement grounded in myth. Thus what purports to be a sentimental evocation of traditional forms can be seen as part of a larger project of constructing and reinforcing a regional or national identity. We might therefore recognize within regionalism not only the potential dangers inherent in all such calls for a regional or national identity, but also the essential complicity of the concept within the cultural conditions of late capitalism. For regionalism is presented as a movement that has arisen in opposition to the homogenized space of late capitalism. The very placelessness of contemporary society has prompted a fresh interest in 'place' as 'difference'. But against this it could be argued – in line with Fredric Jameson – that it is late capitalism itself that has in part sanctioned these developments (Jameson, 1994: 189–205). In a world dominated by all-consuming capitalism 'difference' itself can be seen to be a product of the market. As such, Jameson's views can be understood within the framework of Lyotard's remarks on the *domus*. Postmodern calls for 'place' echo postmodern calls for the *domus*. If the countryside – the realm of the *domus* – is seen increasingly in terms of tourism and vacation, then 'place' as difference could be understood in equally cynical, ironic terms, as the site of the 'exotic'. Just as the call for difference can be understood as spawned by – and not resistant to – global capitalism, so 'place' becomes another commodity in the marketplace.

These values are particularly suspect in an age when there has been a fundamental shift in the ways in which we relate to the world. Not only must we question the primacy of a concept such as 'dwelling' as a source of identification, but we must also ask whether a concept that is so place-specific can any longer retain much authority.

For Lyotard, in the age of the megalopolis even the concept of dwelling is marked by a form of passage. 'Lost behind our thoughts, the *domus* is also a mirage in front, the impossible dwelling', so that we are trapped in a form of passage between an awakening, in the form of a phantom-like remembrance of the lost *domus*, and the re-inscription of this awakening in the future: 'So only transit, transfer, translation and difference. It is not the house passing away, like a mobile home or the shepherd's hut, *it is in passing that we dwell*' [italics added] (Lyotard, 1988: 198). Thus for Lyotard it is not the mobility of the house per se so much as the endless re-inscription of the concept that constitutes the 'passage' of dwelling. To claim otherwise would be to subscribe to the myth of the *domus*. Yet equally one might point towards more concrete manifestations of the transiency of dwelling. For it could also be said that the 'mobile home' remains the condition of the present, if by 'mobile homes' we understand a flexible range of indexical markers on which identity might be cathected as a form of symbolic 'grounding'. Not only has the home been largely redefined as property, so that what was once a stable point of origin has become a commodity, exchangeable in the marketplace – located within a price range, if no longer constrained by place – but, arguably, there has also been a shift in the way in which we relate to the world.

The possibility of such a shift is afforded by an age that constitutes its identity less through notions of place - place of origin, birthplace etc. – and increasingly through more transitory phenomena, such as jobs and possessions. These possessions may include even technological objects, such as cars and computers. Indeed technology, far from being the necessary source of alienation, as Heidegger had supposed, may itself offer mechanisms of symbolic identification. For what thinkers such as Heidegger overlook is the fundamental capacity of human beings to accommodate and adapt to new conditions. This chameleon-like tendency ensures that human beings eventually absorb technology as part of their symbolic background, to the point where they may grow attached to and identify with technological objects.

Furthermore, advances in technology have themselves influenced the way that we relate to 'place'. Technological developments in transportation have caused physical distance to be largely displaced by 'time distance'. Meanwhile, developments in communications technology have deeply affected the space of interpersonal relationships. In an age when the actual space of the crossroads is giving way to the virtual space of the Internet, the hegemony of the physical is being progressively eroded (Virilio, 1991). This is not to deny the necessity of place. Rather it is to recognize the possibility of a shift in mechanisms of symbolic identification. In a society that is constantly mobile, and whose archetypal space is the transport interchange or the airport lounge, identity can be defined increasingly in terms of departures and impending arrivals. The concept of the *domus* as the stable site of 'dwelling' therefore comes across not only as a myth, but as a *nostalgic* myth.

Indeed, calls for the *domus* and for regionalism share something of the nostalgia for a lost tradition – a lost paradise – that is embodied in other contemporary projects to recapture the past. In an age whose fashions are often dominated by 'retro' imagery, reproduction itself – whether furniture, clothes or architecture – must be viewed within this context. Hence the distinction between 'authentic' reproduction and postmodern 'retro' pastiche begins to be effaced. Indeed it is precisely against the charge of 'inauthenticity' that so-called 'authentic' appeals to the past must defend themselves most virulently, while – paradoxically – claiming their authority in their very 'authenticity'.

Inevitably any architectural approach that is grounded in a Heideggerian framework must be based on terms such as 'authenticity'. Yet it is precisely for its 'jargon of authenticity' that Theodor Adorno criticizes the whole of Heidegger's work (Adorno, 1964).[5] For Adorno, 'authenticity' in Heidegger amounts to little more than the aura of authenticity – the myth of the authentic. This evocation of 'authenticity' becomes particularly suspect in our contemporary cultural condition if, as Fredric Jameson has argued, 'authenticity' is prone to collapse into its opposite (Jameson, 1999). Calls for an 'authentic' regionalism may themselves share something of the 'inauthenticity' of Disneyland, and other patently artificial worlds. And it is precisely the model of Disneyland that offers us a crucial insight into the mechanisms at play in this evocation of 'authenticity'. For Disneyland, in Jean Baudrillard's eyes, is complicit within a broader deception. By declaring itself 'unreal' in opposition to the 'real' world outside, Disneyland is presented as a device to lend authority to that 'reality'. Yet, as Baudrillard argues, Disneyland is in fact precisely part of the reality – or hyper-reality – of the world outside (Baudrillard, 1985: 12). A similar mechanism in reverse underpins contemporary claims of 'authenticity' or 'reality'. By positing themselves in opposition to the 'inauthentic' or 'unreal', they claim an authority that is itself suspect. So calls for regional identity can themselves be seen to be the mythic products of a postmodern age. Questions will always remain as to what constitutes an 'authentic' architectural tradition – the distant past or the immediate past – and whether indeed there can ever be any such thing as a 'return' to a tradition of the past. In this context we might ask, for example, whether the concrete tower block does not itself now constitute an 'authentic' architecture for a city such as Hong Kong, and whether attempts to revive vernacular forms are not in themselves 'inauthentic' attempts to reconstruct a mythology of the past.

Figure 4.3
The spring at
Todtnauberg
Photo: Digne Meller
Marcovicz.

TOWARDS THE COSMOPOLIS

What, then, are the consequences of this for architecture? In a tradition of architectural theory that has too often championed the *domus* uncritically – from the simple homestead to an architecture of regional identity – one should be aware of the negative side of this ideal. For the *domus* in the age of the megalopolis –

in the age of performativity – can never be the true *domus*. The *domus* today is but a mirage, a myth of the *domus*. There is much that is seemingly powerful and seductive in this myth of the *domus*, much that responds to fundamental human desires, and that presents itself as the source of genuine comfort. Vaclav Havel evokes this in his 'dream' for the future of the Czech people beyond the 'shock' of freedom:

> Life in the towns and villages will have overcome the legacy of greyness, uniformity, anonymity, and ugliness inherited from the totalitarian era. It will have a genuinely human dimension. Every main street will have at least two bakeries, two sweet-shops, two pubs, and many other small shops, all privately owned and independent. Thus the streets and neighbourhoods will regain their unique face and atmosphere. Small communities will naturally begin to form again, communities centred on the street, the apartment block, or the neighbourhood. People will once more begin to feel the *phenomenon of home*.

> (Havel, 1992: 104, italics added)

Havel depicts a gingerbread world of bakeries, sweetshops and pubs, a world seemingly unsullied by the grim reality of life in the factories, a world where the 'phenomenon of home' is allowed to re-exert itself. Havel's dream reads as a utopian fantasy. Yet it is precisely as a fantasy that - paradoxically- it has most authority. For, as Renata Salecl has argued, a country is always already a kind of fiction, and the homeland a fantasy structure (Salecl, 1994: 87–101). And herein lies the apparent danger, for it is in dreams that the unconscious is most readily revealed, and it is precisely in this dream - the fantasy of the homeland - that the repressed may be unleashed. If, after the events of 1989, freedom itself was a 'shock', there was a greater shock in the unexpected neo-nazi violence that accompanied the rise of nationalism in the East. But it was a shock that might perhaps have been anticipated. Within the *heimlich* of the homeland there lurks the *unheimlich* of nationalism. And the very 'phenomenon of home' contains a potential violence.

For our present society we should be open to an alternative model of architectural theory more congenial to the complexities of modern society, a model that avoids the domination and exclusion implicit in the *domus*, and which can accommodate the more flexible modes of existence that characterize our contemporary condition. Perhaps, then, rather than continuing to champion the *domus* – the architecture of 'dwelling' – which, it has been argued, is the mythical product of a postmodern age, we might look instead to more appropriate models suggested by the megalopolis – the city – itself. And it is to the specific model of the city as cosmopolis that I wish to turn. For just as there is a dark side to the *domus*, the cosmopolis provides an acceptable face to the megalopolis. The cosmopolis as a form of 'city life' offers an ideal that deserves to be reappraised. For the city constitutes the condition of the present; and urbanity, as Iris Marion Young has observed, remains 'the horizon of the modern, not to mention the postmodern condition' (Young, 1990. 237). If, furthermore, we are to understand our current condition as largely that of a transitory, fleeting society, the predominant – if not universal – mode of existence, it could be argued, is often precisely that of the 'wanderer'. The Jew, then, the gypsy, the 'other' of society provides in some senses the model for the contemporary moment – rootless, international, mobile, deterritorialized (Kaplan, 1987; Sanadjian, 1995). This is in opposition to the rooted, the nationalistic and the static. If the *dominus*, the stable and controlling master of the *domus*, is the creature of the traditional community, the 'wanderer' represents the freedom and flux of the city. As such, the 'wanderer' is the archetypal creature of our contemporary condition, a creature whose existence reflects the very transience of the city.

Often commentators of modernity criticized the city as alienating, fragmentary, violent and disordered. Georg Simmel, for example, observed how the metropolis spawned the modern blasé individual, whose disengaged existence within the city evokes the circulation of capital itself. The modern city-dweller has developed a form of anonymity, itself a defensive cocoon against the overstimulation of life in the metropolis. Yet this very anonymity breeds a certain tolerance. The city, for example, tends to accept difference, and to accommodate the 'other'. Traditionally the city has provided a refuge for minorities: it is the city where the Jew, the outsider, the 'wanderer' has often found a haven. 'City life' is the ideal where 'difference' is acceptable and on occasions even celebrated, to the point where minority interest groups have often been spawned by the city. By comparison, the 'community' – the figure of the *domus* – can be seen to be a homogenizing, universalizing model, which absorbs and therefore denies 'difference'. The notion of 'community' is based on a myth of unmediated social

Figure 4.4
Heidegger at home, with a bucket.
Photo: Digne Meller Marcovicz.

relations. It assumes that all subjects are transparent to one another, and that somehow each can fully understand the 'other'. 'Difference' is therefore collapsed into a single totalizing vision, which itself breeds a certain intolerance to whatever does not conform to that vision. It is only when the city mimics the village, when it fragments into 'neighbourhoods' that constitute autonomous individual units, that this model begins to break down. Within 'neighbourhood watch schemes' and other exclusionary mechanisms, the principle of the city – the heterogeneous, open cosmopolis – is supplanted by the principle of the village – the homogeneous, closed *domus*. And, as the extreme of this condition, we might cite past examples of sectarian and political divides within cities such as Belfast, Beirut or indeed Berlin.

'City life' – the life of the cosmopolis – offers an alternative to the model of the *domus*. The cosmopolis retains the germ of an ideal more in tune with our contemporary cultural conditions. It suggests a possible model for living together in a form of interdependence, a model that can allow for the fluidity and flux, the complexities and multi-faceted solidarities of contemporary society, and which is characterized by a non-oppositional, non-hierarchical openness to the 'other'. Writ large, the cosmopolis suggests a model for a pluralistic, open society, free from the exclusions of nationalism.

And if our contemporary society is to be an open, cosmopolitan society, then surely we require an architecture whose language and forms match such an ideal: an architecture that transcends the rigid constraints of the *genius loci* – that 'ultimate ontotheological component of Architecture Appropriated', as Daniel Libeskind has described it – and which resists the nihilistic unfolding of tradition – an 'open' architecture. Perhaps then we should be envisaging not 'architecture' so much as 'architectures' – unpredictable, flexible and hybrid 'architectures', as Libeskind calls for (Libeskind, 1999; Wagner, 1999); architectures that match the fluidity, flux and complexity of contemporary existence, an existence that is epitomized by the cosmopolis; architectures that might therefore be described as 'cosmopolitan architectures'; architectures born of the spirit of the cosmopolis, but not limited to the cosmopolis: cosmopolitan architectures for a cosmopolitan society.

NOTES

1   Editor's note: Heidegger used '*Dasein*' to mean specifically *human* being. Here the word is used in a more everyday sense.

2   Klaus Theweleit argues in the case of German *Freikorps* soldiers that it is often precisely in the underdeveloped and 'not-fully-born' egos of young males within a particular constellation of social and political circumstances that this 'need' is most acute.

3   These questions are discussed at length in Wolin (1993). See especially the exchange of letters between Herbert Marcuse and Martin Heidegger. Other books on this subject include Sluga (1993).

4   For Lyotard, what takes over from the 'control' of the *domus* in the megalopolis is a form of techno-science that offers a new form of control: one that is no longer territorialized and historicized, but computerized.

5   For Adorno, Heidegger's thought hides behind contentless jargon. It represents a self-referential system that, by failing to address the real political and economic framework of society, serves only as an ideological mystification of the actual processes of human domination.

Chapter 5: The Metaphysics of Housework: Patricia Gruben's *The Central Character*

Kathleen Anne McHugh

Patricia Gruben's experimental film *The Central Character* (1977) works with an aspect of housekeeping that I have not had occasion to mention until now: its symbolic function in maintaining the liminal social space of the home. As a cultural border or boundary, the home constitutes a margin between culture and its traditional other, the natural world. Sometimes this "border" is literally represented in the form of a wooded backyard or garden, requiring an attention to landscaping that solicits the natural while taking care to cultivate it. But the increasingly infrequent spatial placement of the home in between nature and culture supports more ideologically based distinctions between these two realms. How, exactly, is the home a liminal social space? The activities that cultural convention dictates should be performed in the home relate to the body and to the provision of physical necessities. As the place where we presumably eat, drink, defecate, rest, have sex, and seek shelter, the home is linked with activities coded as physical and "natural." Yet it also figures as a sign of civilization and its distance from nature; as Oscar Wilde remarked, "If Nature had been comfortable, mankind would never have invented architecture . . . . I prefer houses to the open air" (Wilde, 1968: 117). Thus one task that the home – or, better, the idea of the home – performs is a transformative one: as an interstitial space, it delimits an area in which specific practices create the distinctions between two territories, the natural and the cultural or the physical and the social. Articulating elements of both, the home is neither. Rather it figures as a place of paradox, connoting at once a refuge or area outside the frantic public world and a shelter inside, protected from the natural elements. Housework manages these conflicting significations. Thus, women – as housekeepers, as homemakers, as the agents of this semiotic operation – become identified with its contradictions and effects. Like the home, women are neither nature nor culture; their liminal functions make both them and their work invisible. *The Central Character* literalizes and demonstrates these paradoxes.

Figure 5.1
Domestic upset.
Photo: Hulton-Getty.

In the film, an amorphous protagonist – initially a housewife – is transformed as her voice and persona move from the emphatically organized environment of the kitchen to the organic profusion of the woods. The film sets up an ambiguous relation between its central character, her activities, and the locations through which she moves. While highlighting the ways in which housekeeping practices construct and maintain a domestic environment, Gruben also illustrates the effects this environment has on the highly ambiguous identity of its protagonist. Focusing attention on food, its raising, acquisition, and preparation, the film aligns two functionally similar yet structurally distinct spaces – the kitchen and the garden. It then traces changes in its protagonist as she moves from the kitchen to the garden to the woods. This protagonist never assumes a distinct identity; instead she takes on the "character" of her surroundings. In the kitchen and the garden she concerns herself with order and cleanliness. Once in the woods, however, she becomes diffuse and wild; she literally revels in dirt.

Gruben uses primarily verbal and architectural texts to render the domestic space of the kitchen. The film opens with a woman tonelessly reciting a grocery list on the soundtrack as a text scrolling up a black screen describes her struggle with two bulky grocery bags on her way into the house. The format of a scrolling text recurs, inter-cut with images, giving us fragmentary descriptions of the events and chores that structure a housewife's domestic existence. All these chores involve a struggle between food and dirt, cleanliness and disorder. Over a floor plan of the kitchen's layout, superimposed titles tell us:

> Entropy is the main problem in the modern kitchen, regulating traffic flow, keeping fingerprints, food particles and other unhygienic particles out. A nucleus of order must be maintained. A kitchen is white steel and chrome for earlier detection. Why is it that disorder is more contagious?

A subsequent text notes that as the woman prepares to fix herself a meal, she must be very careful "to remove all the grit"; a recipe scrolls up the screen, followed by instructions for sprouting potatoes. Utilizing a poetic logic, Gruben plays off the organic implications of the word *cultivation* (as vegetal growth) against its culturally oriented meaning of refinement and polish. But the woman's proclivity for cultivation proves to be her undoing. The next text informs us that the potatoes exhibited "phenomenal growth" and "overtook the kitchen." To get to her dishes, the woman "had to pull roots off the cupboard door." The last written text in the film has the character of a fairy tale: needing to find more containers for her plants, it announces, the woman ventures into the woods, sprinkling seeds behind her to mark her way home. But the birds eat the seeds.

The printed passages that punctuate these initial sequences of *The Central Character* mark the film's movement toward disorder. Beginning with the straightforward description of the grocery list, the clinical treatise on the horrors of entropy, and the recipe, the superimposed texts gradually become a fantastic narration detailing the transformation of a certain milieu and of the character who inhabits and maintains it. Initially the images illustrate the texts. After the passage on entropy and fingerprints, we see a hand scrubbing a dirty footprint off a floor. The early sequences of the film use still images to depict the housewife as an unseen agent of order: we see a broom sweeping a patio, then a hand scrubbing a floor, we hear a voice observing that the patio, must be swept "every day." Time-lapse photography of wildly growing roots accompanies her remark that "the natural world takes dictation from science." The first visual representation of "the central character" depicts her lying in a bathtub, a fern frond dangling down toward her floating hair. The organic world invades and contaminates the domestic. The woman goes to the woods to search for "containers."

In the latter half of the film, compelling, enigmatic images predominate. No written texts order this world, and the woman's voice merges with the cacophony of the outdoors. Overexposed high-contrast film depicts her lying in the mud, initially indistinguishable from the ground, perhaps drinking water from a puddle. Discovered by the camera, she bounds off, her bright white clothing

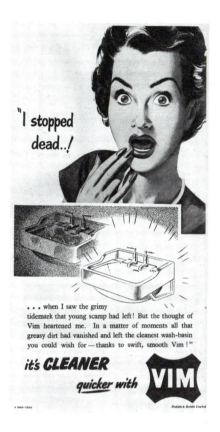

Figure 5.2
"I stopped dead!"
Photo: Hulton-Getty.

patterned with dirt and stains. She peruses domestic artifacts scattered in a field as a voice repeats incessantly, "I only wanted to say, I only wanted to say . . . " Meaning becomes a mantra, a drone blending with the sounds of frogs and insects. Hemmed in by foliage, the woman sets a mock table, placing a worm and a frog on a plate as an almost incoherent, reverberating voice recites the proper placement of knives and spoons.

Gruben contrasts the two halves of her film by whimsically repeating and remotivating certain motifs of order. A high-contrast shot of the woman pushing an empty shopping cart recklessly through a field provides a humorous visual analogue to the opening of the film, where the woman's wrists are described as "white" from the strain of holding bulky grocery bags while she struggles to get into the house. The dull repetition characteristic of housework finds its counterpart in the echoes that render the aural atmosphere of the woods. The pattern of stains on the woman's white blouse visually recalls the dirty footprint so industriously scrubbed off the white floor in an earlier sequence. Much of the play between the two sections derives from Gruben's strategy of recontextualizing the film's motifs. The dresser and shopping cart, embedded in a fairy tale and found in the woods, become objects of curiosity and fascination, deprived of their familiar surroundings and utilitarian functions.

The reverberating instructions for setting a proper table sound ludicrous and strange when we see the woman carefully following the rules as she lays out a table in the forest. Gruben invokes a visual pun as the woman scoops a worm out of a can for dinner. Literally a grub, the worm writhes on the plate as "grub," or food.

Gruben further distinguishes the two worlds of her film by tone or mood. Initially she uses images or texts that consist of abstract, schematic sets of instructions – the floor plan, the carpenter's drawing, the recipe – to represent the ordering of a domestic space. These "objective" or scientific documents function both as instructions and as representations, involving a perspective, a point of view, a way of knowing based on causality, reason, explication, and consensual means of transmitting knowledge. In the woods, however, the film-maker manipulates the images and the soundtrack to articulate a very different kind of textuality. In the first half of the film Gruben documents housework, but in the second half she "plays house." She renders setting a table and pushing a shopping cart fantastic and nonsensical simply by moving them outdoors. If the first section stresses the rationality, the drudgery, and the humorlessness of housework, the second invents a whimsical fantasy from housekeeping practices. There is no center, no emotional quality or coherent subjectivity that unifies the two parts of the film; instead, Gruben moves from one world to the other by following the contradictory imperatives of the housewife's duties – to clean, to feed, to cultivate.

The narrative moves from indoors to outdoors according to a deconstruc-tive logic that illuminates the differing senses of the words *cultivation*, *cultivate*, and *culture*. Deriving from the same Latin stem as *culture* and almost synony-mous with it, *cultivate* means to till the soil, to plough and fertilize, to dig the soil around growing plants. It also means to foster or nourish and, finally, to refine or polish. Gruben uses the differing meanings of this term to reveal para-doxes relating to dirt, to food, to depth and surface, and to indoors and out-doors that all affect the "character" of house-wifery, the home, and, by implication, women who keep house. To cultivate out of doors, as Gruben's film illustrates, involves getting dirty, getting beneath the surface, and concern-ing oneself with growth, roots, and fertility. The cultivation practiced indoors, by contrast, implies ridding oneself of dirt and vulgarity, cleaning and polishing all aspects of one's person (physical, mental, and social), and obsessively con-cerning oneself with surfaces and appearances. While the cultivation one prac-tices outdoors often produces food, indoors one cultivates the intangible nourishments associated with a refined sensibility. Cultivation in its sense of "refinement" implies activities of purification and discrimination; fertility, however, requires the mixing of disparate elements. Beginning with the implied oppositions that structure the opening sequences of the film, between the grocery store and the garden, between the sterility the housewife should strive for within the home and the messy fertility that is a necessary component of nourishment, *The Central Character* playfully explores the plethora of contra-

Figure 5.3
Pastry-making.
Photo: Hulton-Getty.

dictions, both actual and symbolic, that are managed and provisionally effaced by the activities of housework.

The film opens. As stills of the broom sweeping the patio dissolve one on top of the other, the woman's voice informs us that "the patio must be swept every day to reclaim it from the out of doors." Margins are problematic; the patio, outdoors yet part of the home, borders on the woods and requires vigilant daily attention. As the stills of a sweeping broom continue, the housewife notes the superimposition of the patio, of the cultural surface, onto the natural one: "The clay bricks are set directly into the earth in the extensive backyard." This attention to the cultural function of surfaces dominates the first half of the film, the half that concerns the indoors, the domestic; furthermore, most of the early images are flat, two-dimensional (a white floor, a floor plan on graph paper, a drawing of cabinets). These surfaces must be kept clean, free from the material that characterizes the outdoors (dirt), from all residue that indicates the work done in the kitchen (food particles), and from the signs of human presence itself (fingerprints and footprints). Significantly, the presence of the housewife is conveyed strictly by her hand, her voice, or scrolling text.

The housewife performs these tasks of erasure and purification that keep indoors separate from outdoors, activity separate from its effects or residue and the body and traces of the body separate from the work involved in satisfying its needs. One of the housewife's chores is to efface the signs of her own work (food particles) and those of her role as worker (fingerprints). Another is to make manifest a system of spatial distinctions. In this regard her work resembles primitive ritual in that it provides a literal frame for culture. As I have noted in another context, Mary Douglas equates our secular housecleaning with ritual:

> When we honestly reflect on our busy scrubbings and cleanings . . . we know that we are not mainly trying to avoid disease. We are separating, placing boundaries, making visible statements about the home we are intending to create out of the material house.
>
> (Douglas, 1966: 68)

While Gruben's film illustrates the role cleaning plays in establishing cultural boundaries and distinctions, it also suggests the fragility of these boundaries and the profound interdependency of the two realms created by them. The film visually suggests the degree to which the ideas of "nature" and "culture" depend on the practices that maintain this supposedly natural division. Although the housewife creates these distinctions and keeps them "neat," she herself inhabits or comes to embody their paradoxical connection.

As a result of the imperatives of purity implied in various aspects of housework, the housewife is placed in what Mary Douglas would call a "dangerous" cultural position. In order to clean, to separate, to keep dirt (nature) out, the housewife must "get her hands dirty," do the "dirty work." As a cultural cleaning agent, she must come into contact with and handle the very pollutions she protects others from; she therefore runs the risk of being tainted with them herself. But she also must avoid being too clean, or becoming overzealous and maniacal like Craig's wife in Dorother Azner's film (*Craig's Wife*, 1936). Douglas remarks that

Figure 5.4
Telephone conversation.
Photo: Hulton-Getty.

the quest for purity is pursued by rejection . . . [W]hen purity is not a symbol but something lived, it must be poor and barren. Purity is the enemy of change, of ambiguity and compromise . . . it is an attempt to force experience into logical categories of non-contradiction. But experience is not amenable and those who make the attempt find themselves led into contradiction.

(Douglas, 1966: 161–2)

We can see the housewife's liminal and paradoxical situation represented in advertisements for cleansers, soaps, dishwashing liquids, or floor-cleaning products, where the same contradictions between inside and outside, between "nature" and "culture," shape the character of the product. Ad copy stresses that the effects of housework are effects of erasure, yet an erasure that leaves traces in its wake – a gleam, a shine, the scents of lemon or pine. Cleaning products promise not only to evacuate dirt, grime, and germs, aspects of the "natural" that are dirty and dangerous, but also to import the scent and fresh-ness of the outdoors, leaving olfactory traces of vegetal or floral growth.[1] Thus nature or the natural, coded as the source of the dirty and taboo, is also com-modified and chemically reproduced as a signifier of cleanliness that opens up and refreshes indoor domestic space. Significantly, the purity promoted by these ads derives from a complex process of transformations enacted between the "natural" and the "cultural," not from an oppositional relation between them.

As the agent of these paradoxical transformations, the housewife, like the cleaning product, contains contradictory significations that affect the coherence of her identity. Gruben's film shows how a woman's various household duties influence her own (unstable) image. The same instability exists in cultural

Figure 5.5
Childcare.
Photo: Hulton-Getty.

constructions of female gender and sexuality. Historically and culturally relegated to perform tasks that establish the distinctions between the natural and the cultural, women, generalized in the "feminine," come to represent extremes of both.[2] "The feminine" therefore signifies conflicting polarities that articulate not an opposition to a male other but an enclosure, a parenthesis in which "he" figures as norm/neutral/neither. Women, writes Catherine Clément, "are double. They are allied with what is regular, according to the rules, since they are wives and mothers, and allied as well with those natural disturbances, their regular periods, which are the epitome of paradox, order and disorder" (Clément, 1986, 8). While Clément locates the source of this doubling in women's physical, biological functions, Gruben's film argues that the gender coding of certain highly symbolic activities – cleaning, cooking, feeding – also helps create the frame in which we read biological differences. Furthermore, the ideological pressure of such a frame is evident in considerations of housekeepers' and, by inference, women's sexuality.

As a worker whose practices create, police, and maintain the cultural border between purity and impurity, whose actions determine what comes close to the bodies of her family and what is kept at a distance, who supervises what goes in and comes out of those bodies, the housekeeper finds that her own body is subject to stringent limitations and cultural controls. These controls monitor the cleanliness of both her body and her sexuality. If we look at narratives about housewives, we can see that the stories they tell are often marked by a confusion of literal and metaphorical cleanliness. In accounts of bad or mad housewives, the woman is associated either with a "dirty" sexuality and slovenly housewifery or with frigidity and obsessive orderliness. Codes of personal cleanliness and sexuality are bound up with the diverse chores of the housewife, infusing cultural constructions of her sexuality with hygienic concerns: a "slut" is both a slovenly housewife and a promiscuous woman. The housewife's role as cleaner becomes associated with her role as sexual partner, a phenomenon treated in *Craig's Wife* and critiqued in *Jeanne Dielman*. The good housewife must negotiate a position that includes some of both roles and all of neither. She must manage and contain contradiction.

The Central Character exposes the paradoxical character of housekeeping by muddying conventional distinctions between meanings and between spaces. Her poetic meditation on the nature–culture divide adopts this essentialist binary only to deconstruct it on its own terms. In transgressive and playful ways, Gruben's film undercuts the cultural practices that keep things separate by revealing the cracks and contradictions in the language and imagery of housekeeping.

NOTES

1   I am grateful to Jon McKenzie for pointing out the odd significance of the scents of many cleaning products.

2   The woman's alignment with nature in traditional thought is described in Griffin (1978), but the highly cultured is also seen as feminine, as in the stereotype of the effeminate man. See also Jacques Lacan's provocative closure to "Guiding Remarks for a Congress on Feminine Sexuality", in which, commenting on "feminine sexuality and society", he alludes to the particularly refined and cultured quality of groups of women (Lacan, 1982: 88–98).

Chapter 6: "Hi Honey, I'm Home": Weary (Neurasthenic) Businessmen and the Formation of a Serenely Modern Aesthetic

Joyce Henri Robinson

Happy the man who, far from business and affairs,
    Like mortals of the early times,
  May work his father's fields with oxen of his own,
    Exempt from profit, loss, and fee . . .

(Horace, *Epodes*, 2.1–4. In Horace, 65 BC: 99–101).[1]

If we can take Horace at his word, it appears that businessmen have been wearied by the demands of the forum for a very long time. Horace's usurer, who utters this rather plaintive refrain, dreams of returning to the countryside where men work the fields "like mortals of the early times" and are free from the concerns of "profit, loss, and fee." Implicit in every sad song bemoaning the fate of the exhausted merchant is, of course, the denunciation of the workaday world of city life. The inevitable corrective and cultural corollary to the quotidian routine of the forum is the restorative realm of the pastoral which, if not always available to the weary businessman in actuality, has since ancient times been presented to him through the distancing artifice of bucolic poetry and painting. As noted historian of the pastoral Renato Poggioli reminds us, it is when civilization "tires man's heart" that pastoral poetry most often appears and offers the exhausted city dweller "moral relaxation and emotional release" (Poggioli, 1975: 4).

The quest for an uncomplicated moment of felicity in the midst of a highly complicated society is the concomitant to life lived in the city, and since ancient times (as Horace reveals) the onward and increasingly fast-paced march of civilization has been habitually accompanied by the laments of weary sojourners longing for a realm of pastoral calm. This atavistic yearning for the rehabilitative delights of the pastoral is nowhere more provocatively visualized than in Henri Matisse's *Le Bonheur de vivre*, which remains, undoubtedly, modernism's most familiar evocation of an idyllic golden age (Figure 6.1). The painting celebrates humankind's original harmony with nature, a harmony that is expressively com-

Figure 6.1
Henri Matisse, *Le
Bonheur de vivre*, 190–6.
Photo: The Barnes
Foundation.

municated in the gently curving forms of the landscape and the female nude,
that crucial denizen of Arcadia. The image appears to be aesthetically and psychologically fully consonant with Matisse's ideas about his art as expressed in his
1908 essay, "Notes of a Painter", in which the artist includes the weary *homme
d'affaires* among the designated recipients of his serene art:

> What I dream of is an art of balance, of purity and serenity, devoid of troubling or
> depressing subject matter, an art which could be for every mental worker, for the
> businessman as well as the man of letters, for example, a soothing, calming influence on
> the mind, something like a good armchair which provides relaxation from physical
> fatigue . . .

(Matisse, 1908: 35–40)

Matisse's language is both gender and class specific. The beneficiary of his restful
art is the mental or intellectual worker (*travailleur cérébral*): more specifically, the
definitive male bourgeois, the businessman. Why is the *homme d'affaires*, the
businessman, one of the chosen recipients of the pastoral delights of Matisse's
art? Was this merely an entrepreneurial strategy on the artist's part, a bold
announcement of hoped-for patronage?

As Joseph Mashek has shown, Matisse's language and his "prosperously
bourgeois outlook" echo a familiar topos, found in the writings of Reynolds,
Hume, Goethe, and Baudelaire, of the fatigued gentleman whose prosperity
enables him to procure enough refreshment through poetry and art (Mashek,
1975, 1976). What Matisse adds to these earlier aesthetic musings is the understanding of the refectory role assumed by the decorative pastoral landscape in
the creation of a serenely restful art. Though Matisse, in many ways, inaugurated
a modernist attitude toward the production of art in the twentieth century, he
was himself a child of the nineteenth century, and the roots of his pastoral, and I

would argue "domestic" outlook, as expressed in the famous "businessman" passage and in *Le Bonheur de vivre*, are to be found there. This chapter examines the cultural and artistic origins of this serenely *domestic* aesthetic which is indebted to late nineteenth-century writings on interior decoration, domesticity and the housewife, and the decorative landscape.[2] To begin, however, we must investigate that most prominent of Matisse's weary designees: the *homme d'affaires*. Could it be that there is something we don't know about the turn-of-the-century businessman and his need for soothing pastoral interludes to punctuate his frenetic life?

L'HOMME D'AFFAIRES

Medical literature written during the second half of the nineteenth century provides an important clue about weary businessmen and more generally about exhausted "brain-workers". In 1869, the American neurologist George Beard published *A Practical Treatise on Nervous Exhaustion* in which he discussed the symptomology and treatment of the recently identified nervous disorder, neurasthenia. Most simply defined as nervous exhaustion, neurasthenia was believed to result from the overcharging of the nervous system in confrontation with the incessant stimulation of urban existence. An inevitable psychological and physical counterpart to civilization and modernity, neurasthenia was labelled an "American disease" by Beard, and proudly viewed as a kind of medical signifier of America's "advanced" status (Lutz, 1991: 6). Convinced that the disease primarily affected the middle and upper classes, the "higher orders" within American society, Beard singled out male "brain-workers" as especially susceptible to the debilitating condition because of the increased mental exertion demanded by their occupations. Indeed, for Beard, neurasthenia was a "sign of mental superiority" and a natural, even socially acceptable, concomitant to the challenging arena of the marketplace (Drinka, 1984: 208).

Though *A Practical Treatise on Nervous Exhaustion* was not translated into French until 1895, Beard's work was well known to the European medical community and the "*maladie de* Beard" was popularly diagnosed throughout the 1880s and 1890s (Rabinbach, 1990: 153). French neurologists discounted Beard's contention that neurasthenia was a distinctively American phenomenon, citing the increasing number of European cases as ample proof of the condition's universality. Important texts on the mental disorder were published in France throughout the 1890s; each more or less echoed Beard's original findings, though in some cases, additional and more recent scientific evidence was supplied to shore up the author's findings.[3] The symptoms of neurasthenia were multiple and wildly variant and ranged from ticklishness, stomach upset and insomnia to physical enervation, anxiety, and impotence. Cerebral fatigue or "over-pressure" was among the most often-cited neurasthenic complaints and was attributed to the excessive intellectual work demanded of the brain-workers (Rabinbach, 1990: 157).

> Intellectual work is one of the most fatiguing forms of nervous activity . . . Every man of
> average intelligence who exceeds ten hours a day in intellectual work, and, above all,
> who doesn't vary this work and combine it with some sort of physical activity, puts
> himself in the most favorable condition for nervous exhaustion.
>
> (Levillain, 1891: 38–9)

Our author, Fernand Levillain, informs us that it is not only the musical composer, the artist, the writer or the scientific researcher who suffers from nervous exhaustion. "The calculations and strategies of business, preoccupations of a financial nature, political discussions and matters . . . lead to the same result, intellectual fatigue and exhaustion due to an excess of mental excitation."

European writers were generally more willing than Beard to allow for a hereditary component in the development of the nervous disorder. Ultimately, they differentiated two essential types of neurasthenics: accidental or "shock" (typified by the fatigued businessman and the overworked scholar) and degenerative or hereditary (Drinka, 1984: 216).[4] For males, the leading cause of accidental neurasthenia was mental fatigue ("*surmenage intellectuel*"), and the man who dealt with troublesome pecuniary matters on a routine basis, the *homme d'affaires*, was highlighted as the most likely of all intellectual workers to succumb to the debilitating condition. Females, believed more likely to exhibit a natural propensity for the disease, were advised to avoid the excessive intellectual stimulation of the marketplace and counseled to remain within the protective confines of the domestic interior in order to safeguard their fragile nervous systems (Drinka, 1984: 220). One of the primary accidental causes of neurasthenia in women purportedly was the willful violation of their roles as mothers and wives; that is, their willful departure from the calm sanctity of the home.[5]

Fortunately for the fatigued mental worker and the overly ambitious female, shock or accidental neurasthenics responded well to treatment. For the female neurasthenic, there were several recommended cures, the most famous of which was the "rest cure" developed by American neurologist Silas Weir Mitchell in the 1870s (Showalter, 1985: 138).[6] Entailing several weeks of complete isolation and bed rest (often in a country setting), Mitchell's infantilizing cure, which was widely promulgated in French treatises on the disease, apparently was reserved for only the severest cases. For the male brain-worker, the recommended cure was far less punitive, yet equally pastoral in nature.

> Those who work to excess, deskworkers, scientists and men of letters, occasionally
> succumb to bouts of mental depression . . . In general, these forms of neurasthenia are
> not very serious, even less so when hereditary influences are entirely lacking. Rest of the
> overtaxed brain, visits to the countryside or to the mountains, and several weeks of well-
> conducted hydrotherapy, are sufficient to restore the nervous system's equilibrium.
>
> (Bouveret, 1890: 12)

The palliative effect of hydrotherapy, rest, and sojourns in the countryside was forthrightly proclaimed in French treatises on the nervous condition.[7] The rest cure, taking the waters, a day in the country: all were meant to bring serenity to the weary mind and spirit.

While neurasthenic businessmen might on occasion visit the healing waters in Vichy, they could hardly be expected to return to a domestic routine (as many neurasthenic women were advised to do) in order to mitigate the nervous tension produced by the tedious environment of commerce. Popularizing medical treatises from the period were eminently more practical. What was recommended for the weary and overworked businessman was that he retire, after a hard day's work, to a restful domestic environment within the city. In *La Neurasthénie et son traitement*, published in 1895, Emile Laurent tersely stated this prescriptive advice, noting that the "neurasthenic must lead a calm life sheltered from agitation" (Laurent, 1895: 52). For Laurent, a moderate lifestyle was recommended to corroborate the calming influence of the domestic retreat.

> I forbid them to drink, to smoke, even to love . . . in excess, of course. I allow them what one would allow a sensible man who is mildly ill: a half liter of wine daily, one cup of coffee without alcohol, and *Venus once a week*.
>
> (Laurent, 1895; 53, emphasis added)

The pleasures of Venus, while not prohibited, were to be experienced in moderate doses. Other doctors advocated the domestication of the love goddess and recommended that the male neurasthenic procure, as part of his treatment, a *femme au foyer*, a housewife, who would provide for him a serenely calm oasis, a private interior realm for physical and mental rehabilitation.

Advice books for the young mistress of the house written in the final decades of the nineteenth century encouraged her to create a psychologically and emotionally serene environment for her husband. Clearly, this kind of domestic advice participated in the ever-prevalent "ideology of separate spheres" which identified the female's domain as the interior, while the male was inevitably associated with the exterior realm of the forum.[8] Reiterating this commonly held belief in 1892, Jules Simon pronounced that while man was made "to fight and work outside," it was the woman's task "to maintain order in the house and there organize happiness" (Simon, 1892: 67). Like Ruskin's "angel of the house," she provided a shelter from the mental headaches and tribulations of quotidian existence; and, thus, the foyer, the interior, was identified as an important site for male recuperation.[9]

Handbooks and popular articles on interior decoration also aided the housewife in her creation of a quiet and restful enclave within the urban jungle. Implicit in such writings was the belief that the decoration of the home fell within the purview of wifely activities and the related assumption that such domestic activity was undertaken primarily for the benefit of the male occupant of the home. Typical of this pervasive opinion regarding the nineteenth-century female's aesthetic mission is the argument proffered by Jacob von Falke in *Art in the House* (1879):

the husband's occupations necessitate his absence from the house, and call him far away from it. During the day his mind is absorbed in many good and useful ways, in making and acquiring money for instance, and even after the hours of business have passed, they occupy his thoughts. When he returns home tired with work and in need of recreation, he longs for quiet enjoyment, and takes pleasure in the home which his wife has made comfortable and attractive . . . She is the mistress of the house in which she rules, and which she orders like queen. Should it not then be specially her business to add *beauty* to the *order* which she has created?

(Falke, 1879: 315–16, original emphasis).

It is clear from this and other writings on the decorative in the second half of the nineteenth century that order, beauty, and serenity were the pre-eminently desirable qualities in domestic decoration. While public decoration might be expected to challenge the mind and provoke thought, the decor of the home was intended to calm, rather than excite, the mind and nerves of the city dweller.

The *femme de foyer*'s salubrious mission was often referenced in contemporary journals such as *Art et décoration* and *L'Art décoratif*, which featured any number of articles discussing the "psychology of rooms" (Soulier, 1902: 84) and recommending appropriate colors and lines for the creation of a restful and welcoming interior, a wonderfully domestic variant on the modernist expressive self-sufficiency of pictorial elements. The desired goal, simply stated, was the creation of a pastoral realm for physical and mental reflection in which the decor contributed to, rather than detracted from, the refreshing of the weary brain-worker.

The function of décor is not to arouse particular emotions, but to give the milieu a character in accord with the man who must live there, without compelling his thoughts to focus on the image of a concrete reality, without forcing them to be objective when the hour of subjective refuge awaits them.

(Gerdeil, 1901: 126)

Not unexpectedly, this French author had the tired intellectual worker in mind when he advocated the creation of a decor that would not only inspire analysis or force the weary brain to decipher its mysteries. Simply stated, the decor of the home should not encourage or inspire intellectual effort of any kind, since the fatigued businessman was forced to exhaust his mental energies on the diurnal routine of the forum. Concomitantly, paintings destined for the interior, it was believed, should not inspire mental headaches but participate in the restful ambiance of the domestic environment. Arts and crafts architect M.H. Baillie Scott, an advocate of integrated and harmonious home design, ardently expressed this conviction in his *Houses and Gardens* (1906) in which he clearly privileged the place of the (weary) man of the house.

If we imagine, for instance, the tired man of business returning to his suburban home in the evening, it can hardly be supposed that he will be prepared to make the special mental effort involved in an inspection of his pictures; but whatever decorative quality they express in conjunction with their surroundings will at once enfold him as in an atmosphere which soothes and charms like harmonious music.

(Baillie Scott, 1906: 53)

The ubiquity of this belief that interior decoration and paintings destined for the domestic interior should calm the fatigued viewer is further evinced in the writings of the quintessentially world-weary Vincent Van Gogh. Regarding his *Bedroom at Arles*, Van Gogh noted to Theo that color was to be "suggestive of *rest* or of sleep in general." "In a word," he concluded, "looking at the picture ought to rest the brain, or rather the imagination" (Van Gogh, 1888, in Chipp, 1968: 40–1).

Another source for this homely pastoral aesthetic are critical writings from the 1890s on the decorative landscape, a modern genre of landscape whose intent, according to critics, was not to elevate or teach the spirit, but "to make it serene again" (Germain, 1902: 145–6). This mission was made clear in critic Alphonse Germain's article of 1891, "Le paysage décoratif," in which he outlined the transformative power of the decorative landscape and identified the domestic interior as its intended site (Benjamin, 1993; Robinson, 1993).

What better way to transform our depressing hovels into oases where the spirit can rest after the worries of mundane existence . . . Oh, to forget the ugliness of the street when we stand before an idealized landscape . . .

(Germain, 1891a)

The choice of "oasis" to characterize the foyer is clearly purposeful and suggests a transformation of the domestic realm into a place of refuge, a pastoral shelter, as it were, in the idealized landscape. Germain, along with Raymond Bouyer, was the principal critic responsible for formulating the stylistic parameters of this new decorative genre which was envisioned as a kind of modern apparition of the heroic landscape minus the thought-provoking intrusion of didactic subject matter. The primary stipulation for the decorative landscape was that it contain the "skillful lines of the Old Masters," and both Germain and Bouyer recommended that young artists consult Poussin and Claude in their creation of a modern synthetic landscape. Such esteemed ancestry suggests the conservative nature of the decorative landscape as envisioned by Germain and reveals the true intention of his article, which was to ground the nascent decorative landscape tradition in the French past. For Germain, the decorative landscape as practiced by the young Nabis artists, whom he derogatorily labeled "deformers," was merely an ornamental distortion of the natural world (Germain, 1891b; Marlais, 1992: 171–80). The critic scoffed at the *"néo-traditionnisme"* advocated by Maurice Denis, the most vocal proselytizer for the young followers of Gaugin, and excoriated the apologist's primitivizing, non-western definition of the "decorative." Galvanized by Denis' writings, which he believed had effectively co-opted the "decorative" for the modernist agenda and corrupted the term by associating it with Japanese, Byzantine, and Egyptian art, Germain essentially reclaimed the decorative for the French race. Promulgating a far more parochial understanding of the decorative landscape than would Denis or fellow Symbolist critic Albert Aurier, both Germain and Bouyer ultimately defined the genre as the serenely expressive rearrangement of natural forms via the heroic landscape tradition of Poussin.

Germain believed that the *paysage décoratif* could serve as an integral component of a decorative schema within the domestic setting and was convinced of the *affective* power of interior decoration on the mind and soul of the dweller.

> In general, our contemporaries do not give the decoration of the home the importance it merits and are not sufficiently convinced of its influence on character. Lines and hues exert as considerable an influence as that of pure air, spectacles of nature and flowers . . . It is, therefore, necessary to surround oneself with harmonious and serene effects, luminous colors with nuances evoking feelings of happiness and calm, and ornament inspired by nature.
>
> (Germain, 1902: 151–2)

This belief in the expressive autonomy of formal elements (here within the context of interior decoration) and in the power of line and color to influence "character" derives from Charles Blanc's highly influential *Grammaire des arts du dessin* (1867) and from the more contemporary writings of Charles Henry. Germain's short-lived critical support of the Neo-Impressionists in the early 1890s had familiarized him with the psycho-physical system of Henry (which essentially codified and provided scientific verification for Blanc's traditional and vaguely defined ideas: Herbert, 1968: 21), linking linear movement, the emotional value of color, and viewer physiological response. Ultimately, Germain believed that the soothing formal qualities and idyllic theme of the decorative landscape could appease and provide solace for the weary spirit; as such, its destination was the private interior where it participated in the creation of a domestic pastoral oasis.

Throughout the early years of the twentieth century, critics continued to praise the restorative power of the conservative decorative landscape, repeatedly linking the genre, as had Germain, with idyllic pastoral themes. Writing of the little-known painter Jean-Francis Auburtin in 1912, critic Louis Vauxcelles (best remembered for providing the "Fauve" group with its moniker) identified the decorative pastoral landscape as an important means of placing "a little calm joy and hellenic fantasy on the walls of homes." This task was undertaken, not unexpectedly, "to comfort the worried soul of men overtaxed by their miserably frenetic and brutal condition" (Vauxcelles, 1912: 78).[10]

To accomplish this comforting mission, the decorative landscape had to be serene, rather than frenetic, and produce sensations of calm and well-being, not anxiety, if it were to succeed in creating a restful interior for the weary (male) viewer. According to conservative commentators, many decorative landscapes featured in late nineteenth-century interiors were not successful in achieving the requisite state of serenity. A cartoon bearing the caption "Serpentine painting"

École classique.

Modernisme ou artistico-réalisme.

Impressionnisme.

Symbolisme de la Rose + Croix.

Pointillisme.

Tachisme.

Peinture serpentine.

Incohérents.

NOS GRANDES ÉCOLES MODERNES

Figure 6.2
Avelot, *Modern French Painting*, including "Serpentine Painting", [bottom left] from *Revue Illustrée*, 1 May 1894.

from an 1894 issue of *Revue illustrée* underscores the popular perception of the goal of domestic decoration as restful and the failure of the tentacular forms of Art Nouveau interiors in this enterprise (Figure 6.2). In the cartoon we see the typical *petit-bourgeois* male who, on contemplating this "decorative panel for a dining room," has become incapacitated by the undulating movement of the female nudes, over-stimulated, as it were, by this vision of serpentine shrews.

According to historian Debora Silverman, there were artists and writers in *fin-de-siècle* France who created interiors that were deliberately designed to arouse the senses and activate "nervous vibration" (Silverman, 1989: 77). The most notorious example is, of course, Des Esseintes, in Huysmans' *A Rebours*, who crafted his decor around images of Odilon Redon and Gustave Moreau in order to "shake up his nervous system by means of erudite fancies, complicated nightmares, [and] suave and sinister visions" (Huysmans, 1884: 63). Silverman argues that, though the interior did function as a therapeutic refuge from the metropolis throughout the closing years of the nineteenth century, the "over-stimulated citizen . . . transported with him the propensity for animating the interior." "No longer," she concludes, "could the interior be constructed as a stable and static historical setting" (Silverman, 1989: 79).

Silverman's analysis of the *fin-de-siècle* redefinition of interior decoration via the "new psychology" of Charcot and Berheim highlights, I believe, the *effete* (aristocratic) exception which proves the (*bourgeois*) rule. The "peinture serpentine" cartoon encapsulates the pervasive *bourgeois* belief that the interior should provide a stable, calm environment, and humorously demonstrates the conservative reaction to the mentally exhausting *fin-de-siècle* interior. Similar

Figure 6.3
Henry Van de Velde.
Dining Room, Maison de
l'Art Nouveau, Paris,
1895.
Archives et Musée de la
Litterature, Bibliothèque
Royale, Albert Ier,
Brussels.

attitudes are amply evident in the critical response to Siegfried Bing's model rooms in his *Maison de l'Art Nouveau*, which offered the French public a glimpse of the latest in home design in 1895. Featured in Bing's Paris gallery was a dining-room designed by Henry Van de Velde that included decorative paintings by Edouard Vuillard (Figure 6.3). In the Ranson panels the theme of young women working in the fields might certainly be construed as pastoral and, therefore, appropriate for an idyllic decorative landscape; however, the ornamental deformation and contorted meanderings of the trees and human figures (echoing the arabesques of Van de Velde's inlaid copper decoration) made them, it was suggested by more than one observer, inappropriate for the intended domestic setting. René Boylesve commented that in front of such an image he would barely be able to make it to the meat course before having to beat a hasty retreat from the table (Boylesve, 1896: 116), while Camille Pissarro described the Ranson panels as "odious" (Troy, 1991: 25). Perhaps most telling, however, was the response of *Le Figaro* critic Arsène Alexandre who, though he found Ranson's panels "simple and skilled," said of his visit to Bing's gallery: "I left feeling exhausted, sick, exasperated, my nerves on edge and my head full of dancing nightmares" (Silverman, 1989: 278).

The major plaint levelled against Bing's decorative ensemble was its eclecticism, which was identified by the critical press as a sign of its pastiched internationalism. Critics generally agreed that the French innate understanding of decoration – the French taste, that is, for simplicity, moderation, and harmony – had been tainted by the pernicious example of the meandering and menacing forms of foreign art. What had previously been perfunctorily dismissed in this negative critical response to Bing's *Maison* is its inflection by the language of medical discourse. Alexandre's account, which includes terms such as "undigestible" and "unhealthy," suggests a quite visceral and immediate physical response to the undulating environs of this modern interior. Alexandre was especially troubled by Van de Velde's smoking room with its "wall coverings composed of enormous arabesques that enter your head and swirl about" (Silverman, 1989: 278), while Boylesve likened the room to the interior of a yacht, regretfully noting the absence of "the requisite paraphernalia for sea sickness" (Boylesve, 1896: 116). Another critic, André Hallays, deemed the entire Bing salon the product of a "neurasthenic millionaire," furthering the critical assessment of the "unhealthy" influence on the mythical (and unfortunate) dweller of this *Art Nouveau* domicile (Weisberg, 1986: 77).

Implicit in this response is the converse belief in the rectitude of the well-ordered and restful bourgois domestic interior. In the *fin-de siècle* period, there was one universally acclaimed artist who, it was believed, could provide the perfect thematic and formal recipe for the creation of a domestic pastoral decorative art, and that was Pierre Puvis de Chavannes. Serenely divorced from the anxious present, Puvis' idyllic imagery offered viewers suffering from a general "life fatigue" a brief respite from the chaos of the city (Vachon, 1895: 1–2). This notion of Puvis' work as a kind of quiet haven in the midst of the urban maelstrom appears throughout the critical literature in the late 1880s and 1890s. It is noteworthy, and indeed telling, that the catalogue essay for Puvis's important one-man exhibition at Durand-Ruel in 1887 opened with the following:

> You live amidst agitation, noise and the hectic crowd, surrounded by a feverish atmosphere. Suddenly, a drapery parts, and you are in peace and calm; what a sensation of well-being!
>
> (Roger-Ballu, 1887: 7)

For Roger-Ballu, Puvis' "serene work," unlike the militant art of most of his advanced contemporaries, was the perfect panacea for an exhausted and enervated viewing public. It is not unusual that Puvis' art appeared restful and quiet, from "another era," in the words of one critic, in the privacy of the Durand-Ruel gallery. Yet, even at the annual Salon, which Emile Zola likened to a department store and which most commentators characterized as a bustling fair or bazaar, Puvis' entries were said to have had a similar effect. In a survey of contemporary art written some ten years after Puvis' death, Julius Meier-Graefe recalled the throngs who each year fought to see his pictures, despite the "audacities" of the annual event. "When one got to him through the tumult of the rooms, all the trumpets of the big and brutal musicians and all the squealing of the little pipers seemed to cease. It was like coming into a church" (Meier-Graefe, 1908: 48).

Though Puvis was arguably the most visible and esteemed *public* artist of the Third Republic, his art provided both the thematic material and the stylistic formula for a quintessentially private art. Roger Marx was one of many critics who applauded the artist's abstemious classicism as well as the salubrious pastoralism celebrated throughout his decorative oeuvre. In particular, Marx praised *L'Eté*, publicly enshrined in Paris' Hôtel de Ville, for its power to "take us away from ourselves" and to provide a brief respite from the fever and anguish of city life (Figure 6.4). When viewers gather around the Hôtel de Ville panel, Marx writes, they forget the malaise oppressing society, distanced as they are (visually and psychologically speaking) from the vortex of modern affairs, distanced as well, he notes, from "the contagion of modern neurasthenia,"

> one senses that [the panel] was executed in isolation, far from the whirlwind of human affairs and the turmoils of life; the contagion of modern neurasthenia has not broken its spell; healthy and suspended above the world, it counters our pervasive pessimism with the comforting vision of another, better world.
>
> (Marx, 1897: 242)

The decorative pastoral landscape as essayed by Puvis and many of his followers images the bucolic existence enjoyed by an ancient society before the founding of cities and modern commerce. As such, it provided the perfect visual panacea for a neurasthenic age. The nervous disease, after all, was a highly visible signifier of urban modernism and cultural advancement; that is to say, it was intimately linked to modern civilization. Thus, for a world-weary late nineteenth-century audience, the pastoral mode, with its emphasis on the halcyon existence of a

Figure 6.4
Pierre Puvis de
Chavannes, *L'Eté*, Salon
d'arrivée, Hôtel de Ville,
Paris, 1891.
Photo: Roger-Viollet.

pre-civilized world, effectively served as the cultural antidote to *fin-de-siècle* decadence and malaise.

In *L'Eté* we see a serenely pastoral environment and the calm existence of an ancient society before the founding of cities and modern commerce. As befits the nature of the envisioned activity, the surrounding landscape is bucolic and shelters the arcadians from the harsh realities of life beyond this delightful place. In this decorative panel both the necessary labor and earned leisure that accompanied the construction of mankind's earliest societies are incorporated. Befitting its decorative function, the accessible pastoral iconography demands little in the way of mental cerebration from the viewer, and the thematic interest is evenly dispersed across the picture plane. Rather than focusing on one dominant figural group, the spectator's gaze is thus invited to wander unimpeded throughout the comforting environment.

Throughout all of Puvis' pastoral landscapes, women serve two functions: they are presented either as active and robust caretakers of the hearth (*femme au foyer*) or as visual emblems of rest and calm (bathing nymph). Often, as in Puvis' panels at the Musée de Picardie in Amiens, these female realms are in turn contrasted to the male-dominated realm of work on (as opposed to in) the city. Even within this early bucolic society, the workaday world of the "city" is disassociated from "home," the locus of rest and calm stability. In *L'Eté*, leisure and the feminine realm are literally fore-grounded, while the mundane realm of the masculine is effectively removed and is merely a distant backdrop.

Puvis maintains this ideological bifurcation of the male and female spheres – males identified with work, females with home and/or leisure – throughout his decorative landscapes, though it is clear that his allegiance (as a decorative painter) lies with the serene domain of female leisure and rest. In *Doux pays*, a panel painted for the private home of Léon Bonnat in 1882, the identification of the pastoral with females resting in nature is further evidenced (Figure 6.5). Here young male children join the women in their idyllic (homey?) surrounds, while the masculine realm of arduous activity is remotely referenced and serves as a visual antithesis to the feminine realm of pastoral calm. In 1895, Bonnat spoke in glowing terms of the decorative panel recalling that on days when he was "tired and listless," the *Doux pays* brightened his soul and forced his somber imaginings" to evaporate (Bonnat, 1895: 50).[11] This was, in essence, the mission stipulated by Germain in his essay on the decorative landscape, and both he and other critics interested in the genre believed that Puvis' pastoral decorations could indeed restore serenity to the weary spirit. Roger Marx, who applauded Puvis' ability to image a world distanced from the "contagion of modern neurasthenia," similarly recognized the transformative power of the decorative landscape.

> At the sight of so much calm and harmony, our soul [has] to rediscover the secret of lost tranquility, and [falls] back under the illusion of a possible joy of life.
>
> (Marx, 1897: 242)

Puvis' decorative landscapes, like Matisse's *Le Bonheur de vivre*, image a peaceful enclave sheltered from the world of business and mental fatigue; accordingly, they highlight that quintessentially restful denizen of Arcadia, the female nude. At the turn of the century, the female's socially designated role was to provide comfort and rest for her weary (neurasthenic) husband, either as *femme au foyer*, as keeper of a calm, structured interior, or as decorative nymph, that

Figure 6.5
Pierre Puvis de Chavannes, *Doux pays*, 1882.
Photo: Caisse Nationale des Monuments Historiques et des Sites, Paris Musée Bonnat, Bayonne.

gently-curving hieroglyph of serenity. The cultural linkage of these two seemingly disparate female roles is succinctly evidenced in an 1899 advertisement for decorative panels featuring a reclining curvaceous nude intended, presumably, to function as part of the consumer's "Home Decor" (Figure 6.6). In an article entitled "Le Féminisme et le bon sens," written for an 1895 issue of *La Plume*, Victor Joze further demonstrated this linkage in suggesting that the female remain as nature intended her, as "mistress of the house or bacchante" (Joze, 1895: 392). While the nymph reigns supreme in *Le Bonheur de vivre*, both apparitions of the desirable female lurk throughout Matisse's oeuvre. In *Luxe, calme et volupté* (1904–5), they commingle peacefully as the beach at Saint-Tropez is transformed into a modern-day isle of Cythers (Figure 6.7). Many years later, they reappear in

Figure 6.6
Home Décor, from
L'Estampe et L'Affiche,
15 February 1889.
Photo: Musée des Arts
Décoratifs, Paris.

Figure 6.7
Henri Matisse, *Luxe,
calme et volupté*, 1904–5.
Musée d'Orsay, Paris.
Photo: Giraudon.

that paean to domesticity, *The Music Lesson*, their roles neatly juxtaposed within the sheltering protection of the arcadian world of nature. The domestic and pastoral realm of rest and beauty as envisioned by Matisse is, ultimately, a "masculine dreamworld," to borrow one again from Renato Poggioli (Poggioli, 1975: 22). Within this pastoral world of dreams, the female – in either guise – provides domestic comfort and serenity and contributes to the creation of a private interior haven distanced from the neurasthenic chaos of the city.

This dream of a simpler, happier existence away from the "contentious forum" is the real key to understanding the pastoral (Horace, *Epodes*: 2.7). If the nineteenth-century businessman was unable to live the bucolic life as envisioned by Horace's usurer, he could at the very least recreate (or have recreated for him) the pastoral place of delight *chez lui* via the decorative landscape. For the world-weary *homme d'affaires*, the proper domestic interior embodied an ambiance of restful leisure (*otium*), visually and emotionally providing a retreat from the world of business (*negotium*). Arcadian pleasures were, thus, literally close to home, and it is this domestic serenity that we find celebrated in Matisse's modernist aesthetic.

NOTES

1   The author wishes to acknowledge Christopher M.S. Johns and Paul Barolsky for their thoughtful and faithful readings of early drafts of this chapter. Unless otherwise

noted, translations are the author's. My thanks to Mort Guiney for his assistance with the French passages.

2   Any study of Matisse and the "decorative" is indebted to John H. Neff's pioneering work. See especially Neff (1975).

3   Drinka notes that a number of European doctors ran elaborate experiments on humans and animals hoping to discover the true physiological basis of neurasthenia. Charles Féré, a disciple of Jean-Martin Charcot, subjected patients to a variety of sensory stimulations and measured, among other things, muscle strength and blood pressure aided by several specially designed instruments. As Drinka notes, Féré discovered that "intellectual work is accompanied equally by an exaggeration of the circulatory tendency [blood pressure], in the frequency and amplitude of respiration, a greater abundance of secretion, and an increase in the dynametric force" (Drinka, 1984: 214–16). See Rabinbach (1990, chapter six) for a discussion of "fatigue research" undertaken in the 1880s and 1890s. For a related study, see Rabinbach (1982).

4   Drinka cites a case study undertaken by the neuropsychiatrist Georges Gilles de la Tourette in the 1890s in which a 45-year-old businessman was chosen as the exemplary "shock" neurasthenic.

5   Included among the casues of neurasthenia in females were "the abuse of societal pleasures, sexual excess, the loss of one or more children . . . and neuropathic heredity" (Bouveret, 1890: 31). Increased intellectual activity on the part of women was also often cited as a primary cause of nervous exhaustion.

6   A well-known account of the debilitating (and maddening) effects of the "rest cure" is Charlotte Perkins Gilman's "The Yellow Wallpaper", which Showalter labels "a powerful polemic against Mitchell's methods" (Showalter, 1985: 141). See also Bassuk (1985).

7   For a discussion of the increased interest in exercise and the rise of the sports movement in conjunction with the perceived spread of neurasthenia, see Nye (1982).

8. For a discussion of the doctrine of the *femme au foyer* and the ideology of separate spheres in late nineteenth-century France, see McMillan (1981).

9   In "Lilies: Of Queens' Gardens" (1865), Ruskin championed women as keepers of the home and hearth and praised their ability for "ordering, arrangement and decision." Consequently, the domestic interior served as a protective place of refuge for the male dweller after "his rough work in open world." For Ruskin, the home's true function was to provide shelter and a "place of Peace" amidst the chaos of modern life (Ruskin, 1865: 99–100).

10 For a discussion of Auburtin within the context of late nineteenth-century pastoral painting, see Robinson (1990).

11 Bonnat's comments were read aloud in his absence at the 1895 banquet held in Puvis' honor. Quoted in translation in d'Argencourt (1977: 172).

Chapter 7: From *Techne* to Tectonics

Demetri Porphyrios

> Tectonics . . . envelop the bare form of construction with a symbolism of order.
>
> (Bötticher, 1844)

> The roof must no longer support a load but only be supported, and this character of not supporting must be visible on itself: it must be so constructed that it cannot support anything and must therefore terminate at an angle.
>
> (Hegel, 1835–8: II, 670–1)

FORM AND KNOWLEDGE

We all know from our experience that the craft of making a chair or a table is very different from the fine arts, say, of sculpture or painting. And yet, on closer examination, we find the same procedure in the activity of the cabinet maker and the sculptor or of the weaver and the painter. The making of a utensil or tool and the making of a statue both require craftsmanship. In fact, craftsmen and artists alike have always valued very highly the mastery of their craft.

It should not surprise us, therefore, that the Greeks, who gave a lot of attention and thought to their works of art, used the same word for both art and craft, namely *techne* (τεχνη). Craftsmen and artists alike were all thought of as *technites* (τεχνιτες), that is men who had a *techne* and knew how to practice it. And yet, in sharp contrast to Greek practice, our everyday experience tells us that there is a difference between craft and art. In these circumstances we must not hastily dismiss either our everyday experience or that of the ancients but we must rather consider further the meaning of the concept of *techne*.

In Greek, *techne* refers neither to craft nor to art and it does not have the sense of the technical or of technique as we may otherwise assume. In other words, it does not refer merely to a kind of practical facility in performance or dexterity in execution. Quintilian makes this point clear when he recounts that of all Hellenistic painters, Antiphilos was the most accomplished in 'ease of execution', or *facilitas*, translating in this manner the Greek term *hexis* (εξις), which means a trained skill. But such mere skill in draughtsmanship does not comprise the *techne*, say, of painting.

Instead, the Greek word *techne* refers to a kind of knowledge. It implies method and consistency and it represents man's reasoned intelligence put into practice. *Techne* is an ordered application of knowledge that is intended to produce a specific product, or achieve a predetermined goal. Formerly, the various kinds of work demanding special skill and knowledge were covered by this word *techne*; and the Greeks applied the term equally to agriculture, medicine, carpentry, pottery, engraving, as well as to painting, sculpture, architecture, music and poetry. This essential meaning of *techne* as reasoned intelligence and knowledge put into practice can be also found in the old German *kunst* or the Swedish *konst* which today stand for art but which originally meant knowledge and skill deriving from the root word *kennen* or *können*, to know, with the sense of a know-how.

Perhaps the most overriding characteristic of this classical concept is that *techne* is frequently opposed to nature (*physis*). In Greek thought it is generally assumed that whereas nature acts out of sheer necessity, *techne* involves a deliberate human intention, a procedure of deliberately achieving a preconceived goal by means of reasoned intelligence and skill. But in order to be purposeful *techne* must follow rational rules. The system of such rules, or the organised body of knowledge related to some kind of production, is an essential part of *techne*. In his *Nicomachean Ethics* Aristotle speaks of *techne* as 'a productive capacity involving a true course of reasoning'. This reasoned intelligence exhibited by a *techne* implies that it is possible to formulate the theory of its practice, and it is this theory which constitutes a form of knowledge that becomes its distinguishing feature.

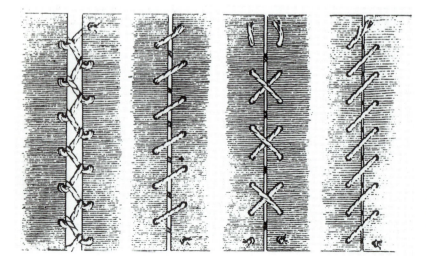

Figure 7.1
Stitching.
From C. Uhde, 1903. *Die Konstructionen und die Kunstformen Architektur.*

Craft, in this sense, is a *techne* in as much as it takes raw nature and transforms it into useful utensils and tools by means of a carefully preconceived and reasoned intelligence. A volcanic island by contrast is something material that has a definite but unintelligible form. What I mean here is that though the volcanic rock might have a shape and form, it nonetheless reveals nothing of the way in which it was made. Even if we were knowledgeable mineralogists the best we could do is give an explanation of its volcanic formation but we could

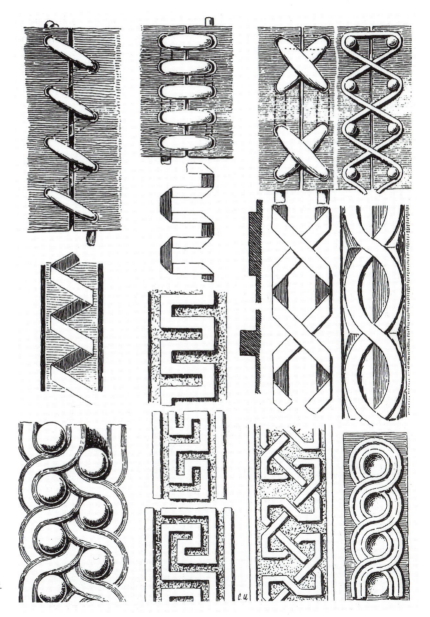

Figure 7.2
Patterns.
From C. Uhde, 1903. *Die Konstructionen und die Kunstformen Architektur*.

offer no explanation of the ultimate purpose of its existence. From this point of view, the volcanic rock is a product of nature in that it has not been intended.

But a coffee pot, an axe, or an automobile exhibit a selection of matter and form that is guided by the respective purpose and usefulness of the artefact. It is in this sense that we say that the utensil or tool is well made, for it fulfils its goal when it is used. Its purpose is to be used in the way which was intended in the first place. It would be ludicrous to claim that a shoe could be worn as a glove or, for that matter, that walls could be horizontal and floors vertical. The utensil or tool as the product of craft fulfils its purpose only when it is used. Once it is no longer useful, either due to failure or obsolescence, it is mute and quite often its form becomes unintelligible. How many times have we not found ourselves staring at some bygone tool or instrument in a museum, struggling to decipher its intended use? But as long as the utensil or tool, as the product of a craft, is still useful and is being used (such as a barrel, for example, that is soundly made and will not disintegrate under the pressure of the liquid contained) then its form, which was the outcome of pure necessity and usefulness in the first place, now becomes a *typical* form. In other words, it becomes a form by which the intended use is recognised. Similarly the rope, the plaited band or the wicker basket have forms which point to their usefulness, while showing explicitly the *techne* that guided their making. In fact, on certain occasions, utensils made by craftsmen exclusively for practical use transcend their purpose as useful objects and acquire, through their familiar form, the status of a symbol.

How is this possible and what do we mean here by the word 'symbol'? Originally in Greek it stood for a mark or a token, an outward sign through which the host could recognise his visitors and guests. Symbols were the broken pieces of a plate or an urn that the host gave to his guests as mementoes. Once these symbols were pieced together the whole could be reconstructed in an act of acknowledgement or recognition. The symbol (from the Greek *symballein*, συμβαλλειν, to put together) takes form, therefore, far from its origins in useful-ness and into the realm of uselessness. This is a uselessness, however, which serves to celebrate remembrance by means of convention.

The stylised bands which adorn many clay vases are but symbolic allusions to the early forms of the stitched seam and the rope. Although this decorative adornment is useless, it is nonetheless highly pleasurable, for it makes us relate back to an anterior mode of construction; be that of the flask with its seams binding the hide or of the barrel tied together by wicker ropes. When habitually encoded, such symbols become accepted decorative motifs that afford recogni-tion of man as *homo faber*. The artist is a *technites* not because he is a craftsman who works with his hands, but because he possesses the knowledge and skill that serve to deepen our understanding of ourselves as makers, as *homo faber*, and thus our familiarity with the world.

NECESSITY AND FREEDOM

Keeping in mind these observations, let us now consider the case of what 'building' means. Words for 'building' are in part connected with verbs for 'dwell' through the notion of remaining in a place. Heidegger's seminal essay, 'Building, Dwelling, Thinking' lovingly argued this case (Heidegger, 1954).

The Old English and High German word for building, *büan*, means to dwell on and till the land. The same idea is found in the Dutch *bouwen* and the Danish *bygge* or Swedish *bygga*, which mean to settle. Heidegger, to his credit, was the first to explore this existential meaning of building as dwelling. But at the same time he appears to have suppressed (for reasons which must be the subject of another study) a whole other group of words for building which reflect the activity, skill or knowledge of constructing.

Whereas the Old English and High German word *büan*, to build, means to dwell, the Greek word *oekodomeo* (οικοδομεω) 'to build', derives from *oekos*, meaning house or dwelling, and the root of the verb *demo* (δεμω), meaning to tie and put together, to construct. What is so significant about this? Fundamentally that the Greek word *oekodomeo* distinguishes between the act of dwelling (as in *oekos*), and the act of constructing a dwelling. In fact this sense of putting together and constructing of the Greek *demo* is so strong that it gives rise to an alternative word for house, namely *domos* (δομος). Thus in Greek there are two words for house: *Oekos*, from the verb *oeko*, to dwell, which stresses the sense of house as dwelling, and *domos*, from the verb *demo*, to construct, which highlights the sense of house as a constructed entity.

This archaeology of language becomes even more fascinating when one probes further into the original meaning of the verb *demo*, to construct, for it appears that it derives from the sanskrit *dama* and the Indo-European root *dem*, which mean 'to build' but formerly also carried the meaning of 'joining and fitting together'. In this sense the Greek word *oekodomeo*, to build, points to a specific mode of making one's house, namely that of joining and fitting together the pieces that will make a place for dwelling.

This emphasis on the particular method of constructing one's house is not found simply in the Greek *oekodomeo* but also in the language of other cultures that had much to do with the *techne* of building. Thus the Latin *aedificare*, to build, derives from *aedes*, house or temple, and the verb *facere*, to make. But we should not forget that *facere* does not generally mean 'to make' but indicates a specific manner of making, namely that of fashioning and moulding, as in the Latin *fingera*. In this sense the Latin *aedificare*, to build, points to a specific mode of making one's house, namely that of moulding the clay by hand.

Similarly, the French *bâtir* and Old French *bastir*, to build, derive from the Old High German word *bestan*, to bind. Building, in the sense of binding, however, is still further qualified when we probe into the root of the word *bestan*, which comes from *bass*, referring to the inner bark of trees frequently used for plaiting wickerwork. In this sense the French word *bâtir*, to build, also

Figure 7.3
Alvar Aalto, sauna at the
Villa Mairea,
Noormarkku, 1937–8.
Photo: Demetri
Porphyrios.

points to a specific mode of building, that of binding together by plaiting. The same is true of the Welsh *adeilad*, to build, which derives from the root *ail* and literally means plaited work and wattling – the structure of interwoven sticks and twigs used for fences and walls. This latter sense of building suits, of course, the historical description of the hut of Romulus on the Forum in Rome and a similar hut on the Aeropagus in Athens, both referred to by Vitruvius.

I do not want you to think, however, that I am trying to prove by means of linguistics that the origins of building lie in the rustic hut. This was debated so thoroughly by the *Querelle* that I doubt that those who are still undecided will ever make up their minds. Instead, my interest here is to probe into the essential meaning of building as constructing and thereby come closer to the *techne*, that is to the body of knowledge, which was formerly required for building.

Originally the builder was a builder in timber – a carpenter – and only later was he to become a builder in stone or a mason. This is well illustrated by the Greek word for builder, *tecton* (τεκτων) from which tectonics, and eventually architecture, derive their meaning within the context of Western civilisation. The *tecton* was first of all an artisan in wood – a carpenter. In Plutarch *tecton* means carpenter and Thucydides distinguishes between *tectones* (carpenters) and *lithourgoi* (masons). This meaning of *tecton* as carpenter is found as late as in the New Testament where Matthew refers to Christ as *o tou tektonos yios* (ο του τεκτονος υιος), the son of a carpenter.

If the builder, therefore, as *tecton*, is primarily a carpenter and only by later extension an artisan working in metal, stone, clay, paint, etc, his *techne* – that is the organised body of knowledge related to his production – is surely superseded by *tectonike*, carpentry, from which the word tectonics derives. In its original Greek sense the term tectonics, *tectonike*, describes the knowledge of carpentry.

But what are we to make of this? Surely it could not be that all building is carpentry nor that we ought to trace all buildings back to their original timber ancestors. In any event, even if we had the patience to compile an exhaustive list of the comparative genealogy of all building elements, the best we could hope to prove is that all building derives from carpentry.

However, this is not the significant point in the meaning of *tectonike* as the *techne* of carpentry. Much more essential is the realisation that tectonics invoke a potential order which is defined by the form-giving capacity of the material used. Thus in carpentry, timber as matter is not shapeless but is suggestive of form. At the same time timber has a finite length and width and therefore invites the artisan to treat construction in a dimensional and scalar sense. In addition, timber is discontinuous and so it begs the skill and knowledge of jointing.

Tectonics, as the *techne* of carpentry, while speaking of the particular skill and knowledge of timber construction, at the same time delineates the ontological experience of construction. The concern of tectonics is threefold. First, the

Figure 7.4
Window of an Ionian
house.
From Viollet le Duc, 1876.
*Histoire de l'habitation
humaine.*

finite nature and formal properties of constructional materials, be those timber, brick, stone, steel, etc. Second, the procedures of jointing, which is the way that elements of construction are put together. Third, the visual statics of form, that is the way by which the eye is satisfied about stability, unity and balance and their variations or opposites.

This means that in any encounter with building it is not the particular exigencies of construction, but rather, the ontological experience of tectonics that is brought to bear. *Tectonike* stands as the highest fulfilment of all construction. It makes construction speak out in the sense of revealing the ontology of constructing. For this reason it seems to me that any aesthetic theory which interprets tectonics simply as a set of signifying gestures added onto everyday practices of construction is thoroughly misleading. In some instances, this may well be the case (as for example, with the theory of the decorated shed adopted by Postmodern Classicism and Postmodern Modernism) and yet a few pilasters or some riveted joints thrown in as referential signs of a constructional order are not enough to give a building a tectonic presence.

Whenever we feel something is lacking in a building it is because it does not hang together. It is because we feel that there is no sense of the necessary, no sense of something that needs to be said and can only be said in that way. A tectonic experience, however, conveys both a sense of the necessary and freedom. It conveys a sense of the necessary because order is delimited by the form-giving capacity of the materials used. The form, say, of a panelled door speaks of its constructional assembly. The forms of the voussoir or the corbel are bound to a sense of necessary structural behaviour. The consistency, say, of roofing materials one finds in most vernacular towns derives from the exclusive use of indigenous materials and, by extension, from the absence of 'options'. In these and all similar cases, building technology is concerned with the useful and the necessary. Technology and tectonics here become synonymous, for there is no interest in mere gadgetry. The sham experience of gadgetry appears only when a contradiction is inserted between form and the necessary in the name of ostentation or as a sales incentive. Instead, the sense of the necessary and the inevitable that a tectonic experience conveys always derives from the construction, structure, or the materials used for shelter.

At the same time a tectonic experience conveys a sense of freedom. What I mean here is better understood using an analogy with play. We are familiar with play as being outside ordinary or 'real' life. Much the same way, tectonic order is a stepping out of 'real' construction and shelter. Much like play, tectonic order pretends it constructs shelter. Standing outside the realm of the necessary, it does not have to satisfy the engineer's calculations nor the performance requirements of the building trade. Yet, it sets its own rules as an image and make believe of real construction and shelter.

Once the rules of tectonics are set up, they become a treasure to be retained in memory and transmitted. We speak, therefore, of the traditions, say, of Classical, Gothic, Chinese, or Romanesque tectonics. And as is the case with all artistic fictions, tectonic fiction creates its own supreme order where the least deviation 'spoils the game'. Consider the analogy with, say, chess. We play a game of chess not out of necessity but of our own free will. And yet we are expected to follow the rules of the game which, in fact, have not been laid down by us. It would be absurd to claim that there should be three knights or two queens; not because the claim would contradict any pragmatic fact or necessity but simply because such a claim falls outside the rules of chess. In fact, such rules are never experienced as a constraint but rather as a mutually acceptable ordering framework within which we can exhibit our ingenuity as chess players.

This profound affinity between play and order is what makes the analogy with tectonics plausible. Tectonic order is indeed a fiction removed from the contingencies of construction and shelter, yet invested with the experience of stability, unity and balance which construction and shelter describe in the first place. The rules of a tectonic order are binding. 'No scepticism is possible,' wrote Paul Valéry, 'where the rules of play are concerned for they are unshakeable truths.' He who might wish to rob tectonic order of its rules is a spoil-sport.

We have now come full circle. Whenever we admire a building it is because it conveys both a sense of the necessary and freedom. It conveys a sense of the necessary because order is delimited by the form-giving capacity of the materials used; and a sense of freedom because it is bound by rules which are made as tokens of recognition of ourselves as *homo faber*. This is what classical antiquity taught and it is precisely this that we seem to have forgotten.

Chapter 8: Bötticher, Semper and the Tectonic: Core Form and Art Form

Kenneth Frampton

Soon after Schinkel's death in 1841, the primary ideological text of the Bauakademie in Berlin came to be Karl Bötticher's *Die Tektonik der Hellenen* (The Tectonic of the Hellenes), published in two volumes in 1844 and 1852. Bötticher first attended the Bauakademie as a student in 1827, studied with both Beuth and Schinkel, and became a member of the faculty after his qualification as an architect in 1844. Influenced by Hübsch's structural rationalism and by Hirt's unwavering faith in the symbolic superiority of Greek form, but simultaneously denying both the materialism of the former and the traditionalism of the latter, Bötticher sought to resolve the dichotomy between classicism and romanticism through the specific hieratic procedures exemplified in Schinkel's buildings Neuer Packhof and Bauakademie. Taking Schinkel's *Architektonisches Lehrbuch* as his point of departure, Bötticher sought a synthesis between the ontological status of the structure and the representational role of the ornament. Antithetical to all forms of eclecticism, be it Gothic Revival or neo-Renaissance, and equally susceptible to both the rational (Kant) and the anti-rational (Herder) lines in Enlightenment thought, Bötticher respectively assimilated the representational to the Greek and the ontological to the Gothic.

Influenced, through the writings of Christian Weisse, by Arthur Schopenhauer's thesis that architecture could only express its essential form and significance through the dramatic interaction of support and load (*Stütze und Last*; Schopenhauer, 1819: 131–3), Bötticher insisted on the corporeality of architecture and on the interstitial spatiality of its ligaments at every conceivable scale. Taking his cue in part from Herder's tactile sculptural aesthetic and in part from Schinkel's articulated method, Bötticher maintained that the symbolic revetment of a work must never be allowed to obscure its fundamental, constructional form. Thus, as Mitchell Schwarzer has written:

> Bötticher's attempt to harmonize the muscular passion of architectural materiality and
> statics with the objectivity of art was quite different from Kant and Schiller's concept of

Architektonik beauty as the marshalling of the subjective senses towards an objective reality . . . [Bötticher] proposed that the beauty of architecture was precisely the explanation of mechanical concepts. As much as its artistic demands related to the imagination, the constructive demands of the *Tektonik* argued against the autonomy of architectural from extrinsic ends

(Schwarzer, 1993: 276).

Bötticher envisaged a kind of reciprocally expressive joint that comes into being through the appropriate interlocking of construction elements. At once articulate and integrated, these joints were seen as *Körperbilden*, not only permitting constructions to be achieved but also enabling these assemblies to become the symbolic components of an expressive system. In addition to this syntactical/constructional concept, Bötticher distinguished between the *Kernform* and the *Kunstform*, the latter having the task of representing the constructional and/or institutional status of the former. He wrote: "The concept of each part can be thought of as being realized by two elements: the core-form and the art-form. The core-form of each part is the mechanically necessary and statically functional structure; the art-form, on the other hand, is only the characterization by which the mechanical-statical function is made apparent" (Bötticher, in Herrmann, 1984: 141). According to Bötticher, the shell of the *Kunstform* should be capable of revealing and augmenting the essence of the constructional nucleus. At the same time, he insisted that one must always try to distinguish and express the difference between the constructional form and its enrichment, irrespective of whether this last manifests itself as cladding or ornament. He wrote that the art form "is only a covering and a symbolic attribute of the part – decoration, κοσμοϛÿ (Herrmann, 1984: 141).

Bötticher was as much influenced by Schelling's natural philosophy as was Schinkel, above all by Schelling's view that architecture transcends the mere pragmatism of building by virtue of assuming symbolic significance. For Schelling and Bötticher alike, the inorganic had no symbolic meaning and hence structural form could only acquire symbolic status by virtue of its capacity to engender analogies between tectonic and organic form. Direct imitation of natural form was to be avoided, however, for like Schelling, Bötticher held the view that architecture was an imitative art only to the extent that it imitated itself. Nevertheless, unlike Schinkel, Bötticher tended to distance himself theoretically from an opportunistic borrowing of historical form.

A fuller development of Bötticher's theory came with his 1846 *Schinkelfest* address entitled "The Principles of the Hellenic and German Way of Building," in which, after praising the tradition of the Bauakademie and above all Schinkel as the initiator of "architectural science," Bötticher proceeded to posit, in somewhat Hegelian manner, the future possibility of an unnamed third style capable of engendering a new cultural entity, synthesizing thereby the dual Germanic legacy of the Gothic and the Greek.[1] For Bötticher the true tectonic tradition, what he refers to as the "eclecticism of the spirit," resides not in the appearance of any one style but rather in the essence that lies behind the appearance. While he condones the adaptation of traditional stylistic formats to new situations, he is categorically against any form of arbitrary stylistic selection, such as the *Rundbogenstil* advocated by Hübsch. Bötticher will argue that any new spatial system or future style will have to be brought into being by a new structural principle, and not the other way round. Thus, in a manner that anticipates Viollet-le-Duc, we find him writing:

> Our contention that the manner of covering determines every style and its ultimate development is confirmed by the monuments of all styles. Equally evident is the truth that from the earliest and roughest attempts to cover spaces by using stone, to the culmination represented by the *Spitzbogen* vault, and down to the present time, all the ways in which stone could possibly be used to span a space have been exploited, and they have completely exhausted the possible structural applications of this material. No longer can stone alone form a new structural system of a higher stage of development. The reactive, as well as relative, strength of stone has been completely exhausted . . . a new and so far unknown system of covering (which will of course bring in its train a new world of art-forms) can appear only with the adoption of an unknown material, or rather a material that so far has not been used as a guiding principle. It will have to be a material with physical properties that will permit wider spans, with less weight and greater reliability, than are possible when using stone alone. With regard to spatial design and construction, it must be such as will meet any conceivable spatial or planning need. A minimal quantity of material should be needed for the walls, thus rendering the bulky and ponderous buttresses of the *Spitzbodenstil* completely superflous. The whole weight of the covering system would be confined to vertical pressure, that is, to the reactive strength of walls and supports. Of course, this does not mean that the indirect use of stone vaulting, especially the system of ribbed and stellar vaulting, will be excluded; on the contrary, the latter will be widely used. But it does mean that, for those parts on which the whole system rests, another material will be used, one that makes it possible to transfer their structural function to other parts in which a different principle operates. It makes no difference whether the members to be replaced are buttresses or members that support the ceiling, such as ribs, bands, etc.
>
> Such a material is iron, which has already been used for this purpose in our century. Further testing and greater knowledge of its structural properties will ensure that iron will become the basis for the covering system of the future and that structurally it will in time come to be as superior to the Hellenic and medieval systems as the arcuated medieval system was to the monolithic trabeated system of antiquity. Disregarding the fragile wooden ceiling (which in any case cannot serve as a comparison) and using mathematical terms, one can say that iron is indeed the material whose principle, yet unutilized, will introduce into architecture the last of three forces, namely absolute strength.
>
> (Bötticher, 1846: 158)

As in the later theory of Viollet-le-Duc, Bötticher foresees the essential complementary role to be played by the absolute strength of iron tie rods, thereby enabling the relative strength of stone vaulting greatly to increase its capacity to span. Yet unlike the French structural rationalist, he insists that the tectonic expressivity of such an unprecedented system will have to model its representational form on some kind of reinterpretation of the principles of Hellenic architecture. Through this assertion, based on attributing some measure of symbolic universality to the classical, Bötticher already anticipates the semiotic transformations of the Jugendstil in its crystallizing phase, particularly as one encounters this at the turn of the century in the work of Otto Wagner (Bötticher, 1846: 159). Implicitly acknowledging the difficulty of superimposing traditional stereotomic symbolism onto unprecedented lightweight, skeletonal structure, Bötticher looked to the organic as a fundamental form force by which to synthesize the mechanical and the natural and in so doing to reinterpret and transform the received iconography of classical form. Thus he will argue in the 1846 address:

> Pictorial art cannot represent an idea as such, but must represent it through a symbol and thus embody it. Architecture follows the same method. It takes its symbols and art-forms only from those natural objects that embody an idea analogous to the one inherent in the members of the architectural system. Therefore, an idea for which no analogue exists in the external world cannot be represented by pictorial art nor for that matter by architecture. The essence of pictorial art and its relation to nature rests in this interaction between concept and object, between invention and imitation.

(Bötticher, 1846: 163)

In 1825, after having studied mathematics in the University of Göttingen, Gottfried Semper appears to have attended architectural classes at the Munich Academy of Fine Arts before fleeing to France in 1826 as the result of a duel. In Paris he studied with Franz Christian Gau, who may have introduced him to the controversy then raging over the original polychromatic rendering of Greek temples.[2] Between 1830 and 1833 Semper traveled in Italy and Greece to see for himself, returning to Germany in 1834 to become architectural director at the Royal Academy in Dresden on Gau's recommendation. His first major commissions following from this appointment were the first Dresden Opera House, completed in 1841, and the Picture Gallery, erected between 1847 and 1854. His participation in the 1848–9 revolution brought him to exile himself first in France, then in England, where he became part of the Crystal Palace circle around Henry Cole and Richard Redgrave, and then to Zurich where he became head of the Polyteknikum in 1855.

The theoretical elaboration of Semper's *Die vier Elemente der Baukunst* (The Four Elements of Architecture), largely written in 1850, parallels in certain respects some of the arguments advanced by Bötticher in his *Die Tektonik der Hellenen*, the first volume of which Semper did not read until after 1852, following the publication of his *Four Elements* in 1851. The notion of the seminal role played by the internal carpet wall in the evolution of classical architecture seems to have developed independently by both men. Close to such anthropological insights lay the tectonic theories of Karl Otfried Müller, whose work Semper studied assiduously in 1834 in preparation for his lectures at the Dresden Academy. Another early influence on Semper was the ethnographer Gustav Klemm, who as Royal Librarian was attached to the imperial court at Dresden during the period of Semper's tenure there. That Klemm was seminal for Semper is suggested by his *Allgemeine Kultur-Geschichte des Menschheit* (General Cultural History of Mankind), published in nine volumes between 1843 and 1851, the fourth volume of which accorded particular import to a description of a Pacific Island hut that Klemm had derived from a late eighteenth-century account of a German explorer who had accompanied Captain Cook to the South Seas. Klemm's gloss on this account gave prominence to the same elements as would later make up Semper's model of the primordial dwelling. While Semper would only refer to Klemm on two occasions, he was nonetheless also indebted to him for his theory of cultural transformation in which southern passive races are succeeded by northern nomadic, active, warlike tribes, with the aboriginal dwelling becoming modified according to climate and the racial origin of the nomads as they settle down. As Harry Mallgrave has observed, this pacifying process will give rise to "southern" building types in masonry that, for Semper, formed the historical beginning of architecture, attaining their apotheosis, so to speak, in the dynastic order of Egypt, wherein a warm climate and geograpical isolation will allow architecture to develop into a courtyard style of building. The core of the temple complex, for instance, was the hidden *sekos* or tabernacle from which evolved a series of processional yards, formerly open and later covered either with canvas or with a permanent roof. One may see this as similar to the transposition in which a tectonic hut eventually becomes transformed into the stereotomic Greek *megaron* surrounded by columns (Mallgrave, 1985: 76).

Corroborated by evidence of the Caribbean hut that he saw in the Crystal Palace Exhibition of 1851, Semper's four elements represent a fundamental break with the Vitruvian triad of *utilitas, firmitas, venustas*. The empirical fact of this promordial shelter prompted Semper to propose an anthropological counterthesis to Laugier's primitive hut of 1753. In its place, he proposed a more articulated model comprising (1) a hearth, (2) an earthwork, (3) a framework/roof, and (4) an enclosing membrane.

While challenging the authority of Laugier's primitive hut, Semper gave primacy to the tensile frame and its infill as opposed to the compressive earthwork or load-bearing mass. Thus, while Schinkel and Semper made exclusive use of load-bearing masonry in their architecture, they nonetheless conceived of their form as a phenomenally transparent grid, structured about a hierarchical articulation of discrete parts. Nevertheless what Semper added to this hieratic assembly was an emphasis upon the earthwork as a stereotomic, topographic mass upon which the more ephemeral form of the tectonic frame literally took its ground.

The emphasis on the earthwork had a number of consequences. On the one hand, it complemented the universal nomadic textile culture that Semper regarded as the ultimate *Urkunst*; on the other hand, as Rosemarie Bletter has

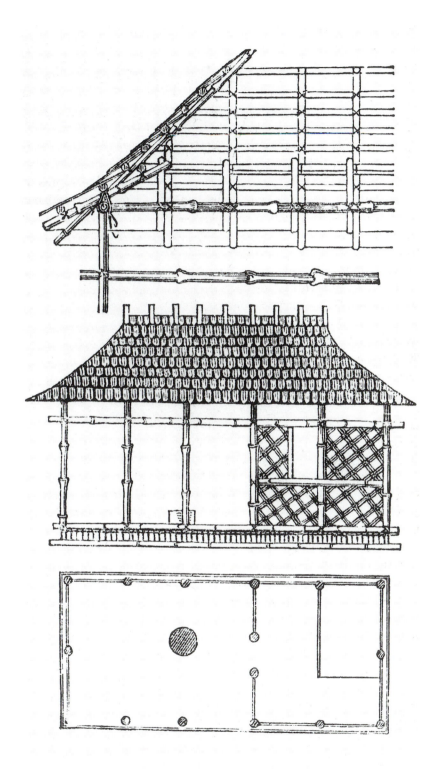

Figure 8.1
Caribbean hut.
From Semper (1863).

Figure 8.2
Knots, from Semper
(1860).

remarked, it gave new importance to a nonspatial element, namely the hearth, which was an inseparable part of the earthwork (Bletter, 1974: 148). For Semper, this last was the irreducible *raison d'être* of architecture in that it incorporated in a single element the public and spiritual nexus of the built domain. At the same time, his four elements were possessed of significant etymological ramifications. Thus the Latin term *reredos* was open to a dichotomous reading; on the one hand it signified the back of an altar; on the other, the back of a hearth. Meanwhile the term "hearth" itself carried with it certain civic implications in as much as the Latin root *aedificare*, from which the word "edifice" derives, means literally to make a hearth. The institutional connotations of both hearth and edifice are further amplified by the verb "to edify," which means *to educate, strengthen, and instruct.* Semper went on to rationalize a great deal of his ethnographic theory on a similar etymological basis. Thus, he would distinguish the massiveness of the fortified wall, as indicated by the word *die Mauer*, from the light screenlike enclosure signified by the term *die Wand*. Both terms imply enclosure, but the latter is related to the German word for dress, *Gewand*, and to the verb *winden*, which means *to embroider*. Semper maintained that the earliest basic structural artifact was the knot, from which follows the primary nomadic building culture of the tent and its textile fabric.[3] Here again, one encounters significant etymological connotations of which Semper was fully aware, above all the curious archaic conjunction of *knot* and *joint*, the former being indicated by *der Knoten* and the latter by *die Naht*. In modern German, both words are connected to the concept *die Verbindung*, binding. Thus, for Semper, the most significant basic tectonic element was the joint or the knot. As Joseph Rykwert has written:

> By a curious use of word-play, Semper foreshadows his later reference to the knot as the essential work of art quite early in the textile chapter, when he considers the term *Naht*: the seam, the joining. It is, he says, an expedient, a *Nothbehelf* for the joining of two planes of similar or dissimilar material. But the very juxtaposition of *Noth* and *Naht* suggests a connection.
>
> (Rykwert, 1976: 77–8)

Of Semper's characterization of the knot as "the oldest tectonic, cosmogonic symbol," Rykwert notes that

> the word-play might have seemed so facile as to be meaningless; though the connection between *Naht* and knot (*Knoten, noeud, nodus*) seemed to him in some way related to

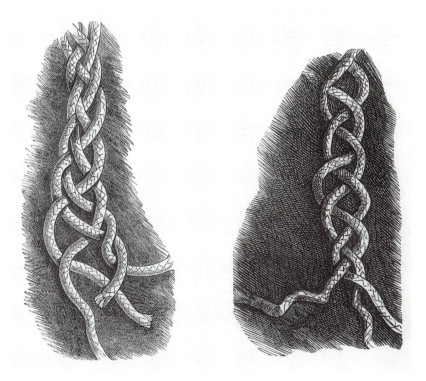

Figure 8.3
More knots
From Semper (1860).

the Greek ανακη, *force*, necessity. Presumably he had made himself familiar with the articles *Knoten*, *Naht*, etc. in Jakob and Wilhelm Grimm's German dictionary. However, he found the answer to his problem after he had written this passage in the work on linguistics by Albert Höfer, a disciple of von Humboldt. Höfer justified the word-play, and pointed out the relation of such words to the Indo-european root *noc*, Latin *nec-o*, *nexus*, *necessitas*, *nectere*, νεω (to spin).

(Rykwert, 1976: 72)

Semper's emphasis on the joint implies that a fundamental syntactical transition is expressed as one passes from the stereotomic base of a building to its tectonic frame, and that such transitions are of the very essence of architecture.

In his later two-volume *Der Stil in den technischen und tektonischen Künsten, oder praktische Aethetik* (Style in the Technical and Tectonic Arts, or Practical Aesthetics, 1860–3), Semper assigned certain tectonic crafts to each of the four elements: textiles pertained to the art of enclosure and thus to the side walls and roof, carpentry to the basic structural frame, masonry to the earth-work, and metallurgy and ceramics to the hearth. In the same text, Semper also outlined his *Stoffwechseltheorie*, that is to say his theory of symbolic conservation, in which the mythical-cum-spiritual values attaching to certain structural elements cause them to be translated into petrified compressive forms, even when they were originally of tensile construction. Semper cited sacred Greek architecture as exemplifying the persistence of certain symbolic motifs that had been transformed from a nomadic wooden framework with textile covering to the permanence of stone. According to Semper, this would explain the transposition of textile motifs into the polychromatic ornamental dressings of the triglyphs

Figure 8.4
Textile façade: the tomb
of Midas.
From Semper (1860).

and metopes in the Doric order. Contrary to the Abbé Laugier, Semper did not feel that such forms arose from the petrification of timber construction, of beam ends and rafters, but rather from features used to tie down the textile fabric covering the roof.

In reference to his own historical period, however, Semper felt that the cheap industrial simulation of one material by another, above all through casting, stamping, and molding, paradoxically undermined the principle of symbolic conservation, largely because these substitutions were expedient and secular and were thus conceptually indifferent to the symbolic continuity essential to the recreation of tectonic form. The various synthetic substances and processes exhibited at the 1851 Great Exhibition had been an object lesson for Semper, for here he had seen cast iron and gutta-percha employed for the simulation of stone and wood respectively.

In his essay "Wissenschaft, Industrie und Kunst" (Science, Industry, and Art) of 1852, Semper argued that the general crisis of style had arisen out of three different causes: first the alienation of the arts from their original motifs, second the devaluation of material and labor, and third the loss of the ability of the art form to exercise a specific function in relation to the historical moment. Semper sought to counter this degeneration by reasserting the ethnographic origins of the various manufacturing procedures, together with their material references and corresponding forms. In this respect he emphasized the task of the form and the process of fabrication over the specific nature of any given material. Thus, while he regarded clay as the primary molding material or *Urstoff*, this did not prevent him from seeing facing brick or tile as a "dressing," a kind of petrified fabric and hence a transformation of nomadic textile forms into a more permanent material.

Taking something of his taxonomic discourse from the writings of Alexander von Humboldt, Semper, like Hübsch, wanted to transcend the classical paradigm successively advanced by Winckelmann, Hirt, and Bötticher. Like Hübsch he envisaged a return to the "interrupted" style of the Romanesque; to the same style that the American architect H.H. Richardson would assume as his point of departure in 1870. This swerve away from the classical led Semper to ground his theory in the universality of making, placing the burden of tectonic proof on the evolution of the crafts and the industrial arts. There are, in Semper's system, as Rykwert has written,

> two primary archetypes: the hearth and the cloth, the *Urherd* and the *Urtuch*. They were the first mark of settlement and the first fabrication; but although they seem to have the same reality for Semper as the *Urpflanze* (original plant) had for Goethe (1788), yet they were not reducible to a single root phenomenon as Goethe would presumably have wanted them, nor do the other root-actions, that of jointing and of heaping, ever merge into each other, but they always, even when they overlap, retain their character, through representation and symbolization.
>
> (Rykwert, 1976: 72)

For Semper, the ultimate cultural model was linguistic, and in this too, like Böt-ticher, he was indebted to Willhelm von Humboldt's insistence that language is not just a description of things but rather a vocalization of action. Linguists of Humboldt's generation saw speech as displaying the will of the people, almost as a Hegelian manifestation of collectivity. In much the same vein, Semper saw artistic culture as an evolving language in which certain root forms and opera-tions are transposed over time.

Semper was a late romantic to the degree that he inherited the epistemologi-cal and political project of the Aufklärung, and in this regard his participation in the unsuccessful liberal revolution of 1849 is symptomatic. He was Hegelian to the extent that he saw Greek classical architecture as sculptural rather than tectonic in its manner of deploying stone. At the same time he challenged Hegel's triadic scheme of symbolic, classic, and romantic by insisting that the monumental art of architecture derives its formal elaboration from the so-called industrial arts and above all from the craft of textiles, to which Semper would devote the entire first volume of *Der Stil*, according some 480 pages to textiles as opposed to the 200 for ceramics, 132 for carpentry, and 120 for masonry that together make up the second volume. Semper recognized the material and technological ramifications of his four elements by grounding them in different material properties and in corre-spondingly different crafts. In this vein he would discriminate between the elasticity of textiles, the softness of ceramics, the ductility of carpentry, and the hardness of masonry. Semper saw the articulation of craft capacity in relation to these materials as the evolution of technical skill, in which the hand gradually increases its ability to work a given material to the full extent of its expressive scope.

The emphasis that Semper placed on textiles assumed the form of an obsession, and in one text after another, from his first London lecture of 1853 to his lecture "*Über Baustyle*" given in Zurich in 1869, he would demonstrate, through anthropological evidence, the symbolic primacy of textile sheathing, as opposed to the corporeality of the form to which it is applied, either as surface decoration or as a shallow, three-dimensional relief. Semper revealed himself a romantic in the Hegelian sense in as much as his *Bekleidung* theory became a model for the progressive dematerialization of architecture, liberating the mind from the stereotomic obtuseness of matter and focusing it instead on a reticula-tion of surface and thus on a dematerialization that, as in the Crystal Palace, aspired to the dissolution of form into light.[4]

In his "Theorie des Formell-Schönen" (Theory of Formal Beauty) of 1856, he will no longer classify architecture with painting and sculpture as a plastic art but rather with dance and music as a cosmic art, as an ontological, world-making art evocative of nature in action rather than as the static substance of two- and three-dimensional form. Semper regarded the performing arts as cosmic not only because they were symbolic but also because they embodied man's underlying erotic-ludic urge, that is to say the impulse to decorate accord-ing to a rhythmic urge, that is to say the impulse to decorate according to a rhythmic law.

This anthropological insight exposes the conceptual schism running through the entire body of Semperian theory. This split manifests itself, at many different scales, as a representational/ontological division that may be seen as an irreducible aspect of architecture. I am alluding here to the difference between the representational face of a building's surface and the phenomenological (ontic) depth of its space. And while the two may be more easily reconciled in a pantheistic world, this becomes problematic in a secular age, as August Schmarsow was prompt to recognize in his fundamental critique of Semper's *Bekleidung* theory which he saw, in 1893, as having placed an undue emphasis on the experiential body of the building considered as a whole.

Notwithstanding the rationally articulated structural logic of his early work as epitomized in his first Dresden Opera House of 1841, Semper would acknowledge in 1869 that an authentic style of the epoch had failed to emerge and that until such a time as it did one would have to make do with the old styles as best one could. It is just this acceptance of eclecticism, made in the name of pragmatic reality and the representation of the bourgeois state, that made him so vulnerable to criticism in the last quarter of the nineteenth century; first from Konrad Fiedler, who saw his architecture as uninspired historicism, overburdened by erudition, second from Otto Wagner, who saw Semper as lacking sufficient courage to push his own tectonic insights to their logical conclusion, namely that a new style must depend of necessity on a new means of construction,[5] and last but not least from Schmarsow, who, however indebted, would regard Semper's architecture as unduly mesmerized by incrusted surface expression and as insufficiently concerned with spatial depth. Semper for his part felt that architecture had lost its cosmic dimension due to secularization and that this loss left his own time with no alternative but to reproduce historical forms, preferably those of the Renaissance that, for him, were symbolic of democracy.

It was left to the next generation of Semperians to pursue the technical and tectonic consequences of his theoretical corpus, together with the legacy of his scientific, architectural realism. Of the many who followed him in this regard, two in particular merit our attention; first the Austrian Otto Wagner, whose work came closest to demonstrating a precise relationship between an articulated skin and the development of a building in depth, and second Georg Heuser, who, in a number of essays written between 1881 and 1894, would assert that architectural realism was more a matter of principle than of style (Berry, 1989).[6] Heuser believed that ultimately architecture could only evolve through constructive rather than decorative innovation. As if to prove the point, he developed an entire typology of composite, rolled and plated iron supports that, according to him, could be used for different constructive *and* expressive ends, depending on the situation. While he shared Semper's antipathy to excessive dematerialization, as this had already been demonstrated, so to speak, by the Crystal Palace and by all the ferro-vitreous structures that followed in its wake, he tried to evolve the substance of an iron architecture that had its own corporeal being. To this end he attempted to adduce a strictly tectonic, one might say paleotechnological, equivalent of the classical orders. While Heuser was aware that such built-up elements could only realize their full cultural potential if they were assimilated by the society in everyday practice, he seems to have been among the first to acclaim the riveted steel frame as the new industrial vernacular of the machine age.

If there is a single heir at the turn of the century to the line of Gilly, Schinkel, Bötticher, and Semper, then it is surely Wagner, who, despite the limitations of his practice, attempted to apply the tectonic legacy of the *Aufklärung* to the modernizing realities of the twentieth-century metropolis. This much is already manifest in the pages of his major theoretical text, *Moderne Architektur*, first published in 1896 and later reissued, in slightly modified versions, in 1889, 1902, and 1914. The changed title of the last edition – *Die Baukunst unserer Zeit* – testifies to Wagner's allegiance to the so-called realist approach of such writers as Hermann Muthesius (*Stilarchitektur und Baukunst*, 1902) and Karl Scheffler (*Moderne Baukunst*, 1907). The term *Baukunst* (building art) indicated an approach that was more *sachlich*, in the sense that it responded objectively to the socio-technical building task of everyday life rather than to the ideals of high art. Nevertheless, despite his mature affinity for the real, Wagner never relinquished his aspirations for the ideal, not even at the peak of his career as an engineer/architect in the service of the Viennese *Stadtbahn*, as we may judge from the 1914 edition of *Moderne Architektur*, published some four years before his death in 1918. Here a series of capitalized aphorisms dotted throughout the text highlight the major tenets of his theoretical position, particularly in the seminal fourth chapter dedicated to "Construction" in which we may read the following six apodictic statements:

> Every architectural form has risen in construction and has successivley become an art-form. It is therefore certain that new purposes must give birth to new methods of construction and by this reasoning also to new forms. The architect always has to develop the art-form, but only the structural calculation and the expense will therefore speak a language unsympathetic to man, while on the other hand, the architect's mode of expression will remain unintelligible if in the creation of the art-form he does not start from construction. Well conceived construction not only is the prerequisite of every architectural work, but also, and this cannot be repeated often enough, provides the modern creative architect with a number of positive ideas for creating new forms – in the fullest meaning of this word. Without the knowledge and experience of construction, the concept "architect" is unthinkable.
>
> (Wagner, 1902: 91–9)

While all of this supported Bötticher's thesis that a new *Kunstform* could only arise out of a new *Werkform*,[7] it makes no reference to Semper's *Bekleidung* theory, which Wagner assumed for its capacity to synthesize lightweight panel construction in both stone and metal. At this juncture, Wagner seems to have embraced the metaphor of the mask of which Semper had written in *Der Stil*, with a certain ambiguity: "Masking does not help, however, when *behind* the mask the thing is false" (Semper, 1860: 257–8). By "masking" Semper did not intend falsehood, but rather the creation of a tectonic veil through which and by which it would be possible to perceive the spiritual significance of the structural form, as it lay suspended, as it were, between the pragmatic world of fact and the symbolic world of value. No-one has perhaps written more perceptively of Wagner's contribution in this regard than Fritz Neumeyer:

> Like the then floating garment that clothes the female body in ancient Greek sculpture, revealing as much beauty as it conceals, Wagner's treatment of the structure and construction exploits a similar kind of delicate, sensuous play that was probably only evident to a connoisseur of a certain age and experience. Exactly this principle gives the interior of the Postparkasse its quality of silk-like transparency. The glass veil is lifted up on iron stilts that carefully cut into its skin and gently disappear. Semper's theory of "dressing" could find no more ingenious interpretation because here an artist, not a theoretician, generously appealed to it to mask his own interests and obsessions.
>
> (Neumeyer, 1993: 135)

Influenced by the *fin-de-siècle* theory of empathy, *Einfühlung*, by which the "form force" of an artwork becomes by association an analogue for corporeal movement and states of bodily being, Wagner found his way back to Bötticher's double articulation of the tectonic, in which the classical legacy of the *Kunstform* would come to be inseminated by the dynamism of the *Werkform* as an inorganically articulated structural invention (Schwarzer, 1993: 280).[8]

NOTES

1   There is a difference between the position adopted in *Die Tektonik der Hellenen* and the 1846 essay. In the former the fusion of Hellenic and Germanic styles is solely as a matter of cultural synthesis; in the later text it is made dependent on the new material, iron.

2   The issue of polychromy in antique Greek sculpture had first been raised by the publication of Quatremère de Quincy's text "Le Jupiter Olympien" in 1816. However, Quatremère resisted the idea of polychromy in architecture except in so far as it arose out of the natural color of the materials themselves. The possibility that the Greeks painted their temples was advanced again by Leo von Klenze's colored reconstruction of the temple at Aegina in Hittorf's *L'Architecture polychrome chez les Grecs* of 1827 and by Henri Labrouste's *envoi* from the French Academy in Rome in 1828 consisting of his reconstruction of the Greek temples at Paestum.

3   Quatremère de Quincy, in *De l'architecture égyptienne* (his 1803 rewriting of his 1785 entry to the competition of the Académie Royale des Inscriptions et Belles-Lettres) posited a triadic origin to all building: the tent, the cave, and the hut. See Lavin (1992).

4   However, as for Ruskin and Pugin, the Crystal Palace was a traumatic form for Semper. He saw it as a vacuum enclosed by glass and thereafter thought it essential that the use of iron should be tempered by the deployment of masonry forms.

5 Benedetto Gravagnuolo cites those various fragmented passages in *Moderne Architektur* in which Wagner criticizes Semper for not having insisted sufficiently that architecture always derives from the principle of construction and that new constructional means must eventually produce new constructional forms (Gravagnuolo, 1987: 34).

6 I am totally indebted to Duncan Berry for his study of Georg Heuser.

7 I am indebted to Mitchell Schwarzer for drawing my attention to Bötticher's later use of the term Werkform to refer to technically innovative constructional form (Schwarzer, 1993: 278–80).

8 Of the part played by *Einfühlung* implicitly in Wagner and by anticipation, so to speak, in the case of Bötticher, Schwarzer writes (with regard to Richard Streiter's critique of Bötticher's *Tektonik* in 1896): "Bötticher's theory represents an ideological bridge between the speculative aesthetics of Sulzer, Moritz and Schelling and the ideas of projective visuality and *Einfühlung* (empathy) that later appeared in the writings of Conrad Fiedler, Adolf Hildebrand and Theodor Lipps."

Chapter 9: The Dislocation of the Architectural Self

David Goldblatt

> Work on philosophy – like work *in* architecture in many respects – is really more work on oneself.
>
> (Wittgenstein, 1980a: 24e)

> They often call me Speedo,
> But my real name is Mr Earl.
>
> (From *Speedo* by the Cadillacs, 1955)

> The child when it appears is a countless crowd, which life reduces soon enough to a single individual.
>
> (Valéry, 1921: 109–10)

Enjoying a mild rejuvenation on the contemporary American drug scene, our word 'ecstasy,' like the English words 'derange' and 'delirium,' has its history in spatial terms. The Greek *ecstasis* meaning to put outside, to put out of place, led to the notion of being beside oneself, of being transported.[1] In moral theory (I have Kant in mind) the idea of acting against ourselves is often seen as imperative and the problem of distancing, if not removing ourselves from our passions and other inclinations is compounded by our own questionable ability to recognize just when we have succeeded. In art, too, *ecstasis* has had its own place especially as the self encounters itself as quotidian being. In this chapter I should like to say something, at least in outline, about what I believe is the role of *ecstasis* in recent architectural practice, specifically in the work of the American architect Peter Eisenman.

Peter Eisenman's architecture recognizes and reflects a paradox regarding the architectural self: that the architect creates institutions, e.g. the home, the city, but as an inventive force, the architect also must resist the very process of institutionalizing what he/she is commissioned to do. As Eisenman puts it, "In order to be, it must always resist being . . . This is the paradox of architecture. Thus, in order to reinvent a site . . . the idea of site must be freed from its traditional places, histories, and systems of meaning. This involves the dislocation of the traditional interpretation of its elements" (Eisenman, 1987: 18). Eisenman's work constitutes an architecture that is somehow removed from an unreinvented architectural milieu, one requiring an architect who will break with architecture's own hierarchical presuppositions.

Under these provisional assumptions rests a deeper difficulty: breaking with such presuppositions cannot simply be a matter of the architect's choosing to do so. The architect is coimplicated in the tradition of architecture, through schooling, apprenticeship and professional reward as well as by the usual devices of enculturation. The architect comes to understand and to respect architecture as traditionally conceived. And since architecture *qua* artform is also inextricably meshed with everyday life, the impact of culture is also an everyday, ingraining phenomenon. Some, like Alan Colquhoun, appreciate at least part of the negotiated condition of architecture if only as a matter of degrees of distinction from other arts: "With architecture so bound to the sources of finance and power, it is much more difficult for the architect than for other artists to operate within an apparently autonomous subculture or to retain independence from bourgeois taste that has been the ambition of art since the early nineteenth century" (Colquhoun, 1988: 7–8). To name oneself as architect is to pose within the context of a tradition, one constituted by expectations, privileges and obligations. I am calling the self that works within the context of a traditional architecture, an architecture of everyday practice, "the architectural self." By definition, the architectural self does not feel the force of Eisenman's paradox. Eisenman's concern is not so much about whether good or interesting work can be produced within architecture's traditional presuppositions; rather, he is skeptical about whether a more "speculative," exploratory architecture, an architecture that investigates its own assumptions, can be designed by a self whose work is an expression of traditional tastes, beliefs, principles.

On the basis of Eisenman's understanding of the architect's situation, the architect ought to attempt employment of a *strategy* that removes that aspect of the coimplicated self from his/her architecture. It is a matter of the self's not being able to trust the self, in the manner of Kant's heteronymous will being an unreliable trustee for the moral restraint upon desire. Part of the problem, Eisenman has come to suspect, is that there may be "a powerful anthropomorphism operating at the level of the unconscious wish," in entrenched architectural practice. As Jeffrey Kipnis has put it, "Architecture in the service of institution is architecture in the service of man as he wants to see himself and to continue seeing himself. As such, it is a denial of architecture as a, perhaps the, vehicle of becoming" (Kipnis, 1986: 46). An architectural process that does not privilege those features that assumes "man" as the measure of all things architectural may be a way of revealing what the architecture of tradition and the traditional self has repressed, a way, in Derrida's phrase of "letting other voices speak" (Derrida, 1989: 11). A strategy is needed to remove the architect as a source of resistance to non-traditional architecture so that design can begin from a dislocated vantage point. I would like to consider *one* strategy Eisenman uses to achieve this dislocation, a series of architectural moves that make use of the notion of "arbitrary text." Eisenman uses the arbitrary text in order to initiate design subsequent to the interruption of the self's usual propensities while doing architecture. It might be helpful to keep in mind a certain representational consequence of Eisenman's work, one that is part of a general anti-idealism: "Some architecture is built as a representation of an ideal state, the condition of the possibility of the ideality of the world. The Greek temple is one instance. My work here is the converse of this, a condition that represents the impossibility of the ideal."[2] This stance, relative to a *telos* of architecture, may lead us to a link with Nietzsche.

In the course of analyzing what ought to happen to the self of the architect in the context of this strategy I will be looking at other sources such as the Nietzsche of *The Birth of Tragedy*, and some neglected but provocative ideas from the final chapter of Arthur Danto's *The Transfiguration of the Commonplace*, a book itself indebted in more ways than one to Nietzsche. Danto, Nietzsche and Eisenman discuss the dislocation of some version of a *commonplace* self dislocated by a mechanism analytically related to art with the result in each case being some *extraordinary* self-situation. For Danto and Eisenman the dislocation takes place by means of an "outside" text and can be attributed to some aspect of that text that is metaphorical in structure. Although Danto uses the commonplace/extraordinary dichotomy and although he gives it a central place in his analysis, I want to show among other things that that distinction only instantiates selves that are substantially different from each other. Danto's dislocation is the result of an arbitrary intersection of one "life" metaphorically brought to bear upon some status quo self, e.g. a reader of texts, ordinary or not. Peter Eisenman, on the other hand, seeks the arbitrary in his architecture in order to dislocate the coimplicated self of the traditional architect by virtue of the kind of metaphorical structure recognized by Danto, a metaphorical structure that, in its limiting and most arbitrary case is *catachresis*. The early Nietzsche, like Eisenman, is interested in shaking off the anthrocentric in order to latch onto a power repressed by an externalized quotidian life, a power according to Nietzsche, internally related to the self of the artist. But first for some background and for a characterization of the problem at hand.

I

The summer of 1988 saw New York's Museum of Modern Art host an exhibit called, "Deconstructivist Architecture." "Deconstructivist Architecture" was curated by Philip Johnson and Mark Wigley in Johnson's first major museum project since his 1932 landmark show that introduced the International Style to America. The new exhibit intended to bring under one umbrella seven important architects that by some stretch of the imagination could be called "deconstructivists" (not merely a variation of "deconstructionist" the term indicates the art born in pre-revolutionary Russia) since they commonly challenged some of the more central traditional aspects of architecture, among them unity, stability, harmony, comfort and function. Deconstruction in architecture has come to be seen as a vital response to the historically necessary, but much more facile, architectural postmodernism as well as to classical/modern architecture in a broad sense of those terms. But it must be kept in mind that far from being the name of an architectural movement or school, 'deconstructivism' refers at best to the practices of a loose set of diverse members many of whom would justifiably resist that or any other label. Peter Eisenman, one of two Americans in the MOMA show (the other was Frank Gehry), is no exception.

As an example of an attempt to deny the privileging of one or more of the traditional aspects of architecture consider an unbuilt Eisenman project, his award-winning Guardiola House. Proposed for a site high above the Atlantic on the Spanish Costa de la Luz near Cadiz it is a startling but also beautiful weekend residence for a single father and his grown son. It has windows in the floor and floors that are unlevel. It is sometimes necessary to go outside to get into another room and the house itself is split by an exterior stairway rising from the sea. The Guardiola House appears fragmented if not tortured and shaky.

According to Eisenman, the Guardiola design researches the meaning of place or *topos* as part of "the breakdown of the traditional forms of place," and results in something "between place and object, between container and contained." This "simultaneity of two traditionally contradictory states" is to be found in the *Timaeus* in Plato's definition of the receptacle (*chora*), which is, roughly, like a holding place or office (as in political office) but does not exist as a sensible or even intelligible thing itself. Recently, Derrida has written an essay entitled, "Chora" and Eisenman's "research" here exemplifies the usual Derridian breakdown of binary oppositions which he, Eisenman, sometimes expresses as *betweeness*. Working *between* can be characterized as suspending the privilege of one member of a binary opposition at the expense or the devaluation of another. Eisenman, whose architecture has put into use a network of concepts taken from the writings of Jacques Derrida, has collaborated with Derrida on the design of a garden in Bernard Tschumi's Parc de la Villette in Paris, 1985). The contemporary philosophical critique of foundational binary oppositions by postmodern thinkers following the lead of Heidegger or Derrida has been given an architectural context by Eisenman: "traditional opposition between structure and decoration, abstraction and figuration, figure and ground, form and function could be dissolved. Architecture could begin an exploration of the 'between' within these categories" (Eisenman, quoted in Derrida, 1989: 7). Eisenman's Wexner Center for the Visual Arts at the Ohio State University in Columbus, explores the betweeness of architectural binary opposition (Figure 9.1). For example, the 516-foot-long, white, uncovered, three-dimensional grid, running almost the entire length of the site, at full-building scale, as "scaffolding" (the temporary, tentative construction apparatus) that at Wexner remains prominently and permanently after the structure is completed, falls somewhere between

Figure 9.1
Wexner Center, aerial
view.
Photo: Eisenman
architects.

process and product, past and present, shelter and non-shelter, structure and form, structure and ornament, building and non-building, exterior and interior (Figure 9.2).

Although Eisenman's projects tend to look significantly different from other architectures, Eisenman does not aim at avant-gardism, nor does he direct his projects towards the manipulation of forms, or toward work that pleases aesthetically. Architecture, according to Eisenman, has the potential to join other artists in a deep exploration of meaning. In the unconcealing or opening of meanings that are often hidden beneath a commonplace traditional surface or among the relationships between traditional objects – that which is not laid bare is often if not always that which is repressed by traditional forms of meaning. An architecture that is not merely emblematic of *status quo* interests or desires, one that can "let other voices speak", is as capable as painting or literature of engaging in the tensions between tradition and innovation. A non-traditional architecture can "surgically open up the Classical and the Modern to find what is repressed" (Eisenman, quoted in Derrida, 1989: 7).

Indeed for Eisenman the differences between classical and modern architecture are insignificant; in fact, Eisenman often thinks of modernism as merely another form of classicism. Traditional architecture, then, will include the work of modernists such as Mies, Corbusier and Loos, despite their reputation to the contrary. Eisenman is clear on the reduction of the modern to the classical tradition:

> [I]n trying to reduce architectural form to its essence, to a pure reality, the moderns
> assumed they were transforming the field of referential figuration to that of

Figure 9.2
Wexner Center, lobby.
Photo: Eisenman
architects.

non-referential "objectivity." In reality, however, their "objective" forms never left the classical tradition. They were simply stripped down classical forms, or forms referring to a new set of givens (function, technology). Thus Corbusier's houses that look like modern steamships or biplanes exhibit the same referential attitude toward representation as a Renaissance or "classical" building.

(Eisenman, 1989: 157)

Eisenman's dislocation from the traditional architectural self, then, in such projects as the Wexner Center, includes dislocation from the self that works in the mode of modern architecture, which Eisenman sees as significantly classical even in the period of its inception. Appearances aside, the differences on his view do not run deep. According to Eisenman, then, the metaphysical presuppositions of architecture, architectural essence as traditionally conceived, are the same for modernism as they are for classicism.

The Wexner Center and the Guardiola House instantiate one general problem/solution facing Eisenman: how to make architecture that is unhierarchical, one that avoids the "powerful anthrocentrism" mentioned above. Such an architecture would refuse to acknowledge the stability of the concept of architecture which is buttressed by a grounding metaphysics of essentiality and which in turn allows for the appearance of the timeless self-evidence of architecture's "essential" features. "Deconstruction," Derrida has said, "is first and foremost a suspicion directed against just that kind of thinking – "what is . . . ?" "what is the essence of . . . ?" (Derrida, 1989: 9) The seeming self-evidence of such features constitute what Kipnis has called, "a resistance, a received value-structure by which architecture is repressed" (Kipnis, 1986: 7). Eisenman's aim is to refuse the privilege rendered in these anthrocentric features, to deny their centrality, their favored position, in the *praxis* of design. But this task is only compounded by the situation of the self when the self is making architecture. The traditional architectural self is inclined not only to celebrate and express the anthrocentric essentials of traditional architecture, it also has a propensity toward making architecture that looks and feels like traditional architecture, i.e. toward being pleased and feeling perceptually and emotionally satisfied by what is "designed" by his or her own labor. The problem at hand is not to be underestimated.

If the quotidian architectural self is itself suspect, it follows that it will not do to *express* that self, a self that makes design merely a matter of taste or preference. "A major displacement," Eisenman says

> concerns the role of the architect/designer and the design process. Something may be designed which can be called displacing, but it may be only an expressionism, a mannerist distortion of an essentially stable language. It may not displace the stable language, but on the contrary further stabilize its normative condition. This can be seen in many examples of current architectural fashion. There is a need for process other than an intuition – "I like this," or "I like that." When the process is intuitive it will already be known, and therefore complicit with the repressions inherent in architectural "knowledge."
>
> (Eisenman, 1989: 42)

Architects, then, like to "design," to make buildings that are visually pleasing, to join and further entrench the history of architecture; to make "architecture." Derrida says, "Let us never forget that there is an architecture of architecture. Down even to its archaic foundation, the most fundamental concept of architecture has been constructed . . . " He continues:

> This architecture of architecture has a history, it is historical through and through. Its heritage inaugurates the intimacy of our economy, the law of our hearth (*oikos*), our familial, religious and political 'oikonomy,' all the places of birth and death, temple, school, stadium, agora, square, sepulchre. It goes right through us (*nous transit*) to the point that we forget its very historicity: we take it for nature. It is common sense itself.
>
> (Derrida, 1986: 65)

According to Derrida then, the commonsensicality of a *certain* metaphysics of architecture has come to present itself as *architecture itself* masking the correct view that the concept of architecture is itself a construct. Once this is understood it is possible, if not yet practical, for the architect to question stability and to explore and initiate other architectures. But practical autonomy in architecture requires something else. "Autonomy," Eisenman says in his *Houses of Cards*, ". . . depends on distancing both the architect from the design process and the object from a traditional history" (Eisenman, 1987: 174). But since the architect is already coimplicated, perhaps as an unwitting party to the process of design, it cannot *simply* be a matter of choosing to do so. The issue of distancing oneself from the process of architecture is the problem of distancing oneself from oneself, the issue of *ecstasis*.

II

It is part of my purpose in presenting ecstatic themes in Nietzsche and Danto to undercut resistance to utilizing so dramatic a concept as ecstasis by citing precedents in art-theoretical contexts other than the one I am rendering for Eisenman. Although I hope to identify certain similarities among these views I am in no way claiming that ecstasis functions identically in each different circumstance in which it is invoked. Indeed, I have hoped to emphasize just how differently ecstasis is used by Nietzsche and Danto, and how Peter Eisenman's use of this notion is distinct from either of them.

In what follows I would like to emphasize the role of ecstasis in Nietzsche whose *Birth of Tragedy* has been correctly understood as a critical response to the eighteenth/nineteenth-century construct "Classical Greece" in which the Greek character is represented as one of noble simplicity and serene greatness and where "the expression in Greek figures reveals greatness and composure of soul in the throes of whatever passions" (Winckelmann, 1774). By contrast Nietzsche's first book emphasizes the centrality of the Dionysian in Greek life, manifested paradigmatically in Bacchian ritual, and characterized by the kind of frenzy and intoxication that the Germanic Greece sought to repress. Out of such rites came "a complete sexual promiscuity overriding every form of established tribal law; (where) all the savage urges of the mind were unleashed . . . " Nietzsche locates precedents of dramatic tragedy in what he calls "the Dionysian ecstatic artist."[3]

Architecture is an unlikely candidate for the Dionysian "vortex." Greek architecture, for Nietzsche, especially the Doric, stood in the foreground of the Apollonian representation of austerity and control, which Nietzsche saw as necessary but far from sufficient for tragedy, that dramatic form which takes as its theme the ultimate destruction of an individual.

> The only way I am able to view Doric art and the Doric state is as a perpetual military
> encampment of the Apollonian forces. An art so defiantly austere, so ringed about with

fortifications – an education so military and exacting – a polity so ruthlessly cruel – could endure only in a continual state of resistance against the titanic and barbaric menace of Dionysos.

(Nietzsche, 1872: 35)

E.R. Dodds, in a passage cited by Silk and Stern, describes the ecstatic role of a decidedly democratic Dionysos: "Apollo moved only in the best society, aristocratic athletes; but Dionysos was at all periods *demotikos*, a god of the people . . . Dionysus . . . is *Lusios*, 'the Liberator' – the god who enables you for a short time to *stop being yourself*, and thereby sets you free" (Silk and Stern, 1981: 182). This is the very advice Nietzsche offers the dramatist: "To be a dramatist all one needs is the urge to transform oneself and speak out of strange bodies and souls" (Nietzsche, 1872: 55). During the Dionysian excitation of the Bacchic rituals, when the *principium individuationis* is dropped, this is precisely what happens in the dramatic chorus and constitutes for Nietzsche "the primary *dramatic* phenomenon" namely, "projecting oneself outside the self and then acting as though one had really entered another body, another character . . . what we have here is the individual effacing himself through entering a strange being" (Nietzsche, 1872: 55).

As *anamnesis* or *recollection* played its role for Socrates in the recapturing of knowledge, *forgetting* is the mechanism at work for Nietzsche in the self's abrogation. What is negated by virtue of forgetting is "one's civic past and social rank," one's everyday or commonplace self. And since in Nietzsche's unreified notion of Will, it is analytic that willing is willing towards an end, "our personal interest in *purposes*," the dropping of such civil or social ends is also the negation of the will. The artist of *The Birth of Tragedy* is without will, replaced perhaps by impulse, in unmediated contact with some kind of primordial being or "original Oneness" and becomes identified with it. The artist becomes "exempt from the embarrassing task of copying reality" (Nietzsche, 1872: 50). "He . . . strides with the same elation and ecstasy as the gods he has seen in his dreams. No longer the *artist*, he has himself become a *work of art*: the productive power of the whole universe is now manifested in his transport . . ." (Nietzsche, 1872: 24–5). Nothing much in this chapter turns on this early romantic notion of being in direct touch with some thing-in-itself, a view Nietzsche was later to reject. Rather, the point to be emphasized here is that some self has been dislocated from the ordinary self by art, in some manner or other.

Not entirely arbitrary "this mystical un-selving" is "a world sanctioned by myth and ritual" and stands in definite contrast with the commonplace. For Nietzsche the "receptacle" in early tragedy for the intersection of artist, artwork and audience was the chorus, the *chora* within which those divisions were dropped. For Nietzsche, ". . . the subjective artist is simply the bad artist . . . since we demand above all, in every genre and range of art, a triumph over subjectivity, deliverance from the self, the silencing of every personal will and desire . . . " (Nietzsche, 1872: 37). Art, in this early Nietzschean account, is not a matter of the expression of the traditional self, but of its removal.

In this Nietzschean scenario the emptied, formerly commonplace self becomes a receptacle, a placeholder (not unlike the *chora*) not in order to enhance one's will or replace one will with another but rather to negate it and to fill its place with former repressions. What the ecstatic self experiences is often unpalatable to the formerly repressed civic self: the violent, the ugly, the "unnatural." Analogously, Peter Eisenman claims that in striving for the conventionally beautiful, architecture also represses the grotesque or confines it to the peripheries: "the grotesque was acceptable as long as it was as decoration; in the form of gargoyles, and frescoes. This is because the grotesque introduces the idea of the ugly, the deformed, the supposedly unnatural as an always present in the beautiful. It is this condition of the always present or the already within, that the beautiful in architecture attempts to repress" (Eisenman, 1989: 42). The return of the will following the Bacchic ritual, is the return of civic and social interests from Dionysian to quotidian reality. "But," says Nietzsche, "as soon as that quotidian reality enters consciousness once more it is viewed with loathing, and the consequence is an ascetic, abulic state of mind" (Nietzsche, 1872: 51).[4]

In broader terms this early Nietzschean account recognizes minimally that the everyday, reasonable self is significantly incomplete and that the perfecting of the quotidian "artistic" self through traditional forms of practice only leads one further from an authentic pursuit of art. In the words of Habermas,

> The critique of the Western emphasis on *logos* inspired by Nietzsche proceeds in a destructive manner. It demonstrates that the embodied, speaking and acting subject is not master in its own house; it draws from this the conclusion that the subject positing itself in knowledge is in fact dependent upon something prior, anonymous, and transsubjective . . . Once the defenses of subject-centered reason are razed, *logos*, which for so long had held together an interiority protected by power, hollow within and aggressive without, will collapse into itself. It has to be delivered over to its other, whatever that may be.
>
> (Habermas, 1985: 310)

For Nietzsche this "other" constitutes an unqualified original, precisely the sort of entity that Derrida and Eisenman deny. But on the need for the dislocation of the traditional self in order to dissolve repressions of that traditional self they agree.

III

At this point I would like to consider some of Arthur Danto's ideas on the relationship between self and art, in particular good if not great art. Although Danto is concerned with the self as auditor rather than as artist, his ideas about self-identity in his chapter on "Metaphor, Expression and Style" are pertinent to what I am calling the dislocation of the self, what Danto refers to as "being taken out of oneself by art."

Much has been written about Danto's consideration of art objects: how objects with certain well-entrenched ontologies take on new, additional ontologies and, correspondingly, how objects with predicates of certain sorts take on new and different sets of predicates without necessarily abandoning the old ones. Not only Duchampian readymades have this "double citizenship" but all artworks which are also so much "materiality," e.g. paint on canvas on frame. Indeed, more broadly, all representations are (at least) dually ontologized in this way. And lest one think that Danto's ontological considerations regarding perceptual indiscernibles apply to artworld concerns alone, one need but think of the grand pairs of look-the-sames pervading the history of philosophy: the waking experience and the dream, a deterministic world and a world of accidents, a world in which God exists and one in which God is absent, language and scribble, persons and bodies. For Danto, the initial task of philosophy has been to explain such differences if differences do not lie in perception alone.

Towards the end of *The Transfiguration of the Commonplace* Danto turns his attention away from the transfiguration of objects to the transfiguration of selves. Here he presents a provocative thesis about what happens to *auditors* and *spectators* of artworks in the course of being engaged with them. Parallel to his account of transfigured objects, Danto's account is an explanation of how selves take on new art-relevant identities in a way that is both temporary and uncommonplace while somehow retaining their old ones. The "spectator," Danto says, "identifies himself with the represented character: and sees his or her life in terms of the depicted: it is oneself as Anna Karenina, or Isabelle Archer, or Elizabeth Bennett, or O: oneself sipping lime tea; in the Marabar Caves; in the waters off East Egg; in the Red Chamber ... where the artwork becomes a metaphor for life and life is transfigured" (Danto, 1981: 172). Here, the possibilities for the transfiguration of the self are closely tied to the notion of what the self believes the self to be, if only for a temporary period of time:

> You cannot altogether separate from your identity your beliefs about what that identity is: to believe yourself to be Anna is to be Anna for the time you believe it, to see your life as a sexual trap and yourself as a victim of duty and passion. Art, if a metaphor at times on life, entails that the not unfamiliar experience of *being taken out of oneself by art* – the familiar artistic illusion – is virtually the enactment of a metaphoric transformation with oneself as subject: you are what the work is ultimately about, a commonplace person transfigured into an amazing woman.
>
> (Danto, 1981: 173, my emphasis)

Thus, according to Danto: if a reader, R, is metaphorically transformed (transfigured) by (reading about) C, where C is a fictional character, then there is a metaphor, CM, whose relevant analogical features are also features that are part of the life of C, and that by virtue of CM, R sees his or her life a new way, at least for the time that he or she "believes" those relevant analogical features to be part of his or her own life. On some accounts of metaphor C is just CM and on some accounts of belief R's belief includes a suspending of disbelief.

For Danto, the removal of self from self happens by virtue of metaphor (whose Greek root, it is worth recalling, means 'to transport') with the Aristotelian notions of analogy and new perspective (which includes belief) as part of the means. I think it is important to note, for my purposes here and in order to properly understand Danto's position, that the notion of "being commonplace" is logically independent of the notion of "being a candidate for transfiguration," although the transfiguration of a commonplace object into one that is somehow uncommonplace may be his most striking example. But there is nothing in Danto's notion of transfiguration that precludes the ontological transition from objects already interpreted (a necessary condition for artworks according to him) to those that also require new ones. Even interpreted objects can be takeover targets. And for Danto, it is part of the logic of *transfiguration* (as opposed to transformation) that earlier identities remain intact. Whether commonplace objects are really interpreted objects but so familiar that we do not notice the interpretation, is another matter and one that will not concern me here. So then, it is merely a working assumption rather than a necessary condition that the self that is transfigured through artworks is a commonplace self, humble with respect to the extraordinary personal circumstance waiting in artworks for the interpreter/self to pay respects.

What *is* relevant to Danto's scheme for the dislocation of self is difference – difference of sufficient significance that ontological identities change during the course of the reader's metaphorical confrontation with the network of properties and relationships that constitute fictional characters. The commonplace/extraordinary dichotomy, while it brings for some a kind of worthwhileness to the enterprise of reading, is only an instantiation of this ontological differential.

Although Danto's own examples for an artistically transfigured self come from the fictional portrayal of persons, there is no difficulty in imagining that sort of transfiguration taking place by virtue of architecture – the self transfigured by powerful buildings. For example, it is easy to imagine the native Indian transfigured into a member of the British Empire, or the private bourgeois into the patriot/citizen, or the indifferent believer into the awestruck theist and so forth, each transfiguration respectively initiated by the self's presence to a meaningful structure.

For the time being, I would like to note only that, at least in the kind of literary examples Danto uses, there is a certain degree of unpredictability about the self's new location – that in the course of reading a novel there is a certain arbitrary abandonment of oneself to the text's protagonist in an accidental intersection and super-imposition of lives. There is something arbitrary too, in that at the outset of the novel the reader is unaware of the full future consequences to his/her self, of seeing the world from another perspective, even if those consequences are innocent and short-lived.

IV

In the wake of two decades or so of literature on the subject, Eisenman views architecture as *textual* and his own architectural strategies as textual strategies.

Traditional architecture, in Eisenman's view, begins with certain traditional texts. One might say, for example, that a typical program (an account of client requirements) is a determining or relevant architectural text. So too, a specific site can be "read" with respect to access to surrounding buildings or opportunity of view. The history of architecture is also a text replete with meanings. For example, what a church, or home, or stadium means includes what it has looked like through the ages until the present.

In addition, *formal typologies*, simple abstract geometrical configurations, which, according to Rafael Moneo, allow for "the possibility of grouping objects by certain inherent structural similarities" (Moneo, 1978: 23), are architectural instruments that are available as architectural texts. The instantiations of formal types in real architectural practice on actual sites are usually distorted or otherwise modified so that architecture can address "both their singleness and their shared features" (Moneo, 1978: 44). It is not obvious that there is anything inherently architectural in the *abstracted* geometricality of formal typologies. But the *use* of simple types of geometrical forms in the process of design has incorporated those forms textually into the history of architecture. Eisenman sees these texts as part of traditional or, as he sometimes call it, "classical" architecture, architecture that accepts the anthropological metaphysics of architecture. The kind of "singleness" or newness mentioned by Moneo, for example, leaves unscathed the foundational assumptions of architecture including the traditional essence/accident opposition.

The dislocation of the architectural self requires a strategy, and one such strategy includes positing a text that will bring into question those architectural assumptions. But such a text cannot be one of the traditional texts of architecture. Instead, Eisenman reaches for an outside text, one that, relative to some particular current project, is accidental or arbitrary.

V

The history of the meaning of the word "arbitrary" seems to have undergone a reversal of sorts with respect to the idea of the will. Once meaning that which was a result of the preference *or* will of an arbiter, in contrast to being governed or determined by rule or law alone, 'arbitrary' now seems to designate, at least in some domains, the quality of being selected by preference or impulse only, but not really chosen; i.e. not a product of the will. The notion of an arbitrary text continues to include the idea of being generated by an arbiter, a textual arbiter which, like a law, stands *outside* its object of application. Such a textual arbiter may even be selected more *or less* at random and not itself really the product of the will of the selector. This needs certain qualification but means that although the selector does not know the full consequences of the text for the architectural project beforehand he or she is nevertheless willing to accept those consequences even if they violate the architect's good, traditional sense, his/her tastes or preferences or those characteristics such as function or harmony, which are traditionally understood to constitute essential architectural conditions.

Wittgenstein said in 1931 that, " 'Arbitrary' as we normally use it always has reference to some practical end: e.g. if I want to make an efficient boiler I *must* fulfil certain specifications, but it is quite arbitrary what colour I paint it" (Wittgenstein, 1980b: 60). Since willing in traditional architecture tends to be willing toward the constructed metaphysical essentials of entrenched architectural practice, it is possible to say that Eisenman, by virtue of the arbitrary text, is reversing, for a specified period during an architectural project, the usual opposition between essence and accident. A reversal of the relationship between traditional architectural essence and accident does not necessarily result in the absence of a traditionally essential quality, say shelter, from an architectural project any more than Wittgenstein's boiler is uncolored. Accidents (in a double sense of that word) are incorporated into the project as practical ends, and traditional essences now become accidents of the project. Acting as the result of some arbitrary text helps remove the architect as a source of resistance toward *establishing* essential/traditional ends as privileged architectural goals including one of a pair of the sets of binary oppositions now held in suspension.

The idea behind an arbitrary text in the context of the dislocation of the self is to remove the hands from the hands of the architect, to eliminate a major motivation from a highly motivated self in order to place the self in a new position regarding its own work. By removing an initiating constituent in the traditional design process the outside text diminishes, but does not eliminate, the architect's role overall in making well-entrenched architecture. The arbitrary text is a text lifted from its own home, its own context, rationale and motivation, its own traditional place and utilized in some materially applicable respect. In a certain sense then, the arbitrary text is context-free; i.e. it is free of the context of the project at hand. Eisenman has used the Derridian notion of *grafting* to express the transplanting of this "other" text onto a particular architectural project.

It seems to me that there are at least two relevant senses in which a text can be context-free. First, a text can be free of or outside architecture as traditionally understood; i.e. a non-architectural text; and second, it can stand outside the traditional subject matter of the project at hand. Eisenman's use of DNA in his Bio-Centrum research laboratories at the J.W. Goethe University, Frankfurt-am-Main is an example of the former, while his use of scaffolding for the Columbus city grid in the design for the Wexner Center comes at least close to being an example of the latter. Let me call a text that is arbitrary in both of the above senses a *strongly* arbitrary text and a text that is arbitrary in only one of those senses arbitrary in the *weak* sense. It must be said that to the best of my knowledge, Eisenman has never made use of an arbitrary text in the strong sense outside of studio exercises.[5]

The arbitrary text works by the architect's choosing some *materially applicable* aspect of that text, by juxtaposing it to the usual texts of architecture and assigning it more or less equal influence in the final design. In a theoretically limiting case neither will dominate, and the result will be the *betweeness* mentioned earlier. Those aspects then make their appearance in the design as "traces," fragmented signs that indicate but do not image the arbitrary text.[6] The "architect" then also will be *between* in a sense: between the architect coimplicated in the institutional history of architecture and an other if non-characterized self, dislocated but ready to begin to work with design possibilities that intersect the immediate project but are accidental relative to it.

The arbitrary text functions analogically, which implies that only certain of its aspects are contextually transplanted by the architect. The applied aspects of the arbitrary text may surface in the architectural project more or less obviously but in any case are themselves chosen from the text by the architect. There is, then, by virtue of certain shared features, an analogical relationship between the project and the arbitrary text. But the analogy is a peculiar one since the consequences of its use are not entirely worked out. It works, for a time at least, like a metaphor postponed. Since the analogous features of the arbitrary text, now analogue, have not yet been considered, the new insight or vision essential to metaphor is incomplete or open. In the case of the strongly arbitrary text the relationship between new architectural text and arbitrary text may be uninterpretable, the connection not or not yet bearing the metaphorical fruit of novelty or insight. If it does not, *catachresis* takes place; i.e. an abuse of words, a misuse of words, a "forced metaphor", something with the structure of metaphor but metaphor when it misses its mark.

As the result of the imposition of a metaphorical structure on a traditional project by virtue of an arbitrary text, catachresis generates what is traditionally inappropriate. In the practice of architecture it holds before the architect a new value, a polar absence whose possibility of meaning must fall between the initial and the catachretic. Forced metaphor provides a greater "hang time" (to borrow from the sporting life) than ordinary metaphor where familiarity and propriety lubricate the closure of the activity (the *energeia*) initiated by metaphoric introduction. It is the tension and the possibility for play along this detour towards and away from meaning that prompt Derrida to think of catachreses as "*revelation*, unveiling, bringing to light, truth," and why its role is so central for philosophy (Derrida, 1982).

In the case of the strongly arbitrary text there is no guarantee that interesting connections or meaningful relationships will result between new architecture and outside text although configurational similarities in the form of traces might prevail. Whether these similarities are meaningful at the time of application is out of the control of the no-longer-designing architectural self. But it is precisely this juxtaposition of entities that creates a tension outside the traditional limitations of meaning channeling thought somewhere between the two. Not unlike the Apollonian imposition upon the Dionysian, it is, in the words of Eisenman, "a controlled accident." It is metaphor without an end or goal produced by removing the self from its original pursuit of meaning and purpose.

While the architect *chooses* the arbitrary text, the choice is made without deliberation and without knowingly exploiting its potentially metaphorical features for the project. It is an act of conscious disavowal on the part of the self. So that even if the architect chooses the text by the aforementioned tastes and preferences, the arbitrary text replaces the architect in the role of arbiter (worker). In the Wexner Center, for example, which is in part determined by two different sets of intersecting axes (city and campus grids at $12\frac{1}{4}$-degree angles) a column is allowed to fall on the steps of a major stairway and a dominant enclosed form determined in part by those axes in conjunction with the three-dimensional use of Eisenman's permanent "scaffolding," has no practical function whatsoever; i.e. it is not a space in which anything happens. (Campus lingo has dubbed it "student housing.") A commitment to the arbitrary text on the part of the architect assures that traditional texts are violated. It will sometimes call for compromises with those traditionally essential features of architecture such as function or shelter even if the result will be inconvenience or discomfort (or the appearance or representation of such) to the inhabitants of the dwelling.

The employment of the arbitrary text is part of a strategy to undermine the search for origin, to work with "starting points without value," as Eisenman puts it. " '[N]ot-classical' origins," he says, "can be strictly arbitrary." Once the self-evident characteristic of architecture is dismissed, "architecture is seen as having no a priori origins – whether functional, divine or natural – alternative fictions for the origin can be proposed: for example, one that is *arbitrary*, one that has no external values derived from meaning, truth or timelessness" (Eisenman, 1984: 168). When Eisenman says that the arbitrary is that without origin or value he has not lost the strong connection with the arbitrary as accidental or unwilled. It is the traditional text that has a place or origin, a meaning that is presupposed by the willer who must know that use or meaning in its proper context. But the unwilled, arbitrary text is outside the tradition, is outside the language-game in which it gains its home or original use. Outside of that it no longer has its original value, carrying only traces of its "original" or traditional meaning, its function as a sign. With apologies to Aristotle, outside these points of traditional obligation, there is nothing but gods and beasts. And they are untrustworthy and unpredictable.

With respect to the Wexner Center, the completed project is itself what Eisenman calls "a non-building – an archaeological earthwork whose essential elements are scaffolding and landscaping." It instantiates his concept of betweeness. Fractured and looking incomplete, the project nevertheless *functions*, *shelters*,[7] etc. but unlike "modern" architecture does not *represent*, or celebrate or monumentalize, function or shelter – does not privilege those elements. And, it is a Center without a center or an obvious front or back and without some single White House-like gestalt. From one look we have no idea what the rest of it is like.[8]

Eisenman's 1996 project, the Aronoff Center for Design and Art (Figure 9.3), an addition to the existing Design, Art, Architecture and Planning (DAAP),

Figure 9.3
Aronoff Center, east
entry.
Photo: Eisenman
architects.

joined a diverse group of buildings at the University of Cincinnati. In DAAP, the
chevron (or zigzag) took on an arbitrary aspect as it manifested itself as a spine
hugging the existing building and creating a work, of which Philip Johnson says,
"There is no equal to it anywhere in the world, from any period of modern architecture" (Eisenman, in Goldblatt, 1996). Its torquing, tipping, leaning walls seem
to twist vertically as well as horizontally and its exterior forms appear to be
sliding off their foundations. Its stairways are more like places of inhabitation or
decks of conversations rather than or in addition to instruments of elevation
(Figure 9.4). Its exteriors utilize pastels as part of a nine-color scheme that is
carried throughout the building. It is a building almost as much about color as it
is about anything else. The colors are notational, not simply gratuitous, leaving
the aspect of color in DAAP, as well as its fragmented surfaces and spaces,
generated by a textual scheme – and undesigned.

Eisenman is perfectly comfortable with the idea that he does not nor would
he want to, live in one of his own houses. He is after all, a commonplace dweller,
a self replete with resistance and repression, a self seeking traditional comforts.
But the issue here is no more one about satisfying human comfort than Kant's
concern about morality was the fulfillment of human desire. And while the cate-
gorical imperative is anything but arbitrary in that it is a paradigm of logocentric
enlightened thinking, it, like the arbitrary text, is *outside* the anthrocentric but
applicable within that sphere. Eisenman's work is an exemplification of what the
Italian philosopher Gianni Vattimo has called, *il piensiero debole* – or weak thinking. In any case, Eisenman's didactic place in contemporary culture should not be
evaluated by what I am calling the "manifesto mentality," a belief that in the

Figure 9.4
Aronoff Center, interior
view
Photo: Eisenman
architects.

best of all possible worlds a given kind of art would replace all other works traditional or otherwise. Fortunately for Eisenman there are those persons and institutions who are interested in consuming an architecture that grows out of a suspicion of Enlightenment values. For Eisenman it is an architecture of betweeness; one that refuses to accept the "self-evidence" of the concept of architecture and one that explores extended modes of architectural meaning.

As explained at the outset, I consider this chapter an outline that mentions numerous issues without always fully recognizing the problematic nature of those raised. Nevertheless, I hope that the breadth achieved here in drawing together a range or architecturally related items will compensate for this unavoidable omission.

VI

Architecture is usually not the paradigm used by philosophers when dealing with artworks. As was the case for Kant, Ruskin and Loos among others, this probably stems from architecture's role in commonplace life, its questionable status as a pure artwork, its position as hybrid. Unlike the Bacchic festivals or the novels and paintings of contemporary life, architecture in a sense is not merely aberration, a deviance from the everyday that we visit but from which we easily extract ourselves. Wherever architecture is, it is enmeshed in forms of life rather than juxtaposed to it. Such a condition simultaneously makes resistance to the hierarchical values of architecture all the more difficult and its overcoming all the more important. Where we no longer ask for feelings of comfort and soothing ideas in other artworks, it still *seems* reasonable to question the need for an architecture that may leave our daily satisfactions shaken or disoriented. But there is also, I suspect, a feeling that architecture lacks a certain capacity to speak that paintings and novels do not. Some recent, important work in architecture should change all that, and Eisenman's work is among it. In any case, Eisenman's architecture is inseparable from philosophical thinking, for example, thinking about the possibilities of self.[9]

NOTES

1   The notion of *ecstasis* has played a certain role in a good deal of philosophy from Pythagoras and Plato to Kierkegaard and Heidegger and so my concerns here are limited.

2   In conversation. See Goldblatt (1996).

3   Nietzsche, uses the German *Rausch* which, in addition to *ecstasy*, means *transport* among other things and has its etymological origins in the Middle High German, *rouch* and the Old High German *rauh* meaning smoke or steam. Francis Golffing is the translator for the edition I am using.

4   There are two different kinds of things going on here with respect to the Dionysian *ecstasis*. *The Birth of Tragedy*, "brimming with artist's secrets," as he says later in his famous preface "Self-Criticism," was offered as advice to artists contemporary with Nietzsche himself. On the other hand, the Bacchic experience was not de facto available for those artists acting alone. In the festival for Dionysus the commonplace self joins a transfiguring community in a well-entrenched ritual where the *raison d'être* was to dissolve, through orgiastic amnesia, a communion experienced *en masse* culminating in the appearance of Dionysus himself. Leaving the commonplace meant joining a common throng, the participants together acting in an uncommon way, sharing an experience that, with respect to the everyday self, was radically dislocating. But for Nietzsche, it was only by virtue of stepping outside the self-in-everyday activity that art could happen. For Nietzsche, one's own will needed to be exteriorized in order to internalize art since the artistic self was not located in the transparent, "common sense" world.

5   These studio exercises have been documented in *Investigations in Architecture: Eisenman Studios at the GSD: 1983–85*.

6   Eisenman makes much greater use of the concept of a trace than I indicate here, a concept used by Husserl and Freud as well as by Derrida.

7   For example, one of the major visual elements, the so-called scaffolding, is actually non-sheltering, an outside passage unscaled to human proportions.

8   It is an *irony* for Eisenman, who intended to distance his self from the aesthetic, that the arbitrary text will have powerful *aesthetic* implications for any architectural project and that, given his anti-avant-garde position, his projects are exciting from an aesthetic point of view. Furthermore, there is no question that Eisenman's work, especially his more recent work, is *not* perceptually indiscernible from traditional architecture.

9   In part, this chapter was made possible by an Occasional Fellowship from the University of Chicago and a Robert C. Good Fellowship from Denison University spent at Harvard Graduate School of Design in the Spring of 1988. I would like to thank Jeffrey Kipnis of the School of Architecture at the Ohio State University whose inspiration would be difficult to overestimate and also Philip Glotzbach, my steadfast general consultant.

Chapter 10: The Pleasure of Architecture

Bernard Tschumi

Functionalist dogmas and the puritan attitudes of the modern movement have often come under attack. Yet the ancient idea of pleasure still seems sacrilegious to contemporary architectural theory. For many generations any architect who aimed for or attempted to experience pleasure in architecture was considered decadent. Politically, the socially conscious have been suspicious of the slightest trace of hedonism in architectural endeavors and have rejected it as a reactionary concern. And in the same way, architectural conservatives have relegated to the Left everything remotely intellectual or political, including the discourse of pleasure. On both sides, the idea that architecture can possibly exist without either moral or functional justification, or even responsibility, has been considered distasteful.

Similar oppositions are reflected throughout the recent history of architecture. The avant-garde has endlessly debated oppositions that are mostly complementary: order and disorder, structure and chaos, ornament and purity, rationality and sensuality. And these simple dialectics have pervaded architectural theory to such an extent that architectural criticism has reflected similar attitudes: the purists' ordering of forms versus art nouveau's organic sensuousness; Behrens's ethic of form versus Olbrich's impulse to the formless.

Often these oppositions have been loaded with moral overtones. Adolf Loos' attack on the criminality of ornament masked his fear of chaos and sensual disorder. And De Stijl's insistence on elementary form was not only a return to some anachronistic purity but also a deliberate regression to a secure order.

So strong were these moral overtones that they even survived Dada's destructive attitudes and the surrealists' abandonment to the unconscious. Tzara's ironical contempt for order found few equivalents among architects too busy replacing the *système des Beaux-Arts* by the modern movement's own set of rules. In 1920 – despite the contradictory presence of Tzara, Richter, Ball, Duchamp, and Breton – Le Corbusier and his contemporaries chose the quiet and acceptable route of purism. Even in the early 1970s, the work of the architectural school circles, with their various brands of irony or self-indulgence, ran counter to the moral reminiscences of '68 radicalism, although both shared a dislike for established values.

Beyond such opposites lie the mythical shadows of Apollo's ethical and spiritual mindscapes versus Dionysius' erotic and sensual impulses. Architectural definitions, in their surgical precision, reinforce and amplify the impossible alternatives: on the one hand, architecture as a thing of the mind, a dematerialized or conceptual discipline with its typological and morphological variations, and on the other, architecture as an empirical event that concentrates on the senses, on the experience of space.

In the following paragraphs, I will attempt to show that today the pleasure of architecture may lie both inside *and* outside such oppositions – both in the dialectic *and* in the disintegration of the dialectic. However, the paradoxical nature of this theme is incompatible with the accepted, rational logic of classical argument; as Roland Barthes puts it in *The Pleasure of the Text*: "pleasure does not readily surrender to analysis," (Barthes, 1973)[1] hence there will be no theses, antitheses, and syntheses here. The text instead is composed of fragments that relate only loosely to one another. These fragments – *geometry*, *mask*, *bond*age, *excess*, *eroticism* – are all to be considered not only within the reality of ideas but also within the reality of the reader's spatial experience: a silent reality that cannot be put on paper.

FRAGMENT 1: A DOUBLE PLEASURE (REMINDER)

The pleasure of space: this cannot be put into words, it is unspoken. Approximately: it is a form of experience – the "presence of absence"; exhilarating differences between the plane and the cavern, between the street and your living-room; symmetries and dissymmetries emphasizing the spatial properties of my body: right and left, up and down. Taken to its extreme, the pleasure of space leans toward the poetics of the unconscious, to the edge of madness.

The pleasure of geometry and, by extension, the pleasure of order – that is, the pleasure of concepts: typical statements on architecture often read like the one in the first edition of the *Encyclopaedia Britannica* of 1773: "architecture, being governed by proportion, requires to be guided by rule and compass." That is, architecture is a "thing of the mind," a geometrical rather than a pictorial or experiential art, so the problem of architecture becomes a problem of ordinance – Doric or Corinthian order, axes or hierarchies, grids or regulating lines, types or models, walls or slabs – and, of course, the grammar and syntax of the architecture's sign become pretexts for sophisticated and pleasurable manipulation. Taken to its extreme, such manipulation leans toward a poetic of frozen signs, detached from reality, into a subtle and frozen pleasure of the mind.

Neither the pleasure of space nor the pleasure of geometry is (on its own) the pleasure of architecture.

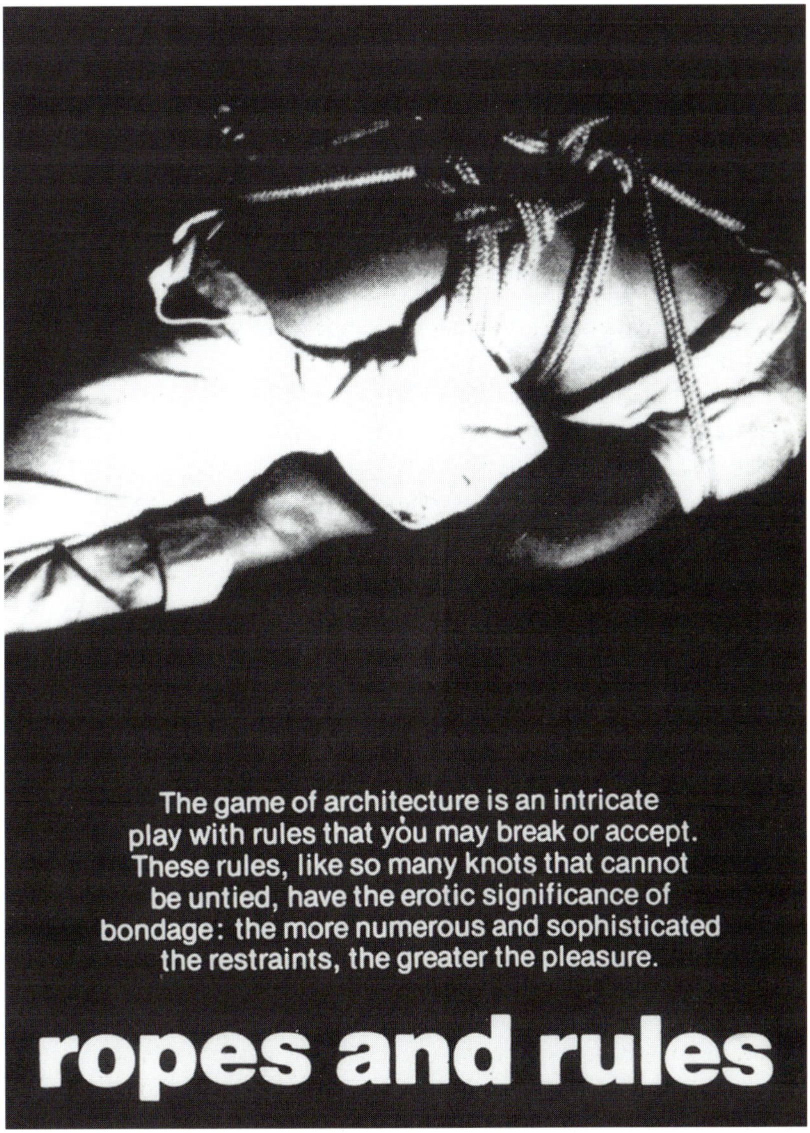

The game of architecture is an intricate play with rules that you may break or accept. These rules, like so many knots that cannot be untied, have the erotic significance of bondage: the more numerous and sophisticated the restraints, the greater the pleasure.

ropes and rules

Figure 10.1
Bernard Tschumi, knots.
From *Advertisements for Architecture*.
Photo: Bernard Tschumi.

FRAGMENT 2: GARDENS OF PLEASURE

In his *Observations sur l'architecture*, published in The Hague in 1765, Abbé Laugier suggested a dramatic deconstruction of architecture and its conventions. He wrote:

> Whoever knows how to design a park well will have no difficulty in tracing the plan for the building of a city according to its given area and situation. There must be regularity and fantasy, relationships and oppositions, and casual, unexpected elements that vary the scene; great order in the details, confusions, uproar, and tumult in the whole.
>
> (Laugier, 1765: 312–13)

Laugier's celebrated comments, together with the dreams of Capability Brown, William Kent, Lequeu, or Piranesi, were not merely a reaction to the Baroque period that preceded them. Rather, the deconstruction of architecture that they suggested was an early venture into the realm of pleasure, against the architectural order of time.

Take Stowe, for example. William Kent's park displays a subtle dialectic between organized landscape and architectural elements: the Egyptian pyramid, the Italian belvedere, the Saxon temple. But these "ruins" are to be read less as elements of a picturesque composition than as the dismantled elements of order. Yet, despite the apparent chaos, order is still present as a necessary counterpart to the sensuality of the winding streams. Without the signs of order, Kent's park would lose all reminder of "reason." Conversely, without the traces of sensuality – trees, hedges, valleys – only symbols would remain, in a silent and frozen fashion.

Gardens have had a strange fate. Their history has almost always anticipated the history of cities. The orchard grid of man's earliest agricultural achievements preceded the layout of the first military cities. The perspectives and diagonals of the Renaissance garden were applied to the squares and colonnades of Renaissance cities. Similarly, the romantic, picturesque parks of English empiricism pre-empted the crescents and arcades of the rich urban design tradition of nineteenth-century English cities.

Built exclusively for delight, gardens are like the earliest experiments in that part of architecture that is so difficult to express with words or drawings; pleasure and eroticism. Whether romantic or classical, gardens merge the sensual pleasure of space with the pleasure of reason, in a most *useless* manner.

FRAGMENT 3: PLEASURE AND NECESSITY

"Uselessness" is associated only reluctantly with architectural matters. Even at a time when pleasure found some theoretical backing ("delight" as well as "commodity" and "firmness"), utility always provided a practical justification. One example among many is Quatremère de Quincy's introduction to the entry on architecture in the *Encyclopédie méthodique* published in Paris in 1778. There you will read a definition of architecture that contends that

> amongst all the arts, those children of *pleasure and necessity*, with which man has
> formed a partnership in order to help him bear the pains of life and transmit his memory
> to future generations, it can certainly not be denied that architecture holds a most
> outstanding place. Considering it only from the point of view of *utility*, architecture
> surpasses all the arts. It provides for the salubrity of cities, guards the health of men,
> protects their property, and works only for the safety, repose and good order of civil life.
>
> (De Quincy, 1778: 109)

If De Quincy's statement was consistent with the architectural ideology of his time, then two hundred years later, the social necessity of architecture has been

Figure 10.2
Bernard Tschumi,
North–South covered
walk, Parc de la Villette,
Paris, 1989.
Photo: Andrew
Ballantyne.

reduced to dreams and nostalgic utopias. The "salubrity of cities" is now determined more by the logic of land economics, while the "good order of civil life" is more often than not the order of corporate markets.

As a result, most architectural endeavors seem caught in a hopeless dilemma. If, on the one hand, architects recognize the ideological and financial dependency of their work, they implicitly accept the constraints of society. If, on the other hand, they sanctuarize themselves, their architecture is accused of elitism. Of course, architecture will save its peculiar nature, but only wherever it questions itself, wherever it denies or disrupts the form that a conservative society expects of it. Once again, if there has lately been some reason to doubt the necessity of architecture, then *the necessity of architecture may well be its non-necessity*. Such totally gratuitous consumption of architecture is ironically *political* in that it disturbs established structures. It is also pleasurable.

FRAGMENT 4: METAPHOR OF ORDER-BONDAGE

Unlike the necessity of mere building, the non-necessity of architecture is undissociable from architectural histories, theories, and other precedents. These bonds enhance pleasure. The most excessive passion is always methodical. In such moments of intense desire, organization invades pleasure to such an extent that it is not always possible to distinguish the organizing constraints from the erotic matter. For example, the Marquis de Sade's heroes enjoyed confining their victims in the strictest convents before mistreating them according to rules carefully laid down with a precise and obsessive logic.

Similarly, the game of architecture is an intricate play with rules that one may accept or reject. Indifferently called *système des Beaux-Arts* or modern movement precepts, this pervasive network of binding laws entangles architectural design. These rules, like so many knots that cannot be untied, are generally a paralyzing constraint. When manipulated, however, they have the erotic significance of bondage. To differentiate between rules or ropes is irrelevant here. What matters is that there is no simple bondage technique: the more numerous and sophisticated the restraints, the greater the pleasure.

FRAGMENT 5: RATIONALITY

In *Architecture and Utopia*, the historian Manfredo Tafuri recalls how the rational excesses of Piranesi's prisons took Laugier's theoretical proposals of "order and tumult" to the extreme (Tafuri, 1973). The classical vocabulary of architecture is Piranesi's chosen form of bondage. Treating classical elements as fragmented and decaying symbols, Piranesi's architecture battles against itself, in that the obsessive rationality of building types was "sadistically" carried to the extremes of irrationality.

FRAGMENT 6: EROTICISM

We have seen that the ambiguous pleasure of rationality and irrational dissolution recalled erotic concerns. A word of warning may be necessary at this stage. Eroticism is used here as a theoretical concept, having little in common with fetishistic formalism and other sexual analogies prompted by the sight of erect skyscrapers or curvaceous doorways. Rather, eroticism is a subtle matter. "The pleasure of excess" requires consciousness as well as voluptuousness. Neither space nor concepts alone are erotic, but the junction between the two is.

The ultimate pleasure of architecture is that impossible moment when an architectural act, brought to excess, reveals both the traces of reason and the immediate experience of space.

FRAGMENT 7: METAPHOR OF SEDUCTION – THE MASK

There is rarely pleasure without seduction, or seduction without illusion. Consider: sometimes you wish to seduce, so you act in the most appropriate way in order to reach your ends. You wear a disguise. Conversely, you may wish to change roles and *be* seduced: you consent to someone else's disguise, you accept his or her assumed personality, for it gives you pleasure, even if you know that it dissimulates "something else."

Architecture is no different. It constantly plays the seducer. Its disguises are numerous: façades, arcades, squares, even architectural concepts become the artifacts of seduction. Like masks, they place a veil between what is assumed to be reality and its participants (you or I). So sometimes you desperately wish to read the reality behind the architectural mask. Soon, however, you realize that

Figure 10.3
Bernard Tschumi,
fragmentation, Parc de la
Villette, Paris, 1989.
Photo: Andrew
Ballantyne.

no single understanding is possible. Once you uncover that which lies behind the mask, it is only to discover another mask. The literal aspect of the disguise (the façade, the street) indicates other systems of knowledge, other ways to read the city: formal masks hide socioeconomic ones, while literal masks hide metaphorical ones. Each system of knowledge obscures another. Masks hide other masks, and each successive level of meaning confirms the impossibility of grasping reality.

Consciously aimed at seduction, masks are, of course, a category of reason. Yet they possess a double role: they simultaneously veil and unveil, simulate and dissimulate. Behind all masks lie dark and unconscious streams that cannot be dissociated from the pleasure of architecture. The mask may exalt appearances. Yet by its very presence, it says that, in the background, there is something else.

FRAGMENT 8: EXCESS

If the mask belongs to the universe of pleasure, pleasure itself is no simple masquerade. The danger of confusing the mask with the face is real enough never to grant refuge to parodies and nostalgia. The need for order is no justification for imitating past orders. Architecture is interesting only when it masters the art of disturbing illusions, creating breaking points that can start and stop at any time.

Certainly, the pleasure of architecture is granted when architecture fulfills one's spatial expectations as well as embodies architectural ideas, concepts, or archetypes with intelligence, invention, sophistication, irony. Yet there is also a special pleasure that results from conflicts: when the sensual pleasure of space conflicts with the pleasure of order.

The recent widespread fascination with the history and theory of architecture does not necessarily mean a return to blind obedience to past dogma. On the contrary, I would suggest that the ultimate pleasure of architecture lies in the most forbidden parts of the architectural act; where limits are perverted and prohibitions *transgressed*. The starting point of architecture is distortion – the dislocation of the universe that surrounds the architect. Yet such a nihilistic stance is only apparently so: we are not dealing with destruction here, but with excess, differences, and left-overs. *Exceeding* functionalist dogmas, semiotic systems, historical precedents, or formalized products of past social or economic constraints is not necessarily a matter of subversion but a matter of preserving the erotic capacity of architecture by disrupting the form that most conservative societies expect of it.

FRAGMENT 9: ARCHITECTURE OF PLEASURE

The architecture of pleasure lies where concept and experience of space abruptly coincide, where architectural fragments collide and merge in delight, where the culture of architecture is endlessly deconstructed and all rules are transgressed. No metaphorical paradise here, but discomfort and the unbalancing of expectations. Such architecture questions academic (and popular) assumptions, disturbs acquired tastes and fond architectural memories. Typologies, morphologies, spatial compressions, logical constructions – all dissolve. Such architecture is perverse because its real significance lies outside utility or purpose and ultimately is not even necessarily aimed at giving pleasure.

Figure 10.4
Bernard Tschumi,
overcome by sensuality.
From *Advertisements for
Architecture*.
Photo: Bernard Tschumi.

The architecture of pleasure depends on a particular feat, which is to keep architecture obsessed with itself in such an ambiguous fashion that it never surrenders to good conscience or parody, to debility or delirious neurosis.

FRAGMENT 10: ADVERTISEMENTS FOR ARCHITECTURE

There is no way to perform architecture in a book. Words and drawings can only produce paper space and not the experience of real space. By definition, paper space is imaginary: it is an image. Yet for those who do not build (whether for circumstantial or ideological reasons – it does not matter), it seems perfectly normal to be satisfied with the representation of those aspects of architecture that belong to mental constructs – to imagination. Such representations inevitably separate the sensual experience of a real space from the appreciation of rational concepts. Among other things, architecture is a function of both. And if either of these two criteria is removed, architecture loses something. It nevertheless seems strange that architects always have to castrate their architecture whenever they do not deal with real spaces. So the question remains: why should the paper space of a book or magazine replace an architectural space?

The answer does not lie in the inevitability of the media or in the way architecture is disseminated. Rather it may lie in the very nature of architecture.

Let's take an example. There are certain things that cannot be reached frontally. These things require analogies, metaphors, or roundabout routes in order to be grasped. For instance, it is through *language* that psychoanalysis uncovers the unconscious. Like a mask, language hints at something else behind itself. It may try to hide it, but it also implies it at the same time.

Architecture resembles a masked figure. It cannot easily be unveiled. It is always hiding: behind drawstrings, behind words, behind precepts, behind habits, behind technical constraints. Yet it is the very difficulty of uncovering architecture that makes it intensely desirable. This unveiling is part of the pleasure of architecture.

In a similar way, reality hides behind advertising. The usual function of advertisements – reproduced again and again, as opposed to the single architectural piece – is to trigger desire for something beyond the page itself. When removed from their customary endorsement of commodity values, advertisements are the ultimate magazine form, even if somehow ironically. And, as there are advertisements for architectural products, why not for the production (and reproduction) of *architecture*?

FRAGMENT 11: DESIRE/FRAGMENTS

There are numerous ways to equate architecture with language. Yet such equations often amount to a *reduction* and an *exclusion*. A reduction, in so far as these equations usually become distorted as soon as architecture tries to produce meaning (which meaning? whose meaning?), and thus end up reducing language to its mere combinatory logic. An exclusion, in so far as these equations generally omit some of the important findings made in Vienna at the beginning of the century, when language was first seen as a condition of the unconscious. Here, dreams were analyzed as language as well as through language; language was called "the main street of the unconscious." Generally speaking, it appeared as a series of *fragments* (the Freudian notion of fragments does not presuppose the breaking of an image, or of a totality, but the dialectical multiplicity of a process).

So, too, architecture when equated with language can only be read as a series of fragments that make up an architectural reality.

Fragments of architecture (bits of walls, of rooms, of streets, of ideas) are all one actually sees. These fragments are like beginnings without ends. There is always a split between fragments that are real and fragments that are virtual, between memory and fantasy. These splits have no existence other than being the passage from one fragment to another. They are relays rather than signs. They are traces. They are in-between.

It is not the clash between these contradictory fragments that counts but the movement between them. And this invisible movement is neither a part of language nor of structure ("language" or "structure" are words specific to a mode of reading architecture that does not fully apply in the context of pleasure); it is nothing but a constant and mobile relationship inside language itself.

How such fragments are organized matters little: volume, height, surface, degree of enclosure, or whatever. These fragments are like sentences between quotation marks. Yet they are not quotations. They simply melt into the work. (We are here at the opposite of the collage technique.) They may be excerpts from different discourses, but this only demonstrates that an architectural project is precisely where differences find an overall expression.

A film of the 1950s had a name for this movement between fragments. It was called desire. Yes, *A Streetcar Named Desire* perfectly simulated the movement toward something constantly missing, toward absence. Each setting, each fragment, was aimed at seduction but always dissolved at the moment it was approached. And then each time it would be substituted by another fragment. Desire was never seen. Yet it remained constant. The same goes for architecture.

In other words, architecture is not of interest because of its fragments and what they represent or do not represent. Nor does it consist in *exteriorizing*, through whatever forms, the unconscious desires of society or its architects. Nor is it a mere representation of those desires through some fantastic architectural image. Rather it can only act as a recipient in which your desires, my desires, can be reflected. Thus a piece of architecture is not architectural because it fulfills some utilitarian function, but because it sets in motion the operations of seduction and the unconscious.

A word of warning. Architecture may very well activate such motions, but it is not a dream (a stage where society's or the individual's unconscious desires can be fulfilled). It cannot satisfy your wildest fantasies, but it may exceed the limits set by them.

NOTE

1   Editor's note. The quotation is not actually from Barthes, but is a paraphrase from Richard Howard's introduction to the English edition, from a point at which he quotes Willa Cather ("a writer Barthes has never heard of") (Barthes, 1973, vi).

Bibliography

Adorno, T. (1964) *Jargon der Eigentlichkeit: Zur deutschen Ideologie*. Frankfurt: Suhrkamp. Translated by K. Tarnowski and F. Will (1973) *The Jargon of Authenticity*. London: Routledge.

Agrest, D., Conway, P. and Kanesweisman, L. (eds) (1996) *The Sex of Architecture*. New York: Abrams.

Alexander, C. (1979) *The Timeless Way of Building*. London: Oxford University Press.

Alexander, C. (1983) Christopher Alexander in debate with Peter Eisenman. In *HGSD News*, March/April 1983.

Alexander, C., Ishikawa, S. and Silverstein, M. (1977) *A Pattern Language: Towns, Building, Construction*. London: Oxford University Press.

Alexandre, A. (1895) L'Art nouveau. *Le Figaro*, 28 December.

Amato, J.A. (2000) *Dust: a History of the Small and the Invisible*. Berkeley: University of California Press.

Aragon, L. (1926) *Le paysan de Paris*. Paris: Gallimard. Translated by S.W. Taylor (1994) *Paris Peasant*. Boston, MA: Exact Change.

Arendt, H. (1958a) *The Human Condition*. Chicago: University of Chicago Press.

Arendt, H. (1958b) *The Origins of Totalitarianism*. New York: Harcourt.

d'Argencourt, L. (1977) *Puvis de Chavannes, 1824–1898*. Ottawa: National Gallery of Canada.

Ashfield, A. and Bolla, P. de (1996) *The Sublime: a Reader in British Eighteenth-Century Aesthetic Theory*. Cambridge: Cambridge University Press.

Bachelard, G. (1958) *La poétique de l'espace*. Paris: Presses Universitaires de France. Translated by M. Jolas (1969) *The Poetics of Space*. Boston: Beacon Press.

Baillie Scott, M.H. (1906) *Houses and Gardens*. London: G. Newnes.

Bajlon, J. (1999) As architecture. In *Architecture and Civilization*, M. Mitias (ed.). Amsterdam: Rodopi, pp. 95–106.

Ballantyne, A. (1993) The face in the cloud: anthropomorphism in architecture. In *The Routledge Companion to Architectural Thought*, B. Farmer and H.J. Louw (eds). London: Routledge, pp. 294–9.

Ballu, R. (1887) *Exposition de Tableaux, Pastels, Dessins par M. Puvis de Chavannes*. Paris: Galerie Durand-Ruel.

Banham, R. (1997) *A Critic Writes*, M. Banham, S. Lyall and C. Price (eds). Berkeley: University of California Press.

Barron, S. (ed.) (1991) *Degenerate Art: The Fate of the Avant-Garde in Nazi Germany*. Los Angeles: Los Angeles County Museum of Art.

Barthes, R. (1970) *L'Empire des signes*. Genève: Skira. Translated by R. Howard (1982) *Empire of Signs*. New York: Farrar, Strauss and Giroux.

Barthes, R. (1973) *Le plaisir du texte*. Paris: Seuil. Translated by R. Miller (1975) *The Pleasure of the Text*. New York: Farrar, Strauss and Giroux.

Bassuk, E.L. (1985) The rest cure: repetition or resolution of Victorian women's conflicts? In *The Female Body in Western Culture*, S.R. Suleiman (ed.). Cambridge, MA: Harvard University Press.

Baudrillard, J. (1985) *Simulacre et simulation*. Paris: Galilée. Translated by S.F. Glaser (1994) *Simulacra and Simulations*. Ann Arbor, MI: Michigan University Press.

Baudrillard, J. (1988) *The Ecstasy of Communication*. New York: Semiotext(e).

Becker, L. (1994) Aspects of art of the Third Reich. In *The Romantic Spirit in German Art 1790–1990*, K. Hartley, H.M. Hughes, P.-K. Schuster and W. Vaughan (eds). London: Hayward Gallery.

Bell, V. (1999) *Performativity and Belonging*. London: Sage.

Benedict, Saint (pre-547) Translated by J. McCann (1952) *The Rule of St Benedict*. London: Sheed and Ward.

Benedikt, M. (1987) *For an Architecture of Reality*. New York: Lumen Books.

Benedikt, M. (1991) *Deconstructing the Kimbell: an Essay on Meaning and Architecture*. New York: Lumen Books.

Benedikt, M. (1997–9) *Value*. 2 vols. Austin: University of Texas.

Benjamin, A. (2000) *Architectural Philosophy*. London: Athlone.

Benjamin, R. (1993) The decorative landscape, Fauvism and the Arabesque of observation. *The Art Bulletin*, 75, 2.

Bennington, G. (1991) *Jacques Derrida*. Chicago: University of Chicago Press.

Berleant, A. (1992) *The Aesthetics of Environment*. Philadelphia: Temple University Press.

Berleant, A. (1994) Architecture and the aesthetics of continuity. In *Philosophy and Architecture*, M. Mitias (ed.). Amsterdam: Rodopi, pp. 21–30.

Berleant, A. (1997) *Living in the Landscape: Toward an Aesthetics of Environment*. Lawrence, KS: University Press of Kansas.

Bermann, M. (1982) *All That Is Solid Melts Into Air: the Experience of Modernity*. New York: Simon and Schuster.

Berry, J.D. (1989) *The Legacy of Gottfried Semper: Studies in Späthistoricismus*. Unpublished PhD dissertation, Brown University.

Betsky, A (1995) *Building Sex: Men, Women, Architecture, and the Construction of Sexuality*. New York: Morrow.

Betsky, A. (1997) *Queer Space: Architecture and Same-Sex Desire*. New York: Morrow.

Bidoue, C. and Kouie, F.H.T. (1974) *Le Vécu des habitants dans leur logement à travers soixante entretiens libres*. Paris: CEREBE.

Blackburn, S. (2000) *Think*. Oxford: Oxford University Press.

Blanc, C. (1867) *Grammaire des arts du dessin*. Paris.

Bletter, R.H. (1974) On Martin Frohlich's Gottfried Semper. *Oppositions*, 4.

Bois, Y.-A. and Krauss, R.E. (1997) *Formless: A User's Guide*. New York: Zone.

Bonnat, L. (1895) *La Plume*, 6, 15 January.

Bötticher, K. (1844) *Die Tektonik der Hellenen*. 2 vols, 1844, 1852. Potsdam: F. Riegel. Second edn (1869). Berlin: Ernst and Korn.

Bötticher, K. (1846) Das Prinzip der hellenischen und germanischen Bauweise hinsichtlich der Übertragung in die Bauweise unserer Tage. In *Allemeine Bauzeitung* 11 [address delivered at the Schinkelfest] translated by W. Herrmann. The Principles of the Hellenic and German Ways of Building, with Regard to their Application to Our Present Way of Building. In (1992) *In What Style Should We Build?: The German Debate on Architectural Style*, W. Herrmann (ed.). Santa Monica: Getty Center.

Bouveret, L. (1890) *La Neurasthénie*. Paris: Baillère.

Boylesve, R. (1896) Les Arts: salon de l'art nouveau, Galerie Bing. In *L'Ermitage*. Paris.

Brent, J. (1998) *Charles Sanders Peirce: A Life*. Second edn. Bloomington: Indiana University Press.

Brunet, N. (1979) Un Pont vers l'acculturation. Ile de Noirmoutiers. Unpublished dissertation (DEA Ethnologie), Université de Paris VII.

Bryden, I. and Floyd, J. (1999) *Domestic Space: Reading the Nineteenth-Century Interior*. Manchester: Manchester University Press.

Burke, E. (1757) *A Philosophical Enquiry into the Origin of our Ideas of the Sublime and Beautiful*. London.

Busch, A. (1999) *Geography of Home: Writings on Where We Live*. Princeton, NJ: Princeton Architectural Press.

Canetti, E. (1976) Hitler, according to Speer. In *Das Gewissen der Worte*. München: Carl Hanser. Translated by J. Neugroschel (1986) *The Conscience of Words*. London: Seabury Press/André Deutsh.

Carlson, A. (1994) Existence, location, and function: the appreciation of architecture. In *Philosophy and Architecture*, M. Mitias (ed.). Amsterdam: Rodopi, pp. 141–64.

Carlson, A. (1999) The aesthetic appreciation of everyday architecture. In *Architecture and Civilization*, M. Mitias (ed.). Amsterdam: Rodopi, pp. 107–21

Carlson, A. (2000) *Aesthetics and the Environment: the Appreciation of Nature, Art and Architecture*. London: Routledge.

Casey, E.S. (1993) *Getting Back into Place: Toward a Renewed Understanding of the Place-World*. Bloomington: Indiana University Press.

Certeau, M. de (1976) Délires et délices de Jérôme Bosch. *Traverses*, 5–6, 37–54.

Certeau, M. de (1980) *L'Invention du quotidian*, vol. 1, *Arts de faire*. Paris: Union Général des Editions. Translated by S. Rendall (1984) *The Practice of Everyday Life*. Berkeley: University of California Press.

Chatwin, B. (1987) *The Songlines*. London: Jonathan Cape.

Chipp, H.B. (1968) *Theories of Modern Art*. Berkeley: University of California Press.

Clement, C. (1986) *The Newly Born Woman*. Translated by B. Wing. Minneapolis, MN: University of Minnesota Press.

Coleman, A. (1990) *Utopia on Trial*. London: Hilary Shipman.

Collingwood, R.G. (1938) *The Principles of Art*. Oxford: Clarendon.

Colomina, B. (ed.) (1992) *Sexuality and Space*. Princeton, NJ: Princeton Architectural Press.

Colquhoun, A. (1988) Postmodernism and structuralism: a retrospective glance. *Assemblage*, 5.

Colvin, H. (1995) *A Biographical Dictionary of British Architects 1600–1840*. Third edn. New Haven: Yale University Press.

Compton-Burnett, I. (1947) *Manservant and Maidservant*. London: Victor Gollancz.

Compton-Burnett, I. (1953) *The Present and the Past*. London: Victor Gollancz.

Cook, C. (1881) *The House Beautiful*. New York: Scribner.

Cook, J.W. and Klotz, H. (1973) *Conversations with Architects*. New York: Praeger.

Crinson, M. and Lubbock, J. (1994) *Architecture: Art or Profession? Three Hundred Years of Architectural Education in Britain*. Manchester: Manchester University Press.

Curtis, W. (1982) *Modern Architecture Since 1900*. London: Phaidon.

Dallmayr, F. (1993) *The Other Heidegger*. Ithaca, NY: Cornell University Press.

Danto, A. (1981) *The Transfiguration of the Commonplace: a Philosophy of Art*. Cambridge, MA: Harvard University Press.

Davidson, C. (ed.) (1997) *Anybody*. Cambridge, MA: MIT Press.

Davis, S. (1994) Is architecture art? In *Philosophy and Architecture*, M. Mitias (ed.). Amsterdam: Rodopi, pp. 31–47.

Decker, R.T. (1994) Tactility and imagination: considerations of aesthetic experience in architecture. In *Philosophy and Architecture*, M. Mitias (ed.). Amsterdam: Rodopi, pp. 203–19.

Deleuze, G. (1953) *Empirisme et subjectivité. Essai sur la nature humaine selon Hume*. Paris: Presses Universitaires de France. Translated by C. Boundas (1991) *Empiricism and Subjectivity, an Essay on Hume's Theory of Human Nature*. New York: Columbia University Press.

Deleuze, G. (1962) *Nietzsche et la philosophie*. Paris: Presses Universitaires de France. Translated by H. Tomlinson (1983) *Nietzsche and Philosophy*. London: Athlone.

Deleuze, G. (1985) *Cinema 2: l'image-temps*. Paris: Minuit. Translated by H. Tomlinson and R. Galeta (1989) *Cinema 2*. London: Athlone.

Deleuze, G. and Foucault, M. (1972) Les intellectuels et le pouvoir. *L'Arc*, 49, 3–10. Translated by D.F. Bouchard and S. Simon (1977) Intellectuals and power. In Foucault, M. (1977) *Language, Counter-Memory, Practice*, D.F. Bouchard (ed.). Ithaca, NY: Cornell University Press, pp. 205–17.

Deleuze, G. and Guattari, F. (1972) *L'Anti-Oedipe*. Paris: Minuit. Translated by R. Hurley, M. Seem and H.R. Lane (1977) *Anti-Oedipus: Capitalism and Schizophrenia*. New York: Viking.

Deleuze, G. and Guattari, F. (1991) *Qu'est-ce que la philosophie?* Paris: Minuit. Translated by H. Tomlinson and G. Burchill (1994) *What is Philosophy?* London: Verso.

De Quincey, T. (1863) The last days of Immanuel Kant. In *De Quincey's Works*, 16 vols. Edinburgh. 3, 99–166.

Derrida, J. (1982) White mythology: metaphor in the context of philosophy. In *Margins of Philosophy*. Chicago: Chicago University Press.

Derrida, J. (1986) Point de folie – maintenant l'architecture. *AA Files*, 12.

Derrida, J. (1989) "Jacques Derrida, In Discussion with Christopher Norris," *Architectural Design*, 58, 1/2.

Descombes, V. (1987) *Proust: philosophie du roman*. Paris: Minuit. Translated by C.C. Macksey (1992) *Proust: Philosophy of the Novel*. Stanford, CA: Stanford University Press.

Diffey, T.J. (1999) Architecture, art and works of art. In *Architecture and Civilization*, M. Mitias (ed.). Amsterdam: Rodopi, pp. 1–23.

Disraeli, B. (1845) *Sybil; or, The Two Nations*. 3 vols. London.

Dixon, R. (1995) *The Baumgarten Corruption: From Sense to Nonsense in Art and Philosophy*. London: Pluto.

Donougho, M. (1994) Spaced out or folded in? Trends in architectural choreography. In *Philosophy and Architecture*, M. Mitias (ed.). Amsterdam: Rodopi, pp. 165–82.

Douglas, M. (1966) *Purity and Danger*. London: Routledge.

Dovey, K. (1999) *Framing Places: Mediating Power in Built Form*. London: Routledge.

Drinka, G.F. (1984) *The Birth of Neurosis: Myth, Malady, and the Victorians*. New York: Simon and Schuster.

Dumézil, G. (1969) *Idées romaines*. Paris: Gallimard.

Dutton, T.A. and Mann, L.H. (eds) (1999) *Reconstructing Architecture: Critical Discourses and Social Practices*. Minneapolis: University of Minnesota Press.

Eisenman, P. (1984) The end of the classical: the end of the beginning, the end of the end. *Perspecta: The Yale Architectural Journal*, 21.

Eisenman, P. (1987a) *Houses of Cards*. London: Oxford University Press.

Eisenman, P. (1987b) Architecture and the problem of the rhetorical figure. *a + u*, 07.

Eisenman, P. (1989) En terror firma: in trails of grotextes. *Architectural Design*, 58, 1/2.

Eliot, T.S. (1920) Tradition and the individual talent. In *The Sacred Wood*. London: Methuen.

Engels, F. (1845) *The Condition of the Working Classes in England in 1844*. Reprint 1973. Moscow: Progress.

Fabbri, P. (1968) Considerations sur la proxémique. *Langages*, 10, 65–75.

Falke, J. von (1879) *Art in the House: Historical, Critical, and Aesthetical Studies on the Decoration and Furnishing of the Dwelling*. Boston: Prang.

Farias, V. (1987) *Heidegger et le Nazism*. Paris: Verdier. Translated by P. Burrell, D. di Benardi and G. Ricci (1989) *Heidegger and Nazism*. Philadephia: Temple University Press.

Farmer, B. and Louw, H.J. (1993) *The Routledge Companion to Architectural Thought*, B. Farmer and H.J. Louw (eds). London: Routledge.

Feher, M. (ed.) (1989) *Fragments for a History of the Human Body*. 3 vols. Cambridge, MA: MIT Press.

Fenner, D. (1999) Pure architecture. In *Architecture and Civilization*, M. Mitias (ed.). Amsterdam: Rodopi, pp. 43–57.

Fielding, H. (1743) *The Life of Mr. Jonathan Wild, The Great*. London.

Fish, S. (1998) Truth and toilets: pragmatism and the practices of life. In *The Revival of Pragmatism: New Essays on Social Thought, Law, and Culture*, M. Dickstein (ed.). Durham: Duke University Press, pp. 418–33.

Fisher, S. (1999) Analytic philosophy of architecture: a course. *Newsletter of the American Society for Aesthetics*, 19, 1–6.

Fisher, T.R. (2000) *In the Scheme of Things: Alternative Thinking on the Practice of Architecture*. Minneapolis: Minnesota University Press.

Foucault, M. (1972) Preface. In *Anti-Oedipus*, G. Deleuze and F. Guattari (eds). Paris: Minuit.

Foucault, M. (1977) *Language, Counter-Memory, Practice*. Ithaca, NY: Cornell University Press.

Frampton, K. (1995) *Studies in Tectonic Culture: the Poetics of Construction*. Cambridge, MA: MIT Press.

Frank, S. (1994) *Peter Eisenman's House VI: The Client's Response*. New York: Witney.

Freud, S. (1985) *Art and Literature*. Translated by J. Strachey. Penguin Freud Library, 14. Harmondsworth: Penguin.

Frontisi-Ducroux, F. (1975) *Dédale. Mythologie de l'artisan en Grèce ancienne*. Paris: Maspero.

Gale, R.M. (1999) *The Divided Self of William James*. Cambridge: Cambridge University Press.

Garreau, J. (1991) *Edge City: Life on the New Frontier*. New York: Doubleday.

Gerdeil, O. (1901) L'intérieur. *L'Art decoratif*, 3.

Germain, A. (1891a) Le paysage décoratif. *L'Ermitage*, 3.

Germain, A. (1891b) Théorie des déformateurs: exposé et refutation. *La Plume*, 3.

Germain, A. (1902) *Le Sentiment de l'art et sa formation par l'étude des oeuvres*. Paris: Bloud et Cie.

Giedion, S. (1941) *Space, Time and Architecture: The Growth of a New Tradition*. Cambridge, MA: Harvard University Press.

Ginsberg, R. (1994) Aesthetics in Hiroshima. In *Architecture and Civilization*, M. Mitias (ed.). Amsterdam: Rodopi, pp. 221–34.

Glymour, C. (1992) *Thinking Things Through: An Introduction to Philosophical Issues and Achievements*. Cambridge, MA: MIT Press.

Goldblatt, D. (1996) The impossibility of the Ideal. *Columbus Alive*, November 13–19.

Goldblatt, D. and Brown L.B. (eds) (1997) *Aesthetics: A Reader in Philosophy of the Arts*. Upper Saddle River, NJ: Prentice Hall.

Goodman, N. (1976) *Languages of Art*. Indianapolis: Hackett.

Goodman, N. (1978) *Ways of Worldmaking*. Indianapolis: Hackett.

Goodman, N. (1985) How buildings mean. *Critical Inquiry*, June, 642–53.

Gorst, T. (1995) *The Buildings Around Us*. London: Spon.

Graham, G. (1989) Art and architecture. *The British Journal of Aethetics*, 29.

Gravagnuolo, B. (1987) Gottfried Semper, architetto e teorico. In *Gottfried Semper: architettura, arte e scienza*. Naples.

Griffin, S. (1978) *Woman and Nature: The Roaring Inside Her*. New York: Harper and Row.

Guattari, F. (1984) Translated by R. Sheed, The micro-politics of fascism. In *Molecular Revolution*. Harmondsworth: Penguin.

Gutting, G. (1999) *Pragmatic Liberalism and the Critique of Modernity*. Cambridge: Cambridge University Press.

Habermas, J. (1985) *Der philosophische Diskurs der Moderne*. Translated by F. Lawrence. (1987) *The Philosophical Discourse of Modernity*. Cambridge, MA: MIT Press.

Hacking, I. (1995) *Rewriting the Soul: Multiple Personality and the Sciences of Memory*. Princeton, NJ: Princeton University Press.

Haldane, J. (1999) Form, meaning and value. *The Journal of Architecture*, 4, 9–20.

Hall, E.T. (1963) Proxemics: the study of man's spatial relations. In *Man's Image in Medicine and Anthropology*, I. Gladston (ed.). New York: International Universities Press.

Hallays, A. (1896) Au jour le jour. *Le Journal des Débats*, 12 January.

Hammad, M. (1973) *Groupe 107: Sémiotique de l'espace*. Paris: DGRST.

Harpham, G.G. (1987) *The Ascetic Imperative in Culture and Criticism*. Chicago: University of Chicago Press.

Harries, K. (1997) *The Ethical Function of Architecture*. Cambridge, MA: MIT Press.

Havel, V. (1992) Translated by P. Wilson. *Summer Meditations*. London: Faber.

Hays, K.M. (ed.) (1998) *Architecture Theory Since 1968*. Cambridge, MA: MIT Press.

Hegel, G.W.F. (1835–8) Translated by T.M. Knox (1975) *Hegel's Aesthetics: Lectures on Fine Art*. 2 vols. Oxford: Oxford University Press.

Heidegger, M. (1926) *Sein und Zeit*. Tübingen: Max Niemeyer. Translated by J. Macquarrie and E. Robinson (1962) *Being and Time*. Oxford: Blackwell.

Heidegger, M. (1933) The self-assertion of the German university. In *The Heidegger Controversy*, R. Wolin (ed.). Cambridge, MA: MIT Press, pp. 29–39.

Heidegger, M. (1950) *Der Ursprung des Kunstwerkes*. Frankfurt: Klosterman. Translated by A. Hofstadter (1971) The origin of the work of art. In *Poetry, Language, Thought*. New York: Harper and Row, pp. 15–87. The same translation is also collected in Heidegger, *Basic Writings, op. cit.* The ideas were in place earlier than the initial date of publication however – Heidegger tells us that the first version was a lecture given at Freiburg in 1935, repeated at Zürich in 1936. See Heidegger, *Poetry, Language, Thought*, p. xxiii.

Heidegger, M. (1954) Bauen Wohnen Denken. In *Vorträge und Aufsätze*. Pfullingen: Neske. Translated by A. Hofstadter (1971) Building, dwelling, thinking. In *Poetry, Language, Thought*. New York: Harper and Row, pp. 143–61. Page references to this edition. The same translation is also in M. Heidegger (1993) *Basic Writings*, D.F. Krell (ed.). London: Routledge, pp. 347–63; and in N. Leach, (ed.) (1997) *Rethinking Architecture: A Reader in Cultural Theory*. London: Routledge, pp. 100–9.

Heidegger, M. (1966) Translated by J.M. Anderson and E.H. Freund. *Discourse on Thinking*. New York: Harper and Row.

Heidegger, M. (1971a) Translated by T.F. O'Meara. Homeland. *Listening*, 6, 231–8.

Heidegger, M. (1971b) *Poetry, Language, Thought*. A. Hofstadter (ed.). New York: Harper and Row.

Heidegger, M. (1981) Schneeberger. In *Heidegger: The Man and the Thinker*, T. Sheehan (ed.). Chicago: Precedent Publishing.

Heidegger, M. (1993) Schlageter. In *The Heidegger Controversy*, R. Wolin (ed.). Cambridge, MA: MIT Press, p. 41.

Heidegger, M. (1993) *Basic Writings*. D.F. Krell (ed.). London: Routledge.

Herbert, R. (1968) *Neo-Impressionism*. New York: Solomon R. Guggenheim Foundation.

Herrmann, W. (1984) *Gottfried Semper; In Search of Architecture*. Cambridge, MA: MIT Press.

Hersey, G. (1988) *The Lost Meaning of Classical Architecture*. Cambridge, MA: MIT Press.

Hersey, G. (1999) *The Monumental Impulse: Architecture's Biological Roots*. Cambridge, MA: MIT Press.

Hill, L. (1993) *Marguerit Duras: Apocalyptic Desires*. London: Routledge.

Hill, R. (2000) *Designs and Their Consequences*. New Haven: Yale University Press.

Horace [Quintus Horatius Flaccus] (65 BC) Epodes. Translated by C.E. Passage (1983) *The Complete Works of Horace*. New York: F. Ungar.

Horsfield, M. (1997) *Biting the Dust: The Joys of Housework*. London: Fourth Estate.

Hume, D. (1777a) Appendix I, Enquiry concerning the Principles of Morals. In *Enquiries Concerning Human Understanding and Concerning the Principles of Morals*. L.A. Selby-Bigge (ed.). (1975) Oxford: Oxford University Press, pp. 283–94.

Hume, D. (1777b) Of the standard of taste. In *Essays Moral, Political and Literary*. E. Miller (ed.) (1985). Indianapolis: Liberty Fund, pp. 226–49.

Hume, D. (1777c) The sceptic. In *Essays Moral, Political and Literary*. E. Miller (ed.) (1985). Indianapolis: Liberty Fund, pp. 159–80.

Huysmans, J.-K. (1884) *A rebours*. Translated by R. Baldick (1959) *Against Nature*. Harmondsworth: Penguin.

James, W. (1907) What pragmatism means. In *Pragmatism: A New Name for Some Old Ways of Thinking*. New York: Longmans Green. Reprinted in *Pragmatism and The Meaning of Truth*. (1975). Cambridge, MA: Harvard University Press, pp. 27–44.

Jameson, F. (1994) *The Seeds of Time*. New York: Columbia University Press.

Jameson, F. (1999) History lessons. In *Architecture and Revolution*, N. Leach (ed.). London: Routledge.

Janet, P. (1928) *L'Evolution de la mémoire et la notion de temps*. Paris: Chahine.

Järvinen, J. (1992) *Reference and Meaning in Architecture*. Tampere, Finland: Datutop.

Jencks, C. (1973) *Modern Movements in Architecture*. Harmondsworth: Penguin.

Jencks, C. (1991) *The Language of Postmodern Architecture*. Sixth edn. London: Academy Editions.

Jones, E.M. (1995) *Living Machines: Bauhaus Architecture as Sexual Ideology*. San Francisco: Ignatius Press.

Jormakka, K. (1991) *Constructing Architecture: Notes on Theory and Criticism in Architecture and the Arts*. Tampere, Finland: Datutop.

Joze, V. (1895) Le Féminisme et le bon sense. *La Plume*, 6, 15 September.

Kahn, L. (1972) An architect speaks his mind. Interview with Beverly Russell. In *Louis I. Kahn: Writings, Lectures, Interviews*, A. Latour (ed.). New York: Rizzoli, pp. 293–7.

Kaplan, C. (1987) Deterritorializations: the rewriting of home and exile in western feminist discourse. *Cultural Critique*, 6, 187–98.

Kaprow, A. (1993) *Essays on the Blurring of Art and Life*. Berkeley: University of California Press.

Kauffmann, F.A. (1941) *Die neue Deutsche Malerei*. In series *Schriftenreihe der Deutschen Informationsstelle, Das Deutschland der Gegenwart*, 11, Berlin. Translated by L. Becker (1994) Aspects of art of the Third Reich. In *The Romantic Spirit in German Art 1790–1990*, K. Hartley, H.M. Hughes, P.-K. Schuster and W. Vaughan (eds). London: Hayward Gallery.

Kimble, G.T.H. (1938) *Geography in the Middle Ages*. London: Methuen.

Kipnis, J. (1986) *Investigations in Architecture: Eisenman Studios at the GSD: 1983–1985*. Cambridge, MA: Harvard University Graduate School of Design.

Koolhaas, R., Office for Metropolitan Architecture and Mau, B. (1995) *S, M, L, XL*, J. Sigler (ed.). New York: Monacelli.

Kostka, A. and Wohlfarth, I. (eds) (1999) *Nietzsche and "An Architecture of Our Minds"*. Santa Monica: Getty Center.

Kostof, S. (1985) *A History of Architecture: Settings and Rituals*. New York: Oxford University Press.

Kristeva, J. (1993) The soul and the image. In *Les Nouvelles maladies de l'âme*. Paris: Fayard. Translated by R. Guberman. (1995) *New Maladies of the Soul*. New York: Columbia University Press, pp. 3–26.

Lacan, J. (1982) Translated by J. Rose. *Feminine Sexuality: Jacques Lacan and the école freudienne*, J. Mitchell and J. Rose (eds). New York: W.W. Norton.

Lacoue-Labarthe, P. (1990) *Heidigger, Art and Politics*. Translated by C. Turner. Oxford: Blackwell.

Lacoue-Labarthe, P. (1993) Translated by C. Turner, *Heidegger, Art and Politics*. Oxford: Blackwell.

Ladurie, E. Le R. (1979) *Le Carnaval de Romans*. Paris: Gallimard. Translated by M. Fenney (1979) *The Carnival at Romans*. New York: George Braziller.

Lahr, J. (1978) *Prick Up Your Ears*. London: Methuen.

Langer, S. (1953) *Form and Feeling*. New York: Scribner.

Last, N. (1998) Transgressions and inhabitations: Wittgensteinian spatial practices between architecture and philosophy. *Assemblage*, 35, 36–47.

Laugier, M.A. (1753) *Essai sur l'architecture*. Paris: Translated by W. Herrmann and A. Herrmann (1977) *An Essay on Architecture*. Los Angeles: Hennessey and Ingalls.

Laugier, M.A. (1765) *Observations sur l'architecture*. The Hague.

Laurent, E. (1895) *La Neurasthénie et son traitement*. Paris: Maloine.

Lavin, S. (1992) *Quatremère de Quincy and the Invention of a Modern Language of Architecture*. Cambridge, MA: MIT Press.

Lawson, B. (1980) *How Designers Think*. London: Architectural Press.

Lawson, N. (2000) *How to be a Domestic Goddess*. London: Chatto and Windus.

Leach, N. (ed.) (1997) *Rethinking Architecture: A Reader in Cultural Theory*. London: Routledge.

Leach, N. (1998) The dark side of the *domus*. *The Journal of Architecture*, 3, 1, 31–42.

Leach, N. (1999a) *The Anaesthetics of Architecture*. Cambridge, MA: MIT Press.

Leach, N. (1999b) *Architecture and Revolution*. London: Routledge.

Leach, N. (2000) Forget Heidegger. *Scroope* 12, 50–9.

Leddy, T. (1994) Dialogical architecture. In *Philosophy and Architecture*, M. Mitias (ed.). Amsterdam: Rodopi, pp. 183–202.

Leddy, T. (1999) Architecture as art. In *Architecture and Civilization*, M. Mitias (ed.). Amsterdam: Rodopi, pp. 25–42.

Levillain, F. (1891) *La Neurasthénie, Maladie de Beard*. Paris: Maloine.

Levine, N (1996) *The Architecture of Frank Lloyd Wright*. Princeton, NJ: Princeton University Press.

Lewis, D. (1999) The aesthetic experience of ambiguity: Athenian acropolis. In *Architecture and Civilization*, M. Mitias (ed.). Amsterdam: Rodopi, pp. 142–64.

Libeskind, D. (1999) Traces of the unborn. In *Architecture and Revolution*, N. Leach (ed.). London: Routledge, pp. 127–9.

Linde, C. and Labov, W. (1975) Spatial networks as a site for the study of language and thought. *Language*, 51, 924–39.

Loos, A. (1929) Translated by M. Mitchell (1998) Ornament and crime. In *Ornament and Crime: Selected Essays*. Riverside, CA: Ariadne Press.

Lotman, I. [note: Lotman's first name is variously transliterated as Iouri, Jüri and Youri] (1973) *La Structure du texte artistique*. Paris: Gallimard. Translated by R. Vroon (1977) *The Structure of the Artistic Text*. Ann Arbor: University of Michigan.

Lotman, I. and Ouspenski, B.A. (eds) (1976) Ecole de Tartu: *Travaux sur les systèmes de signes*. Paris: Presses Universitaires de France. [See also Uspenskii.]

Lutz, T. (1991) *American Nervousness, 1903: An Anecdotal History*. Ithaca: Cornell University Press.

Lyons, J. (1977) *Semantics*. Cambridge: Cambridge University Press.

Lyotard, J.-F. (1988) *L'inhumain: causeries sur le temps*. Paris: Galilée. Translated by G. Bennington and R. Bowlby (1991) *The Inhuman: Reflections on Time*. Cambridge: Polity.

Lyotard, J.-F. (1990) Translated by A. Michel and M. Roberts. *Heidegger and 'the jews'*. Minneapolis: Minnesota University Press.

Mallgrave, H.F. (1985) Gustave Klemm and Gottfried Semper. *Res*, Spring.

Mallgrave, H.F. (1996) *Gottfried Semper: Architect of the Nineteenth Century*. New Haven: Yale University Press.

Marin, L. (1973) *Utopiques: Jeux d'espaces*. Paris: Minuit.

Marlais, M. (1992) *Conservative Echoes in Fin-de-Siècle Parisian Art Criticism*. University Park: Pennsylvania State University Press.

Marx, R. (1897) Cartons d'artistes: Puvis de Chavannes. *L'Image*, July.

Masheck, J. (1975) Embalmed objects: design at the modern. Appendix: art as rest and rehabilitation. *Artforum*, 13, 6, 49–55.

Masheck, J. (1976) The carpet paradigm: critical prolegomena to a theory of flatness. *Arts Magazine*, 51, 1, 82–109.

Masheck, J. (1993) Tired tropes: cathedral versus bicycle shed; 'duck' versus 'decorated shed'. In *Building-Art: Modern Architecture Under Cultural Construction*. Cambridge: Cambridge University Press, pp. 184–221.

Matisse, H. (1908) Notes d'un peintre. *La Grande Revue*, LII, 24, 731–45. Translated by J. Flam (1973) *Matisse on Art*. New York: Phaidon.

Matravers, D. (1998) *Art and Emotion*. Oxford: Clarendon Press.

Matravers, D. (1999) Revising principles of architecture. *The Journal of Architecture*, 4, 39–46.

McAnn, R. (1999) Receptivity to the sensuous: architecture as 'wild being'. In

Architecture and Civilization, M. Mitias (ed.). Amsterdam: Rodopi, pp. 123–41.

McCorquodale, D., Rüedi, K. and Wigglesworth, S. (eds) (1996) *Desiring Practices: Architecture, Gender and the Interdisciplinary*. London: Black Dog.

McHugh, K.A. (1999) *American Domesticity: From How-To Manual to Hollywood Melodrama*. Oxford: Oxford University Press.

McMillan, J.C. (1981) *Housewife or Harlot: The Place of Women in French Society, 1870–1940*. New York: St Martin's Press.

Médam, A. and Augoyard, J.-F. (1976) *Situations et façons d'habiter*. Paris: ESA.

Meier-Graefe, J. (1908) Translated by F. Simmonds and G.W. Chrystal. *Modern Art*, 2 vols. London: Heinemann.

Meiss, P. von (1990) *Elements of Architecture: From Form to Place*. London: Van Nostrand Reinhold.

Merleau-Ponty, M. (1945) *Phénoménologie de la perception*. Paris: Gallimard. Translated by C. Smith (1962) *Phenomenology of Perception*. London: Routledge.

Michelet, J. (n.d.) *La Sorcière*. Paris: Calman-Lévy.

Miller, G.A. and Johnson-Laird, P.N. (1976) *Language and Perception*. Cambridge, MA: Harvard University Press.

Mitias, M. (1994a) Expression in architecture. In *Philosophy and Architecture*, M. Mitias (ed.). Amsterdam: Rodopi, pp. 87–107.

Mitias, M. (1994b) Is meaning in architecture a myth? A response to Ralf Weber. In *Philosophy and Architecture*, M. Mitias (ed.). Amsterdam: Rodopi, pp. 121–38.

Mitias, M. (1999) Is architecture an art of representation? In *Architecture and Civilization*, M. Mitias (ed.). Amsterdam: Rodopi, pp. 59–79.

Moneo, R. (1978) On typology. *Oppositions*, 13.

Monk, R. (1991) *Wittgenstein: The Duty of Genius*. London: Vintage.

Montaigne, M. De (1588) *Essais*. Translated by M.A. Screech (1991) *The Complete Essays*. Harmondsworth: Penguin.

Morgenstern, C. (1965) Der Lattenzaum. In *Gesammelte Werke*. München: Piper.

Mugerauer, R. (1997). Homo Viator Stigmatized. In *Building, Dwelling, Drifting*, S. Cairns and P. Goad (eds). Conference proceedings, University of Melbourne.

Muthesius, H. (1902) *Stilarchitektur und Baukunst: Wandlungen der Architektur im XIX. Jahrhundert und ihr heutiger Standpunkt*. Mülheim an der Ruhr: K. Schimmelpfeng. Translated by S. Anderson (1994) *Style-architecture and Building-Art: Transformations of Architecture in the Nineteenth Century and its Present Condition*. Santa Monica: Getty Center.

Nagel, T. (1986) *The View From Nowhere*. Oxford: Oxford University Press.

Nagel, T. (1995) *Other Minds*. Oxford: Oxford University Press.

Nast, H.J. and Pile, S. (eds) (1998) *Places Through the Body*. London: Routledge.

Nava, L.E. (1998) *Diogenes of Sinope: The Man in the Tub*. Westport, CT: Greenwood.

Neff, J.H. (1975). Matisse and Decoration: An Introduction. *Arts Magazine*, 49, 9, May.

Nehemas, A. (1998) *The Art of Living: Socratic Reflections from Plato to Foucault*. Berkeley: University of California Press.

Nesbit, K. (ed.) (1996) *Theorizing a New Agenda for Architecture*. Princeton, NJ: Princeton Architectural Press.

Neumeyer, F. (1993) Iron and stone: the architecture of the großstadt. In *Otto Wagner: Reflections on the Raiment of Modernity*, H.F. Mallgrave (ed.). Santa Monica: Getty Center, pp. 115–53.

Nietzsche, F. (1872) *Die Geburt der Tragödie aus dem Geiste der Musik*. Leipzig: E.W. Fritzsch. 1886 edn, *Die Geburt der Tragödie. Oder: Griechenthum und Pessimismus*. Translated by F. Golffing (1956) *The Birth of Tragedy, or: Hellenism and Pessimism*. New York: Doubleday.

Nietzsche, F. (1882) *Die Fröhliche Wissenschaft*. Translated by W. Kaufmann (1974) *The Gay Science*. New York: Random House.

Nietzsche, F. (1889) *Götzen-Dämmerung, oder: Wie man mit dem Hammer philosophirt*. Leipzig: Naumann. Translated by R.J. Hollingdale (1968) *Twilight of the Idols, or: How to Philosophize with a Hammer*. Harmondsworth: Penguin.

Nietzsche, F. (1901) *Der Wille zur Macht: Versuch einer Umwerthung aller Werthe*. Leipzig: Naumann. Translated by W. Kaufman and R.J. Hollingdale (1968) *The Will To Power: Attempt at a Revaluation of All Values*. New York: Vintage.

Norberg-Schulz, C. (1979) *Genius Loci – paesaggio, ambiente, architettura*. Milan: Electa. Translated (1980) *Genius Loci: Towards a Phenomenology of Architecture*. New York: Rizzoli.

Norman, D.A. (1998) *The Design of Everyday Things*. New York: Doubleday.

Novitz, D. (1994) Architectural brilliance and the constraints of time. In *Philosophy and Architecture*, M. Mitias (ed.). Amsterdam: Rodopi, pp. 67–85.

Nye, A. (1982) Degeneration, neurasthenia and the culture of sport in *Belle Epoque* France. *Journal of Contemporary History*, 17, 1.

Oliver, P. (1997) *Encyclopaedia of Vernacular Architecture*. 3 vols. Cambridge: Cambridge University Press.

Ott, H. (1994) Translated by A. Blunden, *Martin Heidegger: A Political Life*. London: Harper Collins.

Palahniuk, C. (1999) *Survivor*. New York: Norton.

Papini, G. (1905) Il Pragmatismo Messo in Ordine. *Leonardo*, Milan, April, 47.

Pawson, J. (1996) *Minimum*. London: Phaidon.

Peirce, C.S. (1878) How to make our ideas clear. In *The Essential Peirce*, N. Houser and C. Kleosel (eds), 2 vols. Bloomington: Indiana University Press, 1, pp. 124–41.

Persico, E. (1934) Punto e da capo per l'architettura. *Domus*, 7.

Pevsner, N. (1943) *An Outline of European Architecture*. Page refs. to Seventh edn (1968). Harmondsworth: Pelican.

Poggioli, R. (1975) *The Oaten Flute: Essays on Pastoral Poetry and the Pastoral Ideal*. Cambridge, MA: Harvard University Press.

Pollan, M. (1997) *A Place of My Own: the Education of an Amateur Builder*. New York: Random House.

Porphyrios, D. (1991) *Classical Architecture*. London: Academy Editions.

Pratt, V., Howarth, J. and Brady, E. (2000) *Environment and Philosophy*. London: Routledge.

Proust, M. (1913–27) *A la recherche de temps perdu*. Paris: Grasset. Translated by S. Moncrief, A. Mayor and T. Kilmartin, revised by D.J. Enright (1992) *In Search of Lost Time*. 6 vols. 6, *Time Regained*. London: Chatto and Windus.

Putnam, H. (1995) Was Wittgenstein a pragmatist? In *Pragmatism: An Open Question*. Oxford: Blackwell, pp. 27–56.

Pye, D. (1978) *The Nature and Aesthetics of Design*. London: The Herbert Press.

Quincy, Q. de (1778) *Encyclopédie méthodique*, vol. 1. Paris.

Quincy, Q. de (1803) *De l'architecture égyptienne*. Paris.

Rabinbach, A. (1982) The body without fatigue: a nineteenth-century utopia. In *Political Symbolism in Modern Europe*, S. Drescher, D. Sabean and A. Sharlin (eds). New Brunswick: Transaction Books.

Rabinbach, A. (1990) *The Human Motor: Energy, Fatigue, and the Origins of Modernity*. New York: Basic Books.

Ramírez, J.A. (1999) *The Beehive Metaphor: From Gaudí to Le Corbusier*. London: Reaktion Books.

Rand, A. (1943) *The Fountainhead*. New York: Scribner.

Rapoport, A. (1969) *House, Form and Culture*. Engelwood Cliffs, NJ: Prentice-Hall.

Read, A. (2000) *Architecturally Speaking: Practices of Art, Architecture and the Everyday*. London: Routledge.

Reed, C. (ed.) (1996) *Not at Home: The Suppression of Domesticity in Modern Art and Architecture*. London: Thames and Hudson.

Rhees, R. (ed.) (1984) *Recollections of Wittgenstein*. Oxford: Oxford University Press.

Rilke, R.M. (1902) Eingang. In *Das Buch der Bilder*. Translated by C.F. MacIntyre (1940) Initiation. In *Rilke: Selected Poems*. Berkeley: University of California Press.

Robinson, J.H. (1990) La Représentation de l'Age d'or. In *Jean-Francis Auburtin, 1866–1930*, C. Briend (ed.). Paris: Délégation à l'Action Artistique de la Ville de Paris.

Robinson, J.H. (1993) *A 'Nouvelle Arcadie': Puvis de Chavannes and the Decorative Landscape in Fin-de-Siècle France*. Unpublished PhD dissertation: University of Virginia.

Rorty, R. (1989) *Contingency, Irony, Solidarity*. Cambridge: Cambridge University Press.

Rorty, R. (1991) Heidegger, contingency and pragmatism. In *Essays on Heidegger and Others*. Cambridge: Cambridge University Press, pp. 27–49.

Rorty, R. (1998) Derrida and the philosophical tradition. In *Truth and Progress*. Cambridge: Cambridge University Press, pp. 327–50.

Rorty, R. (1999) *Philosophy and Social Hope*. Harmondsworth: Penguin.

Rossi, A. (1987) *Aldo Rossi: Architect*. U. Barbieri and M.T. Romani (eds). Crane. Milan: Electra.

Rowe, C. (1994) *The Architecture of Good Intentions*. London: Academy Editions.

Ruskin, J. (1849) *The Seven Lamps of Architecture*. London.

Ruskin, J. (1865) Lilies: of Queens' gardens. In *Sesame and Lilies*. London. Page references to 1887 edn. New York: Wiley.

Rybczynski, W. (1989) *The Most Beautiful Home in the World*. New York: Viking.

Rykwert, J. (1976) Semper and the conception of style. In *Gottfried Semper und die Mitte des 19. Jahrhunderts*. Basel and Stuttgart: Birkhäuser. Reprinted in Rykwert, J. (1982) *The Necessity of Artifice*. London: Academy, pp. 122–30.

Rykwert, J. (1996) *The Dancing Column: On Order in Architecture*. Cambridge, MA: MIT Press.

Safranski, R. (1994) *Ein Meister aus Deutschland: Heidegger und seine Zeit*. München: C. Hanser. Translated by E. Osers (1994) *Martin Heidegger: Between Good and Evil*. Cambridge, MA: Harvard University Press.

Saint, A. (1983) The architect as hero and genius. In *The Image of the Architect*. New Haven: Yale University Press, pp. 1–18.

Salecl, R. (1994) The ideology of the mother nation in the Yugoslav conflict. In *Envisioning Eastern Europe*, M. Kennedy (ed.). Ann Arbor, MI: Michigan University Press, pp. 87–101.

Sallis, J. (1994) *Stone*. Bloomington: Indiana University Press.

Sanadjian, M. (1995) Iranians in Germany. *New German Critique*, 64, 3–36.

Sanders, J. (ed.) (1996) *Stud: Architectures of Masculinity*. Princeton, NJ: Princeton Architectural Press.

Sartwell, C. (1999) Written in stone: architectural communication and disintegration. In *Architecture and Civilization*, M. Mitias (ed.). Amsterdam: Rodopi, pp. 165–75.

Scarry, E. (1985) *The Body in Pain: The Making and Unmaking of the World*. Oxford: Oxford University Press.

Scheflen, A.E. and Ashcraft, N. (1976) *Human Territories. How We Behave in Space-Time*. Englewood Cliffs, NJ: Prentice Hall.

Schegloff, A.E. (1972) Notes on a conversational practice: formulating place. In *Studies in Social Interaction*, D. Sudnow (ed.). New York: The Free Press.

Schezen, R. (1996) *Adolf Loos, Architecture 1903–1932*. New York: Monacelli.

Schmarsow, A. (1894). *Das Wesen der architektonischen Schöpfung*. Leipzig: K.W. Hiersemann.

Schopenhauer, A. (1819) *Die Welt als Wille und Vorstellung*. Translated by W. Durant (1955) The world as will and idea. In *The Works of Schopenhauer*. New York: Ungar.

Schultze, F. (1994) *Philip Johnson, Life and Work*. New York: Knopf.

Schwarzer, M. (1993) Ontology and representation in Karl Bötticher's theory of tectonics. *Journal of the Society of Architectural Historians*, 52.

Scruton, R. (1979) *The Aesthetics of Architecture*. London: Methuen.

Scruton, R. (1982) *Kant*. Oxford: Oxford University Press.

Scruton, R. (1994) *The Classical Vernacular: Architectural Principles in an Age of Nihilism*. Manchester: Carcanet.

Seltzer, M. (1992) *Bodies and Machines*. London: Routledge.

Semper, G. (1860) *Der Stil in den technischen und tektonischen Künsten*. 2 vols. 1 (1860): Frankfurt: Verlag für Kunst und Wissenschaft. 2 (1863). München: Friedrich Bruckmanns Verlag.

Semper, G. (1869) *Über Baustyle: Ein Vortrag gehalten auf dem Rathaus in Zürich am 4 Marz 1869*. Zürich: F. Schulthess. Translated in Semper, 1989.

Semper, G. (1989) *The Four Elements and Other Writings*, H. Mallgrave and W. Herrmann (eds). Cambridge: Cambridge University Press.

Sennett, R. (1970) *The Uses of Disorder: Personal Identity and City Life*. New York: Knopf.

Sennett, R. (1991) *The Conscience of the Eye: The Design and Social Life of Cities*. New York: Knopf.

Sennett, R. (1994) *Flesh and Stone: The Body and the City in Western Civilization*. London: Faber.

Sereny, G. (1995) *Albert Speer: His Battle with Truth*. New York: Knopf.

Sheehan, T. (1981) *Heidegger: The Man and the Thinker*. Chicago: Precedent Publishing.

Shepheard, P. (1994) *What is Architecture?: an Essay on Landscapes, Buildings, and Machines*. Cambridge, MA: MIT Press.

Showalter, E. (1985) *The Female Malady: Women, Madness, and English Culture, 1830–1980*. New York: Pantheon Books.

Shusterman, R. (1989) *Analytic Aesthetics*. Oxford: Blackwell.

Shusterman, R. (1992) *Pragmatist Aesthetics: Living Beauty, Rethinking Art*. Oxford: Blackwell.

Silk, M.S. and Stern, J.P. (1981) *Nietzsche on Tragedy*. Cambridge: Cambridge University Press.

Silverman, D.L. (1989) *Art Nouveau in Fin-de-Siècle France: Politics, Psychology, and Style*. Berkeley: University of California Press.

Simon, J. (1892) *La Femme du vingtième siècle*. Paris: Calmann Levy.

Sluga, H. (1993) *Heidegger's Crisis*. Cambridge, MA: Harvard University Press.

Sokal, A. and Bricmont, J. (1997) *Impostures intellectuel*. Paris: Odile Jacob. Translated (1998) *Intellectual Impostures: Postmodern Philosopers' Abuse of Science*. London: Profile Books.

Sorkin, M. (1991) *Exquisite Corpse: Writing on Building*. London: Verso.

Soulier, G. (1902) Une installation de château, *L'Art Decoratif*, 4.

Sparshott, F. (1994) The aesthetics of architecture and the politics of space. In *Philosophy and Architecture*, M. Mitias (ed.). Amsterdam: Rodopi, pp. 3–20.

Stafford, B.M. (1991) *Body Criticism: Imaging the Unseen in Enlightenment Art and Medicine*. Cambridge, MA: MIT Press.

Stecker, R. (1999) Reflections on architecture: buildings as environments, as aesthetic objects and as artworks. In *Architecture and Civilization*, M. Mitias (ed.). Amsterdam: Rodopi, pp. 81–93.

Stevens, G. (1998) *The Favored Circle: The Social Foundations of Architectural Distinction*. Cambridge, MA: MIT Press.

Sudjic, D. (2000) *John Pawson, Works*. London: Phaidon.

Sullivan, L. (1900) The young man in architecture. address to the Architecture League of Chicago. In *Kindergarten Chats and Other Writings*. (1947). New York.

Tafuri, M. (1973) *Progetto e Utopia*. Bari: Guis. Laterza e Figli. Translated by B.L. La Penta (1976) *Architecture and Utopia: Design and Capitalist Development*. Cambridge, MA: MIT Press.

Tavernor, R. (1998) *On Alberti and the Art of Building*. New Haven: Yale University Press.

Taylor, C. (1989) *Sources of the Self: The Making of Modern Identity*. Cambridge: Cambridge University Press.

Thakara, J. (ed.) (1988) *Design After Modernism: Beyond the Object*. London: Thames and Hudson.

Theweleit, K. (1987) Translated by S. Conway. *Male Fantasies, Volume One*. Cambridge: Polity.

Theweleit, K. (1989) Translated by C. Turner and E. Carter. *Male Fantasies, Volume Two*. Cambridge: Polity.

Thiele, L.P. (1991) *Friedrich Nietzsche and the Politics of the Soul: A Study of Heroic Individualism*. Princeton, NJ: Princeton University Press.

Thoreau, H.D. (1854) *Walden*. O. Thomas (ed.) (1966). New York: Norton.

Tilghman, B.R. (1994) Architecture, expression, and the understanding of a culture. In *Philosophy and Architecture*, M. Mitias (ed.). Amsterdam: Rodopi, pp. 51–66.

Tournikiotis, P. (1999) *The Historiography of Modern Architecture*. Cambridge, MA: MIT Press.

Troy, N.J. (1991) *Modernism and the Decorative Arts in France: Art Nouveau to Le Corbusier*. New Haven: Yale University Press.

Tschumi, B. (1994a) *Architecture and Disjunction*. Cambridge, MA: MIT Press.

Tschumi, B. (1994b) *Event-Cities (Praxis)* Cambridge, MA: MIT Press.

Tschumi, B. (2000) *Event-Cities 2*. Cambridge, MA: MIT Press.

Uspenskii, B.A. [see also Lotman and Ouspensky] (1973) *A Poetics of Composition*. Translated by V. Zavarin and S. Witting. Berkeley: University of California Press.

Vachon, M. (1895) *Puvis de Chavannes*. Paris: Braun, Clément.

Vale, B. (1996) Gender and an architecture of environmental responsibility. In *Desiring Practices*, D. McCorquodale *et al.*, (eds). London: Black Dog, pp. 264–73.

Valéry, P. (1921) Eupalinos, ou l'Architecte. Reprinted in *Eupalinos, L'Ame et la danse, Dialogue de l'arbre*. Paris: Gallimard. Translated by W.M. Stewart (1956) New York: Pantheon.

Van Leeuwen, T.A.P. (1986) *The Skyward Trend of Thought: The Metaphysics of the American Skyscraper*. Amsterdam: AHA Books.

Vattimo, G. (1990) Translated by D. Webb. The end of modernity, the end of the project? *Journal of Philosophy and the Visual Arts*, 74–7.

Vauxcelles, L. (1912) Francis Auburtin. *Art et décoration*, 78.

Veblen, T. (1899) *The Theory of the Leisure Class: An Economic Study of Institutions*. New York: Macmillan.

Venturi, R., Scott Brown, D. and Izenour, S. (1977) *Learning From Las Vegas*. Second edn. Cambridge, MA: MIT Press.

Vidler, A. (1992) *The Architectural Uncanny*. Cambridge, MA: MIT Press.

Vidler, A. (2000) *Warped Space: Art, Architecture, and Anxiety in Modern Culture*. Cambridge, MA: MIT Press.

Virilio, P. (1991) Translated by D. Mosheberg. *The Lost Dimension*. New York: Semiotext(e).

Vitruvius, M.P. (First century BC) *De architectura libri x*. Translated by M.H. Morgan (1914, reprinted 1960) *The Ten Books on Architecture*. New York: Dover.

Wagner, A. (1999) Resisting the erasure of history: a conversation with Daniel Libeskind. In *Architecture and Revolution*, N. Leach (ed.). London: Routledge, pp. 130–8.

Wagner, O. (1902) *Moderne Architektur*. Third edn. Vienna: A. Schroll. Translated by H.F. Mallgrave (1988) *Modern Architecture: A Guidebook for his Students to this Field of Art*. Santa Monica: Getty Center.

Ward, J.F. (1995) *Heidegger's Political Thinking*. Amherst: University of Massachusetts Press.

Watkin, D. (1977) *Morality and Architecture*. Oxford: Oxford University Press.

Weber, R. (1994) The myth of meaningful forms. In *Philosophy and Architecture*, M. Mitias (ed.). Amsterdam: Rodopi, pp. 109–19.

Weber, R. (1995) *On the Aesthetics of Architecture: a Psychological Approach to the Structure and the Order of Perceived Architectural Space*. Aldershot: Ashgate.

Weil, S. (1949) *L'Enracinement*. Paris: Gallimard. English translation (1952) *The Need for Roots: Prelude to a Declaration of Duties Towards Mankind*. London: Routledge.

Weisberg, P. (1986) *Art Nouveau Bing: Paris Style 1900*. New York: Abrams.

Welsch, W. (1997) Translated by A. Inkpen. *Undoing Aesthetics*. London: Sage.

Wigley, M. (1992) Heidegger's house: the violence of the domestic. In *D: Columbia Documents in Architecture and Theory*, 91–121.

Wigley, M. (1993) *The Architecture of Deconstruction: Derrida's Haunt*. Cambridge, MA: MIT Press.

Wijdeveld, P. (1994) *Ludwig Wittgenstein, Architect*. Cambridge, MA: MIT Press.

Wilde, O. (1968) The decay of lying. In *Literary Criticism of Oscar Wilde*. Lincoln: University of Nebraska Press.

Wilson, C.St.-J. (1992) *Architectural Reflections: Studies in the Philosophy and Practice of Architecture*. London: Butterworth.

Wilson, C.St.-J. (1995) *The Other Tradition of Modern Architecture*. London: Academy Editions.

Winckelmann, J.-J. (1774) *Geschichte der Kunst des Alterthums*. Dresden. Translated by G.H. Lodge (1881) *The History of Ancient Art*. Two vols. London.

Winters, E. (1991) Technological progress and architectural reponse. *The British Journal of Aesthetics*, 31, 251–8.

Winters, E. (1996) Architecture, meaning and significance. *The Journal of Architecture*, 1, 39–47.

Winters, E. (1999) Architecture and human purposes. *The Journal of Architecture*, 4, 1–8.

Winters, E. (2001) Architecture. In *The Routledge Companion to Aesthetics*, B. Gaut and D. Lopes (eds). London: Routledge, 519–30.

Wittgenstein, L. (1961) *Tractatus Logico-Philosophicus*. Translated by D.F. Pears and B.F. McGuinness. London: Routledge.

Wittgenstein, L. (1980a) *Culture and Value*. G.H. von Wright (ed.). Oxford: Blackwell.

Wittgenstein, L. (1980b) *Wittgenstein's Lectures, Cambridge 1930–1932*. D. Lee (ed.). New York: Rowman and Littlefield.

Wittkower, R. (1949) *Architectural Principles in the Age of Humanism*. Fourth edn (1988). London: Academy Editions.

Wolin, R. (ed.) (1993) *The Heidegger Controversy*. Cambridge, MA: MIT Press.

Wright, F.L. (1932) *Autobiography*. New York: Longmans Green.

Young, I.M. (1990) *Justice and the Politics of Difference*. Princeton, NJ: Princeton University Press.

Zimmerman, M. (1990) *Heidegger's Confrontation with Modernity*. Bloomington: Indiana University Press.

Index